Labor Organizations

LABOR ORGANIZATIONS

A MACRO- AND MICRO-SOCIOLOGICAL ANALYSIS
ON A COMPARATIVE BASIS

Mark van de Vall

Professor of Sociology
State University of New York at Buffalo

CAMBRIDGE
AT THE UNIVERSITY PRESS
1970

Published by the Syndics of the Cambridge University Press
Bentley House, 200 Euston Road, London N.W.1
American Branch: 32 East 57th Street, New York, N.Y. 10022

Library of Congress Catalogue Card Number: 75-100030
Standard Book Number: 521 07637 4

Printed in Great Britain
at the Aberdeen University Press

To Willem van de Vall

TRADE UNION LEADER

Earlier versions of this work appeared in the Netherlands under the title *De Vakbeweging in de Welvaartsstaat*, 1st printing 1964, 2nd printing 1967, and in Germany under the title *Die Gewerkschaften im Wohlfahrtsstaat*, 1966. The English edition has been entirely revised and expanded by the author.

Contents

Appendices

List of figures

List of tables

List of charts

PART I

Macro-sociological analysis

1. The welfare state

INTRODUCTION

The birth of the labor movement is largely explained by such environmental variables as industrialization, nineteenth-century capitalism, and class conflict. Since then, this environment has changed considerably. Small and paternalistic firms have grown into corporations that straddle the world. Urbanization and immigration have brought about new and universal culture patterns. Social systems such as the affluent society and the welfare state, in which manual workers are no longer social outcasts, have emerged since World War II, and there are profound sociopsychological differences between today's status society and the class society of the past.[1]

In this process, the trade unions have also changed. The relationship between trade unions and society, for example, underwent a process of integration. From an opposition movement, trade unions became a recognized institution, deeply rooted in our economic and political system. Changes also occurred at the micro-level, i.e. in the relationship between the trade union and its members. The acceptance by the unions of fresh responsibilities represented objective changes, the fulfillment of which demanded new methods and new leadership. Subjective changes took place in the members' perceptions of the union and in their motives for joining, participating, or leaving. Such psychological factors are fundamental to an organization which is partly voluntary and relatively democratic. Even in the bureaucratic union of the welfare state, it is ultimately the members who determine its position in society.

In view of these alterations, we may ask whether the Western labor movement is still a child of its time, as it was in the last century. In other words, can we still explain the structure and functions of the labor movement in terms of a confrontation with its environment? What are the problems which the threefold process of change in society, in the unions, and in their membership has created? Such a complex question demands a complex answer. Part I, the macro-analysis, first considers the economic, sociological, psychological, and political differences between nineteenth-century society and the modern welfare state. The next chapter considers how the unions' functions have evolved during this

[1] The term 'status society' was used by Peter Drucker at the Forty-seventh Annual Meeting of the American Sociological Society, 3 September 1952.

century and what trends underlie this change. Our macro-analysis ends with a chapter on three problems arising from the transformation of society and labor.

We cannot, however, fully understand the trade union movement from the outside. Part II, the micro-analysis, probes the movement's organizational structure and gives us a picture from within. It explores both the power of trade unions to attract new members and how the character of this attraction is changing. Next, the size and structure of the group of active members is examined along with the personality of the participant and his motives. The sixth chapter considers why the union's ties with its members are declining and the role automation plays in this process.

Our analysis of Western labor's problems will rest basically upon research in Western Europe, using United States data for comparative purposes. Although the American and European labor movements are, in general, coping with the same problems, they are often more manifest in Europe. The class conflict had its origin in Western Europe and had a deeper impact there on management and labor than in the New World. As a result, European unionism acquired stronger Marxist overtones. In historical perspective, European labor has been more deeply rooted in the nineteenth century than its American counterpart.

After World War II, however, this situation was reversed. For example, the creation of the welfare state in Western Europe—predominantly a product of modern unionism—was not preceded but followed by the 'Great Society'. Although both American and European labor unions are in the process of being integrated into the industrial and national economy, the European unions are far ahead. The American unions, in Drucker's terms, are still very much an 'institution against industry', but European unionism has already turned into an integrated institution of the welfare state, i.e. into an 'institution of society'. As a result, European unionism appears now more a product of the twentieth century than American unionism.

Because of this transformation from a socialist counterforce in capitalist society into an integrated institution of the welfare state, European unionism is experiencing labor's problems in extreme forms. This experience is aggravated by the voluntary character of most European unions, which results in their ups and downs being immediately reflected in their membership. We shall discover how this trait facilitates our analysis of the unions' problems.

ECONOMIC ASPECTS

Industry and prosperity

Industrialization leads to prosperity. A century ago, Marx pointed out that greater concentration of the means of production in buildings and machinery leads to increased productivity and wealth. His figures showed that the industrial revolution caused an unprecedented rise in Britain's national income.[1]

Recent confirmation of this law is provided by the Netherlands, where intensive industrialization did not take place until after World War II. Between 1900 and 1929 per capita income at constant market prices (1953 = 100) rose from 60 to 89, falling back to 82 in the 1930s. But between 1948 and 1958, when industrialization was in full swing, it shot up from 86 to 125. During *ten* years of industrialization, therefore, prosperity rose 1.3 times as much as in the first *thirty* years of this century.[2]

In France Fourastié has shown that the average wage earner's purchasing power for manufactured goods is still increasing.[3] This indicates a general and current relationship between industrialization and prosperity.

While this advance in absolute prosperity is in line with Marx's theory, changes in the distribution of wealth contradict his prophecies. When Marx pointed out the relationship between industry and national prosperity, his objection was that most of the new wealth went to the class owning the means of production. He attached such fundamental importance to this accumulation of wealth in the hands of private persons[4] that he attributed the survival of the bourgeoisie largely to this factor. At that time, Marx's observation of the one-sided distribution of wealth was undoubtedly correct. In 1899, Eduard Bernstein confirmed from German tax figures that the rich were growing richer and the poor poorer.[5] The American economist Simon Kuznets also concludes that, in the first phase of the industrial revolution, social inequality became accentuated. He states that there was widespread impoverishment in England between 1780 and 1850 and, again, between 1840 and 1890 in Germany and the United States.[6] So serious was social inequality in the Low Countries around 1870 that it was recognized as *the* social issue of the period.[7] It

---

[1] 'The General Law of Capitalist Accumulation', *Capital*, ed. Fr. Engels, 2nd impression (Moscow, Foreign Languages Publishing House, 1962), Vol. I, Ch. XXV, pp. 612–712.

[2] *Zestig Jaren Statistiek in Tijdreeksen, 1899–1959* (Zeist, De Haan, 1954), p. 100.

[3] J. Fourastié, *Machinisme et Bien-Être* (Paris, Ed. du Minnit, 1951), Ch. 2.

[4] K. Marx, *The Communist Manifesto* (Chicago, Henry Regnery Company, 1965), p. 38.

[5] E. Bernstein, *Evolutionary Socialism* (New York, Schocken Books, 1961), p. 212.

[6] S. Kuznets, 'Economic Growth and Income Inequality', *American Economic Review*, XLV, No. 1 (1955), *passim*.

[7] A. J. C. de Vrankrijker, *Een groeiende gedachte, de ontwikkeling der meningen over de sociale kwestie in de 19e eeuw in Nederland* (Assen, Van Gorcum, 1959), p. 100.

was no mere coincidence that the Western trade union movement, in-
spired by Marx and others, emerged at that time.

What Marx did not foresee, however, was that subsequent phases of
industrialization would produce the opposite pattern. Kuznets writes
that a gradual process of economic leveling began in England as early as
1875 and in Germany and the United States after World War I.[1] In this
process, the less privileged groups saw a relative increase in their share
of the national income, while the more privileged experienced a relative
decline. As a result, the differences between their respective shares were
reduced and social inequality lessened. The following figures suggest that
the process has continued in the West since World War II.

1. The poorest 60 per cent of the *Dutch* population saw their share of
the national income increase by 3 per cent from 1938 to 1949 and by
about 6 per cent from 1949 to 1954, an indication that in Holland economic leveling has progressed faster since World War II.[2]

2. Although Göseke's figures for *Germany* cover only the years
1955–9, his conclusion is that 'the changes during this period—a decrease in the shares of the upper two to four deciles—clearly indicate that
income distribution has become more equal'.[3]

3. In the *United States*, Miller found sharp changes in income distribution between 1940 and 1950, with the largest relative increase accruing
to the lowest-paid occupations and the smallest to the highest-paid ones,
thus narrowing the income range.[4]

4. In *Britain*, Robertson reports that even before taxation, incomes
were more equally distributed in 1958 than in 1938, and that the progressive tax system intensified this leveling process.[5]

5. Few figures are available for *France*, but there, too, Aron concluded
in 1956 that the trend of income distribution was diametrically opposed
to Marx's prophecies.[6]

[1] S. Kuznets, 'Economic Growth', *passim*.
[2] J. W. W. A. Wit, 'De verdeling van de gezinsinkomens in Nederland in de jaren 1949 en 1954', *Statistische en Econometrische Onderzoekingen* (4th Quarter, 1956), p. 174.
[3] G. Göseke, *Verteilung und Schichtung der Einkommen der privaten Haushalte in der Bundesrepublik 1955 bis 1959* (Berlin, Duncker & Humblot, 1963), p. 59.
[4] H. P. Miller, *Income of the American People* (New York, John Wiley & Sons 1955), p. 5. Also, by the same author, *Income Distribution in the United States*, U.S. Dept. of Commerce, Washington, D.C., 1960, Table 1 (10).
[5] D. J. Robertson, *The Economics of Wages and the Distribution of Income* (London, Macmillan & Co., 1961), pp. 154, 168.
[6] 'Dans cette perspective l'évolution serait exactement contraire à celle que Marx anticipait. Au lieu d'un abaissement du niveau de vie, une élévation des rémunérations ouvrières, du moins proportionelle à l'augmentation des ressources collectives.' R. Aron, 'Remarques sur les particularités de l'évolution sociale de la France', *Transactions of the Third World Congress of Sociology*, III (London ,ISA, 1956), p. 44.

Since virtually all blue collar workers are in the lower half of the income scale, we may conclude from these observations that the socioeconomic group over whose interests the Western trade unions have watched for the past century has experienced a relative increase in its share of the national income since World War II; in other words, that Marx's theory of the progressive pauperization of the Proletariat has been contradicted by facts. The changes in the pattern of consumption resulting from the workers' growing prosperity have been partly material and partly psychological, as illustrated by the following examples from Germany and the Netherlands:

1. Family budget research in a West German province shows the following *material* changes: while the gross income of the average employee's family (four persons) rose by 118 per cent from 1950 to 1959, the proportion spent on food fell (in full accord with Engels's law) from 47·5 per cent to 28 per cent. At the same time, the food became more wholesome: the consumption of bread, potatoes, milk, and cheap fat pork declined, but lean meat, poultry, ham, eggs, and fresh semitropical fruits became more popular. The amount spent on education and entertainment went up from DM 19 to DM 57 per month, compared with an increase in cost of 24 per cent. The corresponding amounts for household effects were DM 10 in 1950 and DM 63 in 1959, with a price increase of only 11 per cent.[1]

2. Increasing prosperity produces *psychological* changes, as our inquiry among Dutch housewives revealed. Asked why they bought their groceries from a particular store (Co-op), women in the various age groups mentioned high quality rather than low price in the ratios given in Table 1.

TABLE 1. *Quality versus price by age groups*

	REASON FOR PREFERENCE	
	Low price	High quality
Oldest age group (61 and over)	1	1·7
Middle age group (35–60)	1	3·8
Youngest age group (under 35)	1	10·5

The table shows that the youngest age group attaches more than six times as much importance to quality as the oldest group, which suggests that the housewife's pattern of consumption changes as she is mentally

[1] 'Einkommen und Verbrauch in nordrhein-westfälischen Haushalten 1950–1959', *Beiträge zur Statistik des Landes Nordrhein-Westfalen*, No. 135 (Düsseldorf, 1961), *passim*.

more acclimatized to prosperity. The findings also illustrate how the consumers' movement, as well as the labor movement, must face the social changes brought about by affluence.[1]

The question now arises whether these figures imply that poverty has been entirely banished from modern society. The facts show this interpretation to be overoptimistic. The proportion of the population still living in poverty in Western Germany, Britain, and the United States is no less than 23 per cent, 21 per cent, and 23 per cent respectively.[2] As Galbraith pointed out, however, this modern poverty is becoming more and more 'insular', prevailing among specific and more or less isolated groups.[3] Examples of such islands of poverty are the inhabitants of a worked-out mining district or an isolated mountain area, old persons, invalids, persons from broken homes, and such cultural and racial minorities as Puerto Ricans and Negroes in the United States.

The principal difference between contemporary poverty and that of the nineteenth-century working classes is that the first is confined to well-defined groups, whereas the latter indiscriminately affected the entire working population. The term 'forgotten groups', currently used in Western Europe for the poor, reflects the fact that poverty is no longer synonymous with membership in the working class. The workers of the Western world are now better off, absolutely as well as relatively, than they ever were. In this connection, it should be mentioned that the *relative* increase in prosperity, i.e. the individual's advance in relation to others, is probably more strongly felt than the *absolute* one.[4] This is because it represents progress beyond the worker's own situation in the past *and* towards what others, more well to do, have today. Since relative

---

[1] M. van de Vall, 'Clients, Consommateurs ou Coopérateurs, une enquête Néerlandaise', *Coopération, Idées, Faits, Techniques*, April, May, June 1962, *passim*.

[2] The information for *Germany* is taken from G. Fürst *et al.*, 'Zur Frage der Einkommensschichtung', *Wirtschaft und Statistik*, No. 6 (1954), p. 265; that for *Britain* from D. J. Robertson, *The Economics of Wages*, Table 20, p. 169; that for the *United States* from 'Poverty and Deprivation in the U.S.', *Conference on Economic Progress, Washington, D.C., April, 1962*, p. 19. The poverty line taken for the three countries was: Germany, DM 2,400 per annum; Britain, £250 per annum; United States, $4,000 per annum.

[3] J. K. Galbraith, *The Affluent Society* (New York, Mentor Books, 1958), Ch. 22.

[4] Sometimes another process cuts across this, viz. the replacement of the traditional frame of reference. In the rural districts of Western Europe in the nineteenth century, for instance, incomes in agriculture were the frame of reference for factory workers, craftsmen, civil servants, and others. Anyone whose earnings were the same as those of the farmer was reasonably well off; a man who earned more, well off. Owing to the closer contact between the different groups and the consequent social integration, the pattern of the national labor market became clearer and the local reference group was gradually replaced by a national frame of reference. Although the wage earned by his fellow villager still has the strongest appeal on his imagination, the modern rural worker now keeps a keen eye on city wages. E. W. Hofstee, 'Changes in Rural Stratification in the Netherlands', *Transactions of the Second Congress of Sociology* (London, ISA, 1956), II, Pt. 2, p. 44.

progress is judged by the double frame of reference of both one's own former situation and the present situation of others, the *degree* of redistribution determines how much satisfaction the new prosperity provides. There is little doubt that for most people in the Western world, postwar society is not only a welfare state providing social security but also an affluent society providing both the material and psychological satisfactions of a rising standard of living.

Industry and equalization

A redistribution of national income that lessens social disparities is one of the most important changes that can take place in the trade unions' social environment. We shall now examine the background of the leveling process from this angle and assess, if possible, its future trend. To express this in terms of intensity of change we use the 'pattern of redistribution'.

This 'pattern' is arrived at by taking the rise or fall in each income category's percentage share of the national income over a given period and expressing it as a percentage of the earlier share. The percentages of relative change for all income categories together form the redistribution pattern. For the purposes of this 'pattern', it is convenient to divide the population according to income into five numerically equal groups known as quintiles. If a particular income category, say the lowest quintile, increases its share of the national income from 3 to 4·5 per cent, the relative change is +50 per cent. It should be remembered, however, that although a relative change of +75 per cent in the lowest quintile is 7·5 times as great as a +10 per cent change in the fourth quintile, in absolute terms these figures may represent a smaller additional income for the former than for the latter. Nevertheless, a man whose income goes up by 75 per cent will experience this as a greater change than someone who receives only 10 per cent more.

Substantial differences are revealed by a comparison of the redistribution patterns in three countries: the Netherlands, Denmark (a country less highly industrialized), and the United States (a country more highly industrialized). (See Figure 1.)[1]

In Denmark, which (with 26 per cent of its working population in agriculture) was less industrialized than the Netherlands (with 19·6 per cent), the equalization of incomes has been slowest. Although the share

---

[1] The percentages for *Denmark* are calculated from Kjeld Bjerke, 'Changes in Danish Income Distribution, 1939–1952', *Income and Wealth*, VI (London, 1957), p. 107; those for the *Netherlands* from J. W. W. A. Wit, 'De verdeling van de gezinsinkomens in Nederland'; and those for the *United States* from S. Goldsmith, G. Jaszi, K. Kaitz and M. Liebenberg, 'Size Distribution of Income since the Midthirties', *Review of Economics and Statistics*, XXXVI, No. 1 (1954), p. 9.

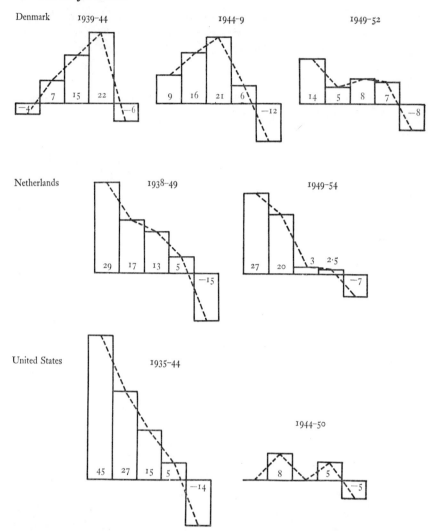

FIGURE I. The redistribution pattern, in quintiles, of national income in three countries with different levels of industrialization.

of the national income of the middle 60 per cent increases between 1939 and 1944, it was at the expense not only of the highest 20 per cent but of the lowest 20 per cent as well. The period that followed in Denmark showed a trend towards the Dutch pattern, though even then the second and third categories benefited most. It was not until 1949 that the lowest income group had the greatest relative increase and that economic leveling took place in the sense described.

There are various factors that may cause the workers' share of national income to increase. For instance, low paid farm workers may be driven to the towns to work in factories for higher wages. Changes in the occupational structure may also lead to redistribution, as when the number of skilled workers increases at the expense of unskilled workers, or when jobs with small wage differentials (such as bench hand, fitter, mechanic, smelter, and charge hand) increase proportionally. Moreover, a drop in unemployment will obviously increase the income of the lowest categories. Lastly, the number of wage earners per family may increase, especially when the wife takes a job. The United States is a striking example of this; there is more than one wage earner in two-thirds of 'middle-income' families with incomes of $6,000 to $8,000 per year against one-third of families in the $10,000 and over income bracket.[1] The greater number of wage earners per family in the lower bracket has a leveling effect between both the two categories.

These factors lead to the question of whether or not economic leveling will continue, as industrialization progresses, until all categories have an *equal* share of the national income. A possible clue is found in the United States, where industrialization has progressed so far that only 6 per cent of the working population are still employed in agriculture.[2] Figure 1 shows that the intensive leveling that took place from 1935 to 1944 was completely halted between 1944 and 1950. Some years later this trend became also apparent in Europe where after 1955 between occupational groups the income inequality ceased to reduce. For wage- and salary-earners recent data even indicate a reversed trend, in the direction of increasing income inequality. Measured among households, the income dispersion is widening most between the poorest group (which includes most pensioners) and the middle income ranges.[3] Both trends bear out Dahrendorf's contention that modern industrial society shows little indication of abolishing income differentials.[4]

If we wish to compare income inequality in the various Western countries, a common criterion is the income of the families forming the top 5 per cent of the income scale, expressed as a percentage of national income. Table 2 gives the figures for seven countries.

[1] H. P. Miller, *Income of the American People*, Ch. 9.
[2] From *Statistical Abstracts of the United States: 1960*. The figures for the agrarian working population in Denmark have been taken from the *International Yearbook of Labor Statistics*, 1960; those for the Netherlands from *Statistisch Zakboekje* (Zeist, De Haan, 1959).
[3] *Incomes in Postwar Europe: A Study of Policies, Growth and Distribution*, prepared by the Secretariat of the Economic Commission for Europe (Geneva, 1967), Ch. 6.
[4] '. . . there is no indication that hierarchies of socio-economic status will disappear in the forseeable future', R. Dahrendorf, *Class and Class Conflict in Industrial Society* (Stanford, Stanford University Press, 1959), p. 70.

TABLE 2. *Proportion of families in the top 5 per cent of the income scale in Western Europe and the United States, after taxation*

(Expressed as a percentage of national income)[1]

	Year	Percentage
United States	1950	20* (19·6 in 1962)
Sweden	1948	20
Denmark	1952	20
United Kingdom	1951–2	21
Italy	1948	24
Western Germany	1950	24* (15·0 in 1962)
Netherlands	1950	25* (17·5 in 1962)

* The 1962 data for the United States, West Germany and the Netherlands were the only ones obtained in a survey by the author among National Census Bureaus in the above countries. The corresponding figure for France in 1962 was 22 per cent. Lack of comparability, due to differences in definition, sampling and computation prohibits drawing conclusions over the 1950–62 period.

In the United States, where the capitalistic structure has undergone comparatively little change, the most prosperous citizens might be expected to receive a much bigger slice of the cake than those in countries like the Netherlands and Sweden, where the trade unions have long had one or more of their leaders in the government. For the top 5 per cent, however, this proves not to be the case.[2] Findings like this, naturally, make one wonder what influence the trade unions really have on the distribution of income.

The Unions and Prosperity

From a consideration of this question, two conclusions can be drawn about the relationship of the trade unions to the income structure. First, there is wide agreement among economists that the *direct* influence on income distribution of the unions' bargaining is slight.[3] There are few indications

[1] These figures were found in the fascinating study by H. P. Miller, *Rich Man, Poor Man* (New York, Crowell, 1964), p. 12, who took them from S. Kuznets, 'Quantitative Aspects of the Economic Growths of Nations', *Economic Development and Cultural Change*, XI, No. 2 (1963), Table 3. The 1962 figure for the US is from Jeanette M. Fitzwilliams, 'Size Distribution of Income in 1963', *Survey of Current Business*, April 1964, p. 8.

[2] Irving B. Kravis, using quintiles as basis for comparison, comes to slightly different conclusions. According to him, Denmark, the Netherlands and Israel (Jewish population only) have less inequality than the U.S., while Great Britain, Japan and Canada have about the same. Irving B. Kravis, *The Structure of Income* (University of Pennsylvania, 1962), p. 252. The theoretical problem, however, remains the same.

[3] The following quotations substantiate this conclusion:
1. 'The conclusions pointed by both the theoretical and empirical analyses are that trade unions have not in fact had an observably important effect on the income share going to labor

that the unions, as a separate economic factor, have increased the real wage level for any length of time. This is partly because of the greater influence of the labor market, partly because wage increases are offset by price increases, and partly because in countries like the Netherlands and Western Germany the unions, in the national interest (in order to remain competitive in international markets and to counter inflation), have limited their wage demands. Although they may have raised the lower limit and caused income redistribution *within* the working population, it is doubtful that this has led to a *general* increase in the workers' wage level.[1] As a result, the trade unions are gradually realizing that, as was thought in the nineteenth century,[2] they are not the only force in society capable of leveling social inequalities. Statements which illustrate this are:

'The Dutch Federation of Trade Unions has concluded that there are limits to the possibility of redistribution: where direct remuneration is concerned some anomalies can be removed, but there are fundamental economic forces governing income distribution which lead an existence of their own.'[3]

'The Director of Research of the Industrial Unions Department of AFL–CIO has found that American white collar workers, though less highly organized, have in recent years been making up their income lag in comparison with the better organized blue collar workers. This shows, in his view, how fundamental economic processes, such as the shortage of white collar workers on the labor market, can bring union policy to nought.'[4]

Can we assume from these observations that the trade union movement

in general, nor their share in the organized employment sectors.' A. M. Cartter, *Theory of Wages and Employment* (Homewood, Ill., Irwin, Inc., 1959), p. 178.

2. 'The preponderant opinion is that union influence has been slight, or even non-existent.' L. G. Reynolds and G. H. Taft, *The Evolution of Wage Structure* (New Haven, Conn., Yale University Press, 1956), p. 190.

3. 'It may be fair to conclude that, except for periods of active new unionism (as 1936–37) and for situations with a closed shop (Building Trades), there is little evidence of a definite upward push by unions on the level of wages', *Wages, Prices, Profits, and Productivity* (American Assembly, Columbia University, June 1959), p. 100.

[1] 1. 'When more complete and continuous data are available on the distribution of personal income by size groups, it may be possible to show that the effect of trade union policy has been to influence primarily the distribution of income *within* the brackets below $2,500. That is, trade union wage policy may have been more instrumental in affecting the distribution of income in lower income brackets than changing the distribution between low and high income brackets.' J. T. Dunlop, *Wage Determination under Trade Unions* (New York, A. M. Kelly, Inc., 1950), p. 190.

2. 'We may therefore suggest that if the trade unions have increased the wage earner's share of the national product, this has been done by pushing up the lower paid in each section of the labor force rather than by raising all wages relative to the returns to other factors.' D. J. Robertson, *The Economics of Wages*, p. 192.

[2] K. Kautsky, *Die proletarische Revolution und ihr Program* (Berlin, 1922), p. 162.

[3] A. H. Kloos, Member of Executive of Dutch Trade Union Federation, *De Metaalkoerier*, No. 19 (23 September 1961).

[4] E. M. Kassalow, 'White Collar Unionism in the United States' (mimeographed 1962, p. 61, and in private communication). E. M. Kassalow is now Professor of Industrial Relations at the University of Wisconsin.

is unable to exert any deliberate influence on the redistribution of national income? Such would indeed be the case if, apart from the direct, economic instrument of collective bargaining, there were no *indirect* and partially political means of influence. Trade union influence in government, for example, can obviously have a leveling effect. The social provisions of the welfare state can keep up the living standards of the unemployed, old people, and invalids; planned industrialization of backward areas can raise local living standards; government employment policies can keep down unemployment; progressive taxation and higher death duties can lessen privileges. And if automation should drastically disrupt the labor market, union-inspired government intervention will probably be the only remedy. As any of these forms of action prevents income differentials from widening or hastens their diminution, our conclusion is that, with regard to income equalization, economic unionism is less effective than political unionism. In Cartter's view, however, union leaders and their opponents are so wrapped up in the spectacular, but illusory, effect of wage increases achieved by collective bargaining that they are unable to assess the true value of these political means.[1] Cartter's comments relate to United States unions; the West European unions with their codetermination at the industrial and national level are, in this respect, undoubtedly well ahead. They are already deeply integrated in the politics of the welfare state.

The second conclusion about the union's relationship to the income structure is that ideological changes in industry and the trade unions have gradually brought their goals closer together since World War II. With the incessant expansion of production, industry has a growing need to expand and stabilize its market. Galbraith has described this trend as the transition from the economics of scarcity to the economics of affluence, with a gradual shift of emphasis from production to selling.[2] Sales are now determined by industrial designers and planners rather than by engineers and technicians,[3] and the techniques of modern want-creation receive as much attention as the techniques of production.

This increasingly urgent need for a steady market, coupled with the realization that the increased share in national income of the poorer half of the population has brought an unprecedented expansion of the market for durable consumer goods, has caused industry to view economic leveling with different eyes. 'Buying power has become the life force of

[1] Cartter, *Theory of Wages*, p. 171.
[2] J. K. Galbraith, *The Affluent Society*, pp. 204, 205, and *passim*.
[3] E. Zahn, *Die Soziologie der Prosperität* (Berlin, 1960), p. 21; for an interesting case study, see R. Nader, 'Profits versus Engineering, the Corvair Story', *The Nation*, Vol. 201, No. 14 (November, 1965), p. 297.

industrial society', reflects a member of the Unilever staff,[1] and, even in the 'laissez-faire, laissez-aller' atmosphere of advertising, further leveling is openly desired.[2] These opinions are heard not only in Western Europe, but in the United States as well. Big-business executives support Great-Society programs, and in *The Powerful Consumer*, Katona writes of industry's gradual realization that the consumer, although despised, misunderstood, and badly organized, is one of the most stabilizing forces in our economy.[3]

But while economic leveling thus meets industry's desire to eliminate risk, it fulfills, at the same time, such trade unions goals as 'supplying wants for the common good' and 'a society providing a proper existence for all'.[4] In this sense, the aims of modern 'Wohlfahrtskapitalismus' or 'sociocapitalism' have shifted toward the ideals of modern labor.

On the other hand, the socialist trade union movement has also seen ideological changes since World War II, and these, too, have helped to lessen social conflict. West European labor has abandoned its efforts toward the nationalization of industry and a fully planned economy so that, in the words of an American observer, 'Socialism tends to become liberal socialism'.[5] Gradually, in both aims and policy, Western trade unionism offers less opposition to the existing economic system, except to remedy specific evils, such as insular poverty, housing shortages, and inflation, or to obtain codetermination. This acceptance, in practice, of sociocapitalism is the chief difference between the trade unions of the affluent society and those of a century ago. Moreover, it implies that the gap between West European and American labor may gradually narrow. In 1954, Lauterbach could still write that American trade union policy operated primarily *within* the framework of the existing economic system, whereas the West European movement rejected the system on principle.[6] With this rejection now constantly diminishing, the distinction between the two movements is gradually becoming smaller, while the possibility of their comparison has grown.[7]

---

[1] E. Zahn, *Die Soziologie der Prosperität*, p. 21.

[2] H. Daudt, 'Wij varen niet zo wel als U denkt', *Ariadne*, No. 11 (20 October 1961), p. 896.

[3] G. Katona, *The Powerful Consumer* (New York, McGraw–Hill, 1961), p. 242.

[4] These quotations are taken from 'Statuten en reglementen van het Nederlands Verbond van Vakverenigingen', *Doel en Beginselen* (1959), p. 1.

[5] A. Sturmthal, *Unity and Diversity in European Labor* (Glencoe, Ill., Free Press, 1953), p. 137.

[6] A. Lauterbach, *Man, Motives and Money: Psychological Frontiers of Economics* (Ithaca, New York, Cornell University Press, 1954), pp. 187–98.

[7] 'With the virtual abandonment of socialism by Western European labor movements and the growing similarity between their economic structures and the American, there is a rising interest in the achievements of unions on this side of the Atlantic.' B. C. Roberts, *Unions in America, a British View*, Industrial Relations Section, Princeton University, Research Series No. 97 (Princeton, N.J., 1959), p. 79.

SOCIOLOGICAL ASPECTS

The white collar labor force

When Marx analyzed the social environment in the third volume of *Das Kapital*, workers, capitalists, and landowners were the only categories he recognized; at that time, there were no empirical reasons to mention the white collar group.[1] But only sixty years after the volumes' posthumous publication, Drucker could justifiably use the term 'employee society' to depict our entire social structure.[2] This is a striking illustration of the tempo at which this segment of society has expanded in comparison with other sections of the population.

In the intervening years, sociologists have paid increasing attention to the so-called 'new middle' class. Whereas in 1883 it was scarcely mentioned by Marx, Kautsky in 1922 devoted a whole chapter to its expansion, even though he considered it relatively unimportant, since this nonbourgeois middle class would both sociologically (in class position) and psychologically (in class consciousness) 'become more and more like the proletariat'.[3] Ten years later, Ijzerman, while retaining the formula 'manual workers + office workers = proletariat', acknowledged the existence of deep-rooted psychological differences between the two categories.[4] In 1947, Kruijt continued this line of thought by empirically establishing that there is a cleavage ('dichotomy', 'segregation') between them in many areas, such as home, education, clubs, way of life, work, religion, and marriage. He views blue and white collar workers as 'two distinct worlds that rarely touch, scarcely know each other and lead their own lives'.[5] This theoretical development was taken to its ultimate conclusion in 1952 by the American sociologist Peter Drucker. In direct contradiction of Kautsky, he described how not the office workers are being absorbed by the proletariat, but how, on the contrary, the manual workers are conforming to the pattern of the new middle class. For him this new class dominates the social structure, with 'employeeship' determining the norms and behavior of our working population.[6] Looked at from this point of view, Marx's victory of the proletariat has resulted in a massive process of blue collar acculturation.

All this has had far-reaching consequences for the trade unions. To get some impression of them, we shall examine, in turn, how much the white

[1] '... wage labourers, capitalists and landowners constitute the three big classes of modern society based upon the capitalist mode of production.' Karl Marx, *Capital*, Vol. III, p. 862.
[2] P. F. Drucker, 'The Employee Society', *American Journal of Sociology*, LVIII (1953), p. 358.
[3] K. Kautsky, *Die proletarische Revolution*, p. 33.
[4] A. W. Ijzerman, 'De groei van de nieuwe middenstand', *De Socialistische Gids* (1934), p. 557.
[5] J. P. Kruijt, 'Arbeiders en nieuwe middenstand', (Amsterdam, De Arbeiderspers, 1947), p. 10.
[6] P. F. Drucker, 'The Employee Society', p. 358.

collar labor force has grown, what factors led to its expansion, and how this twentieth-century group is reacting to labor organizations that originated a century ago.

Increase in white collar work

As the white collar group—made up of clerical and sales staff, technicians, supervisors, employed college graduates, and civil servants—grows in numbers, its rate of growth increases. White collar work seems to create the conditions for its own expansion. The acceleration of this expansion is illustrated by trends in the French processing industry given in Figure 2.[1]

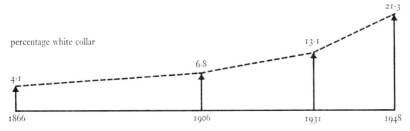

FIGURE 2. The increasing percentage of white collar workers in the French processing industry during the last hundred years.

Since the number of white collar workers increased by 2·7 per cent in the forty years from 1866 to 1906, and by 8·2 per cent in the seventeen years between 1931 and 1948, the graph shows a considerable progression in the growth rate of the new middle class.

There are similar figures for all industrialized countries. In Germany, white collar workers have been increasing faster than blue collar ever since 1907;[2] in Britain, between 1851 and 1951, the percentage of 'clerical labor' in the working population increased from 1·2 per cent to 10·2 per cent;[3] in France and the United States, the proportion of white collar workers in the labor force has in eighty years increased nearly fivefold;[4] and in Sweden, between 1940 and 1950, the number of blue collar workers remained constant, while male white collar workers increased by 70 per cent.[5]

[1] M. Collinet, *Essai sur la condition ouvrière* (Paris, 1951), p. 38; the diagram is based on these figures.

[2] *Verhandlungen des Deutschen Soziologen-Tages* (1948–9), p. 109.

[3] A. Grant, *Socialism and the Middle Classes* (London, Lawrence and Wishart Ltd., 1958), p. 67.

[4] For the United States see B. Solomon, 'The Growth of the White Collar Work Force', *Journal of Business*, XXVII, No. 4 (October 1954), p. 271; for France, see M. Collinet, *Essai sur la condition ouvrière*.

[5] F. Croner, *Die Angestellten in der Gesellschaft* (Frankfurt am Main, Humboldt Verlag, 1954) p. 118.

Predictably, Holland is no exception. Between 1947 and 1959, the white collar group, with a rise in numbers of 58 per cent, grew almost twice as fast as the blue collar group with its 30 per cent increase.[1] This difference in growth rates is seen even more clearly in Figure 3,[2] which shows the rates of increase of white to blue collar workers in Dutch industry between 1953 and 1959.

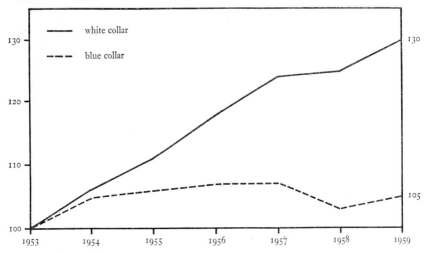

FIGURE 3. The increase of white collar workers in Dutch industry compared with manual workers (1953 = 100).

While the blue collar group in the Dutch working population fell during the period under review from 62 to 58 per cent, the percentage of white collar workers rose from 38 to 42 per cent.[3] This lends support to the prediction that before very long the new middle class will form the majority of Holland's working population, as is already the case in West Germany and the United States. The significance of this for trade unionism is that the working population, whose interests it has traditionally looked after, has completely changed its composition.

Social causes of the change

The white collar group is so heterogeneous in composition that various criteria can be used to subdivide it. According to type of *work*, it can be broken down into technicians and supervisors, clerical and sales staff; according to the nature of *employment*, workers can be classified under

[1] 'Omvang en samenstelling van de Nederlandse beroepsbevolking', (31 October 1959), *Maandschrift van het CBS* (Zeist, De Haan, 1961), Table 5, p. 544.
[2] 'Algemene Industrie Statistiek' (3rd Quarter, 1959), *Maandstatistiek van de Industrie*, I, No. 12 (December 1959), p. 402.
[3] 'Omvang en samenstelling van de Nederlandse beroepsbevolking', *Maandschrift van het CBS*, Table 5, p. 544.

government service, the semipublic sector, and free enterprise. In addition, there are the large categories of *male and female* white collar workers. It would, therefore, seem likely that the sharp increase in the new middle class has more than one cause, and this is confirmed by the facts.

An important factor is that advances in technology increase the need for white collar workers who can design, test, manufacture, and sell processes and equipment. This development has gone furthest in automated firms, which not only have the highest number of technicians but employ no unskilled labor at all. Petrochemical firms in the Rhine delta, for instance, hire on a monthly basis only; unskilled preventive maintenance is carried out by a contractor with workers from outside the firm. In such companies, the 'employee society' has become a concrete reality.

Furthermore, it is not unlikely that the increase in the clerical and sales sectors exceeds that in the technical sector. For example, according to our survey of the 1,700 young white collar workers (males) at the Philips works in Eindhoven, 40 per cent were on the clerical, 15 per cent on the sales, and 45 per cent on the technical staff. In this structure, therefore, 'administration and sales' have overtaken 'development and production'.[1] It is difficult to discuss the factors which have led to this under a single heading. One important element has been the shift in emphasis, already mentioned, from production to sales. Since the 1930s a proper relationship between these two aspects of the economy has become more urgent, the sales force has expanded, and advertising has grown into a want-creation industry, employing white collar personnel almost exclusively.

At the same time, the rise of the limited company, with its obligations to shareholders, and government supervision of taxation and social legislation have led to an extension of the total clerical machinery. Also, when parts of production are passed on to supply companies, there is an accompanying increase in paperwork.

Another group of causes has been described as the 'interpenetration of state and society'. This is most obvious in Western Europe and rather more veiled, but only a little less powerful, in the United States.[2] This

---

[1] M. van de Vall, 'Jonge beambten bij de N.V. Philips' Gloeilampenfabrieken te Eindhoven' (report) (Utrecht, 1959), Table 8, p. 9 (see App. A below). For the United States Melman explains the rise of administrative overhead in manufacturing as partly due to the increasing necessity of coping with more public and private controls. S. Melman, 'The Rise of Administrative Overhead in the Manufacturing Industries of the United States, 1899–1947', *Oxford Economic Papers*, III (1951), pp. 62–112.

[2] For the United States: 'The increasing responsibility of government for economic stability and growth resulted in a rapid rise in the relative importance of the government sector and in a deeper penetration of government into the fabric of economic society in ways that cannot be easily gauged by statistical measures.' S. Kuznets, 'Income Distribution and Changes in Consumption', *The Changing American Population*, ed. H. S. Simpson (New York, Arden House Conference, 1962), p. 57.

interpenetration began in the second half of the last century and has continued. Contemporary Western society is characterized by government manipulation of the business cycle, economic planning, a differential tax policy, and extensive provisions for social security.

As an illustration of the speed with which this government machinery has developed, the number of persons employed in the public services in Germany between 1939 and 1958 rose more than three times as fast as the number in the manufacturing industries; and in the Netherlands, the number of employees in government service increased by 95 per cent between 1947 and 1960, against an increase of 34 per cent in private enterprise.[1] In the United States, state and local government employment is projected to rise between 1965 and 1970 at a rate of nearly 6 per cent a year as compared with about 5 per cent for the 1960–5 period. In comparison, total civil employment is estimated to increase at slightly over 2 per cent a year from 1965 to 1970 as against with about 1·5 per cent between 1960 and 1965.[2]

These statistics point to a general correlation between the rise of the welfare state and the expansion of the white collar group.

A third group of factors is the growth in the West of the 'tertiary' sector. Of the three production sectors distinguished by Fourastié and others, the labor force of the primary one (agriculture) is on the whole diminishing; the secondary one (mining, power, industry, and transport) is growing; but the tertiary sector (services for government, private enterprise and consumers, commerce, banking, and insurance) shows the largest relative increase in manpower.

Comparing the proportions of the labor force employed in the tertiary sector in Western Europe and in the United States for 1950 and 1960, we obtain the trends as shown in Table 3 on p. 19.

Although at first sight markedly different, with the tertiary sector in Britain and the United States almost two times larger than, for example, in Italy and Spain, these figures all exhibit the same trend of expansion. This increase of the tertiary sector has a long history: in some countries it started already in the previous century.

Examining the changes in the three sectors between 1899 and 1959, in the Netherlands, we find that the proportion of the Dutch working population in the primary sector dropped by 19 per cent, the proportion in the secondary sector rose by 8 per cent, while the tertiary sector

[1] German figures based on B. Gleitze, *Wirtschafts- und Sozialstatistisches Handbuch* (Köln, 1960), pp. 36, 38; Dutch figures based on 'Statistisch Zakboek' Den Haag (Staatsuitgeverij, 1966), Table 80, p. 43.

[2] Joseph C. Wakefield, Expanding Functions of State and Local Goverments, 1965–1970', in *Monthly Labor Review*, 1 (July 1967), p. 9.

TABLE 3. *Increase in the proportion of the labor force employed in the tertiary sector in eight Western countries*[1]

	±1950	±1960	1950–60
	%	%	
Spain	26·0 ('50)	27·3 ('60)	+1·3
Italy	21·8 ('51)	29·7 ('61)	+7·9
West Germany	33·9 ('50)	38·0 ('61)	+4·1
France	36·0 ('54)	38·7 ('62)	+2·7
Sweden	38·8 ('50)	41·1 ('60)	+2·3
Netherlands	43·3 ('47)	47·1 ('60)	+3·8
Great Britain	49·4 ('51)	55·9 ('61)	+6·5
United States	50·4 ('50)	55·8 ('60)	+5·4

experienced the greatest increase with 11 per cent.[2] The same picture is seen in Germany, where between 1882 (German Reich) and 1959 (Federal Republic) the primary sector's share of the working population fell by 26 per cent, the secondary sector's share rose by 12 per cent, and the tertiary sector, again showed the biggest increase with 14 per cent.[3]

The trends in Figure 4, based upon Fourastié's computations of the national income, indicate that in this respect Europe is making up its lag behind the United States.[4] Whereas in 1860 France's tertiary sector was far behind that of the United States, it has since expanded faster. If this rate of growth is maintained, the services sector in France will soon cover the same proportion of the national income as in the United States.

Although originating in the nineteenth century, there is little indication that this process has come to an end. On the contrary, the last two decades (1939–61) the number of employees in commerce in West Germany has doubled and the number in banking and insurance has gone up almost 150 per cent.[5] Since banking in Europe is still far from enjoying the popularity which it has in the United States, it is safe to assume that the growth in the tertiary sector will continue there for some time.

[1] The British data are based upon the 'Census of England and Wales', 1951, occupational tables, pp. 1–21, and 1961, occupational tables, pp. 1–6. The other data are based upon the 'Annuaire des Statistiques du Travail', 1954, Bureau International du Travail, Genève, pp. 28–9, pp. 38–9, and pp. 44–7. For the 1960 data upon the 'Yearbook of Labour Statistics', 1966, International Labour Office, Geneva, pp. 84–5; 114–17; 122–5; 128–9. In computing this table the author was assisted by A. J. W. Otten, of the Sociological Institute of the University of Leyden, the Netherlands, and by the Librarians of the Central Bureau of Statistics in The Hague, the Netherlands.
[2] The figures for 1899 are taken from *Zestig Jaren Statistiek in Tijdreeksen*, p. 43. The figures for 1959 are derived from the *Maandschrift van het CBS*, p. 541.
[3] B. Gleitze, *Wirtschafts- und Sozialstatistisches Handbuch*, p. 32. In German statistics, trade is lumped together with commerce, banking and insurance.
[4] Based on J. Fourastié, *Le Grand Espoir du XXe Siècle*, Tables 17 and 18.
[5] Private communication from the Statistisches Bundesamt, Wiesbaden.

Structure of the white collar group

The term 'new middle class' in itself implies that the employees belonging to it are neither manual workers nor entrepreneurs. Within these limits, however, it covers a whole range of ranks and jobs from typist to manager and from policeman to secretary of state. For this reason, it is customary to divide this group into lower, intermediate and higher levels.

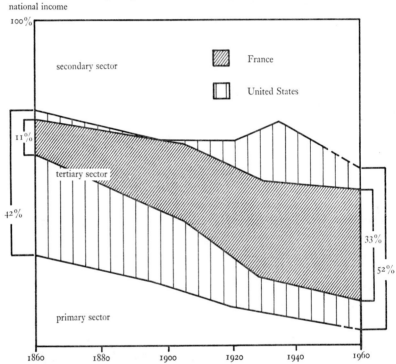

FIGURE 4. The growth of the tertiary sector in France and the United States in the last hundred years.

The lower level

This includes employees who, although their work is exclusively or primarily white collar in nature, are not far above the skilled blue collar worker in their standard of living: storekeepers, costing clerks, lower sales staff, typists and secretaries, filing clerks, lower book-keeping staff, checkers, messengers, porters, foremen and supervisors, 'window clerks', laboratory assistants, opticians' assistants, in fact, everyone performing routine clerical work, simple services, or junior supervisory tasks. This is the group which in Marxist language is termed the 'Stehkragenproletariat', 'black-coated workers', or, when their standard of living is below that of the skilled workman, 'proletaroids'. In most cases, these employees come from blue collar homes, either directly, because, like many foremen and supervisors, they have risen from blue to white collar work in the course of their own careers, or indirectly, because their blue collar parents prepared them for an office job by sending them to high school.

The following processes, all of which have a leveling effect, occur at the lower level of the new middle class.

The introduction of electronic equipment in banking and insurance, wholesale trade, transport, and government agencies has led to increasing displacement of employees performing large-scale, routine clerical operations. An example is banking, where the spread of electronic data-processing has devalued arithmetic skills and reduced the demand for proof and transit clerks, book-keepers, and other routine clerical workers. In the communications industry automatic dial services have diminished the number of telephone operators and other clerical employees.

At the same time, such new jobs as reader-sorter operator, check encoder or inscriber, control clerk and keypunch operator (now being displaced by optical scanning devices) have also been created. In the telephone industry, automated technology has had the effect of increasing the number of linemen, installers and repairmen.

These trends have resulted in the United States after 1957 in a growing amount of dislocation and displacement within the lower white collar ranks, even though the total proportion of white collar occupations in the labor force continued to expand.[1] The data indicate that this usually involves some loss for the displaced workers, e.g. in seniority rights, job protection, rank, savings or wages.[2]

As more women are hired for the lower levels of white collar work, it tends to drop in status. For example, the introduction of women as ticket collectors in public transport soon became a cause, as well as an effect, of male avoidance of this job.

Since there is a tendency to get rid of employees over forty on the sales staff, either for the sake of tradition or because they are too expensive to keep, this group is threatened with unemployment in later life.

In more than one respect, the distinction between the lower level of the new middle class and the higher blue collar levels is becoming blurred.

[1] *Industrial and Occupational Manpower Requirement, 1964–75*, Bureau of Labor Statistics, U.S. Dept. of Labor. Also: Paul Armer, 'Computer Aspects of Technological Change', in *Automation and Economic Progress*, ed. Howard R. Bowen and Garth L. Mangum (Englewood Cliffs, N.J., Prentice Hall, 1966), pp. 68–98; Charles K. Killingworth, 'Structural Unemployment in the United States', in *Employment Problems of Automation and Advanced Technology*, ed. Jack Stieber (New York, St Martin's Press, 1966), pp. 138–40.
[2] William Haber, Louis A. Ferman and James R. Hudson, *The Impact of Technological Change, the American Experiment* (Kalamazoo, Mich., Upjohn Institute for Employment Research, 1963), p. 38.

Skilled manual workers are often more highly paid than junior office staff; collective contracts, once exclusively a blue collar symbol, have been introduced for office workers; and such traditional white collar status symbols as monthly salaries, dispensation from clocking-in, longer holidays, permission to smoke, etc., are now being granted to blue collar workers. Another important point is that while office work is becoming more mechanized, the skilled blue collar worker is gradually doing more clerical work. This latter trend is reaching such proportions that, for skilled blue collar jobs, some firms prefer young workers who have had one or two years' clerical training to vocational school graduates.[1] The contemporary labor market shows a clear tendency toward the formation of a single reservoir of employees who can fill junior white collar and intermediate blue collar jobs.[2]

The intermediate level

Examples of employees at this level are the book-keeper, the trained technologist, the office manager, the journalist, the layout man, and the personnel manager. Higher in the scale are the company's engineers, doctors, economists, and legal staff. These two groups together really comprise the sociological core of the new middle class. One of the fastest growing subgroups is formed by college graduates, who in the United States civilian labor force between 1952 and 1966 increased faster than any other educational group.[3] Within this central group of the new middle class, various social processes are at work with a similar leveling effect. Four of these leveling influences are outlined below.

(*a*) *Material leveling.* When the Communist countries, in which physical and mental work are considered to be of basically equal value, equalize the incomes of blue and white collar workers, it seems normal enough.[4]

---

[1] Between 1952 and 1966 the number of workers, 18 years and over, with a specified number of years of school completed, in the United States civilian labor force, for the groups:

with less than 5 years Elementary School	decreased by 64.4 per cent
with 5 to 8 years Elementary School	decreased by 25.8 per cent
with 1 to 3 years High School	increased by 2.7 per cent
with 4 years High School	increased by 61.6 per cent
with 1 to 3 years College	increased by 54.0 per cent
with *4 years College or more*	increased by *76.9* per cent (!)

Source: *Manpower Report of the President*, U.S. Dept. of Labor, Washington D.C., transmitted to the Congress, April 1967, Table B(9), p. 237.

[2] Mark van de Vall and R. W. Boesjes-Hommes, *Een Onderzoek naar de Situatie van Enkele Lagere Technische Scholen* (Research in Elementary Vocational Schools) (Groningen, Wolters, 1961), p. 13.

[3] Robert K. Burns, 'The Comparative Economic Position of Manual and White Collar Employees', *Journal of Business*, XXVII (October 1954), p. 266.

[4] 'Yugoslav endeavours to overcome contradictions between intellectual and manual work shall be achieved by equalizing the position of intellectual and manual workers in the distribution of income.' A. Deleon, *The Yugoslav Worker* (Belgrade, 1962), pp. 64–5.

There is reason for surprise only when similar leveling occurs in the 'welfare states' of Europe and in the United States, and it indicates that the causes of this leveling are not merely ideological but economic as well.

The trend is quite clear in the United States, where in 1929 the white collar worker's average weekly wage was $7.64 *above* the blue collar worker's, but by 1952 was $2.61 *lower*. Although the incomes of both groups had risen during that period, blue collar incomes rose appreciably faster from 1939 onward (see Table 4). An example of socially consistent leveling is found in Holland, where wages were controlled by centralized bodies, under government influence. There, the combination of an economic process—the changing labor market—and a central policy—regulated wages—led to leveling throughout the entire working population. The Dutch and United States figures are given in Table 4.

TABLE 4. *Material leveling of white collar work in the United States and the Netherlands*

Average weekly income of blue and white collar workers between 1929 and 1952 (1929 = 100) in the United States[1]

Year	Blue collar	White collar
1929	100 ($27.14)	100 ($34.78)
1933	68	85
1937	93	94
1939	94	95
1944	167	125
1946	169	141
1949	209	165
1952	255	191

Gross annual income of blue and white collar workers between 1939 and 1960 (1939 = 100) in the Netherlands[2]

Blue collar	1960 index
Unskilled	476
Semiskilled	447
Skilled	423
White collar	
Fl. 4,000*	289
Fl. 6,000	284
Fl. 8,000	272
Fl. 10,000	256
Fl. 12,000	243
Fl. 15,000	235

*Average annual income in 1939.

[1] R. K. Burns, 'The Comparative Economic Position of Manual and White Collar Employees', p. 260.

[2] These figures are taken from a study of the Dutch CSWV, the country's largest employers' federation.

Although these figures are presented in different ways, they display the same trend. Between 1929 and 1952, blue collar incomes in the United States rose faster than white collar, and the same thing happened in Holland between 1939 and 1960. Although wage statistics for Western Germany cover a shorter period, the same tendency is found there: between 1955 and 1959 the average blue collar income went up by 30·4 per cent, as against 26·5 per cent for the average white collar. This still leaves the average blue collar wage below the average white collar income, but it does indicate a leveling trend.[1]

The Dutch figures actually indicate a twofold leveling of the new middle class; on the one hand, in respect to the entire blue collar group, and, on the other, in respect to its own lower strata. Both processes result in the new middle class having less of a sense of affluence than the blue collar group.[2]

More recently, the United States has seen an 'unleveling' of white-collar work, for between 1950 and 1960 high school trained technologists had a rise in income of 63·7 per cent, as against 38·8 per cent for factory workers. This raises the question of whether the over-all trend is permanent or temporary.[3] In our view, circumstances point towards further leveling. An important factor is the supply of labor: with secondary and higher education open to all, the supply of white collar workers is growing faster than the labor market. In the United States, since 1900, the number of employees with higher education has increased ten times as fast as the entire labor force. The same tendency, though moving at a somewhat slower pace, can be observed in Europe. Then, there is the growing supply of female labor; partly, working wives, partly, women transferring from agricultural or domestic jobs, most of whom are engaged in lower white collar work.[4] All this, together with the upgrading scarcity of skilled manual workers, caused by technological change, will probably lead to further economic leveling between the two groups.

(*b*) *Social leveling.* The intermediate level of the new middle class is experiencing a relative decline of social privileges as well as economic ones. At one time, employed college graduates were appointed mainly to

[1] It should be kept in mind that these figures are relative. The absolute figures give a different picture: between 1955 and 1959, the average white collar income in Western Germany went up from DM 5110 to DM 6465, and the average blue collar income went from DM 3660 to DM 4735. In relative terms, however, blue collar workers had the bigger increase. See 'Die Schichtung der privaten Haushalts-einkommen in der Bundesrepublik', *Wochenbericht des deutschen Instituts für Wirtschaftsforschung* (Berlin, 11 May 1962), XXIX, No. 19, 79.

[2] This does not take into account other factors which can have an upgrading effect for blue collar workers; increased social security, more leisure, mass production of previously limited goods and the increasing availability of education.

[3] E. M. Kassalow, 'White Collar Unionism in the United States'.

[4] R. K. Burns, 'The Comparative Economic Position of Manual and White Collar Employees'.

'line' posts and, by virtue of their close contact with the entrepreneur and the number of their subordinates, they would soon identify themselves with their employer.[1] This reaction, which Merton has termed 'anticipatory socialization',[2] was not without justification in view of their considerable chance of eventually joining management. With the great increase in 'staff' posts in industry, however, this privileged position has, in many instances, been lost. Although company-employed engineers, economists, lawyers, and doctors still have a large measure of autonomy, their chances of rising into management are slight, and they rarely have many subordinates. It has been observed that their direct communication with top management decreases particularly among the younger group.[3]

Another manifestation of social leveling is the fact that the tight labor market forces many European firms into agreements, secret or otherwise, not to accept any of each other's white collar employees who apply for jobs. This threatens to deprive these workers of the greater economic freedom they had by virtue of their specialist occupations and academic qualifications.

(c) *Psychological leveling.* The most marked differences between the intermediate new middle class and lower-level employees are psychological. Because of their intensive education, for instance, the former often identify themselves closely with their profession. This identification can often lead to the rejection of all authority except that of professional colleagues, so that a fellow specialist is more easily accepted as a superior than is a personnel or sales manager. These employees tend to compare their own situation with that of their counterparts in the professional world, and often reveal a distrust of industry and a need to preserve their intellectual independence. Psychological leveling occurs, however, when engineers and other specialists are employed by the hundred in one firm, as is happening more and more frequently as a result of the greater concentration of industry. The authority of fellow specialists then gives way to company discipline, determined mainly by business standards, and independence in one's own job goes by the board. This loss of psychological privilege is often felt as an encroachment on one's personal values and leads sometimes to individual crises.[4]

At a lower level, there will be psychological leveling if West European

[1] H. Verwey-Jonker, 'Commissie Ondernemingsraden, inzake de verenigingen van Hoger Personeel' (Memorandum), *Sociaal Economische Raad* (mimeographed), 5 May 1959.
[2] R. K. Merton and A. S. Kitt, 'Contribution to the theory of reference group behavior', *Continuities in Social Research* (Glencoe, Ill., Free Press, 1950), p. 87.
[3] H. Verwey-Jonker, 'Commissie Ondernemingstraden', pp. 2–3.
[4] G. Homans, *The Human Group* (London, Routledge and Kegan Paul, 1951), Chs. 14 and 15.

industry should abolish the distinction between blue and white collar workers, which is greater there than in either Eastern Europe[1] or the United States.[2] Although status differences in industry are widely accepted,[3] this is decreasingly the case with discrimination against manual work.

There are signs of a move towards equal treatment and, in a study in a European steel firm, we found that most office workers agreed that manual workers were no less reliable than they themselves and they were prepared to accept equal controls.[4]

Both of the above trends, which will probably be completed within a comparatively short time, will have a psychologically leveling effect on the lower and intermediate groups of the new middle class.

(*d*) *Leveling in the civil service.* Finally, civil service work is being leveled along with employment in private enterprise. This is usually felt as a step backward by the civil servants, who at one time occupied a privileged position with regard to social security benefits and promotion prospects. A typical comment from this quarter in Holland is: 'There used to be great differences between the legal, social, and economic provisions for civil servants and those for the employees of private enterprise, but these differences have been dwindling in recent decades, mainly because of measures benefiting the latter.' This relative deprivation has also been observed in the Scandinavian countries, where it is a source of discontent among civil servants.[5] It is probably the reason why, in the United States, unions in the public service area are among the few with increases in the white collar group.[6]

Although these four leveling tendencies are concealed by such trends as the absolute rise in prosperity, the ability to purchase durable consumer

[1] 'In the German Democratic Republic the difference between white and blue collar workers is legally of no significance, since both groups have the same rights and obligations.' 'Angestellten', *Meyers' Neues Lexikon* (Leipzig, 1961), p. 262.

[2] Although there are clear status differences in United States industry, the dichotomy between the blue and white collar worker is less pronounced: the difference in income is smaller and both have finished high school, own a car, and call each other by first name. They may differ in status, but they do not live in two separate worlds.

[3] 'The hours of work symbolize prestige position. Usually the later the worker arrives and the earlier he leaves his job, the higher his status.' 'Usually, the longer and later the lunch hour, the higher the status.' 'The length of vacation, the opportunity to choose the time of the year off, and the number of vacations and holidays off all are indicative of prestige rank.' D. C. Miller and W. H. Form, *Industrial Sociology* (New York, Harper & Row, 1964), pp. 483–6.

[4] M. van de Vall, 'Blue Collar and White Collar Workers in Industry—the Institutionalization of a Dichotomy', Paper presented at the Sixth World Congress of Sociology (Evian, 4–11 September 1966), *passim*.

[5] *Freedom and Welfare, Social Patterns in the Northern Countries of Europe*, ed. G. R. Nelson (Copenhagen, 1953), p. 140.

[6] H. J. Neary, 'American Trade Union Membership in 1962', *Monthly Labor Review* (May 1964), p. 506.

goods, and the individual's increased prospects of upward social mobility, there is undoubtedly a collective and relative retrogression of the white collar group. Their loss of material, social and psychological privileges, as compared with manual workers, and the similar loss by the civil service in comparison with private enterprise, has taken place largely since World War II, and has led to a greater consciousness of their social position on the part of the employees on the intermediate level.

The higher level

Much of what has just been said also applies to the top layer of the new middle class. In fact, the intermediate and upper levels are often difficult to distinguish, and among college graduates the two merge imperceptibly with each other. At this level, we find the civil service department heads, trade union chief executives, university professors, members of parliament, college graduates in industry at the higher income levels, and all others on a par with these. This stratum covers about 5 per cent of the working population and is found mainly in large firms, in banking and insurance, and in businesses employing much high grade personnel. The number of these employees is increasing faster than that of office workers as a whole. In the large corporations, this relatively small group of top executives displays much of the mentality of the entrepreneur, while the civil servants, as representatives of the state, may reveal a dignified conservatism. In small industries, they always work in immediate and personal contact with the entrepreneur, partly because the latter often recruits them from among his own acquaintances. As a result, identification with the firm continues undiminished at the higher level, whereas at the intermediate level it is on the wane. Although material equalization (see Table 4) is hitting this group hardest, its effect is offset by expense accounts, status symbols, a large number of subordinates, and the social power conferred by their position. Unlike what has happened in the intermediate group, the individual character of their work has hardly been reduced at all.

The trade unions and the white collar workers

As more members of the labor force in Western Europe and the United States join the new middle class, the attitude of this social group toward the trade unions is becoming more important and more urgent.

Confounding Kautsky's prediction, today's white collar worker is decidedly *not* noted for a favorable attitude toward manual workers and their organizations. In the first place, this is evident from the fact that he is less often a member of a trade union himself. Only 18 per cent of all white collar workers in the Dutch labor force, for instance, are affiliated with a trade union—the figure is slightly higher in the engineering industry, and, probably, somewhat lower in banking and insurance—as against 40 per cent of blue collar workers. In the United States, 10 per cent of all white collar workers are unionized, in contrast to about 30 per cent of all blue collar workers.[1] A second indication is the fact that when white collar workers do become organized, they sometimes join a different kind of organization, the professional union.

In most European countries, the majority of organized labor belongs to an industrial trade union, i.e. one which includes both blue and white collar workers. In Holland, where 47 per cent of workers are organized, 38 per cent are members of industrial unions. The corresponding figures for Germany are 41 per cent and 33 per cent. Although we find in both countries unions that are exclusively white collar, the majority of organized white collar workers still belong to an industrial union. Business leaders are not always aware of this fact; and it sometimes happens that an employer is prepared to discuss his office worker's problems with a professional organization, but closes the door to industrial organizations.

The professional unions in Western Europe seem to derive most of their support from civil servants. In Germany, 61 per cent of the total membership of these unions is in government service. For Holland, the figure is as high as 88 per cent. Consequently, this kind of union is largely a part of the 'civil service sub-culture'. This means that with regard to the attitude toward middle class trade unionism, we must make a distinction between private enterprise and the state. For whereas white collar workers in industry reject industrial trade unions primarily because they are against *any* form of labor organization, civil servants may reject them because of the greater attraction of professional unions.

A detailed analysis reveals the following differences between these two types of trade union:

(*a*) Although the number of professional unions is often large, many of them are small in size. Sometimes, indeed, their membership is restricted to a specialized and limited occupation, such as harbor pilots, and merchant navy captains, and this adds much to their economic power. A strike of harbor pilots, for instance, can bring shipping to a complete standstill.

(*b*) Professional unions often tend to pass over the interests of the community as a whole and to concern themselves largely with the more limited interests of their own group. The actual statement, 'We fight only for the interests of office workers, nothing else matters to us', is typical of such organizations. This kind of particularist attitude is found less often

[1] H. J. Neary, 'American Trade Union Membership in 1962', pp. 504–6.

in industrial unions with their national responsibilities. It is not unknown, however, in some industrial unions in the United States.[1]

(*c*) Such aims as increasing the occupation's prestige, formulating and watching over professional ethics, furthering and keeping abreast of research, providing special training, instituting professional diplomas, and establishing social links within the profession usually play a larger part in professional than in industrial unions, which are more concerned with material interests. Sometimes the members of a professional white collar organization will bitterly oppose any action that might make it resemble a trade union.[2]

(*d*) Since the professional organization tends to have a less pronounced ideological character, it rarely has ties to a denomination or a political creed. It may even feel that the strongest argument against joining a union federation is that the political commitment of the latter would constitute an unnecessary threat to the unity of the profession.[3] This does not imply, however, that the professional organization never takes part in politics. The most striking example of a politically active professional organization is the American Medical Association (AMA), which, although it has no official link with a political party, is, nevertheless, a politically active and powerful group.[4]

All these qualities combine to increase the number of independent splinter groups in the organizational structure of the new middle class. Often these are sharply opposed to each other. In Europe, there is the opposition between trained technologists and graduate engineers and between dentists and dental technicians, in the United States between physicians and chiropractors, and between academically and hospital-trained nurses. Using the division into lower, intermediate, and upper levels, the organizational structure of the new middle class will now be analyzed more closely.

[1] Briefs quotes the similar view of a well-known American union leader: 'My job is to look after the miners; general prosperity is the government's affair.' G. Briefs, *Das Gewerkschafts-problem, Gestern und Heute* (Frankfurt am Main, Fritz Knapp Verlag, 1955), p. 84.

[2] A. L. Strauss and L. Rainwater, *The Professional Scientist, A Study of American Chemists* (Chicago, Aldine Publishing Co., 1962), pp. 180–1.

[3] In Britain: 'Probably the main reason why the "National and Local Government Officers' Association" and the "National Union of Teachers" and some other unions have remained outside the TUC is the dislike of many of their members for its political associations.' E. Wigham, *What's Wrong with the Unions?* (London, Penguin Books, 1961), p. 66. In Holland with its Socialist, Catholic and Protestant trade unions, many professional organizations object to affiliation with the traditional union federations because they fear it would cause their organization and its members to split into three groups divided by religion. This was the main reason, for example, why the small and weak union of opticians' assistants did not join any of the big federations.

[4] Stanley Kelley Jr., *Professional Public Relations and Political Power* (Baltimore, Johns Hopkins Press, 1966), Ch. 3, 'Medical Economics and Doctor Politics', pp. 67–106.

Lower level and trade union

The consequences for the unions of the transition from a blue collar to a lower white collar level are illustrated clearly by the situation in a number of automated firms which now only employ salaried workers. The following comments were written by a union leader in one such company:

> Our union branch finds that this policy makes it very difficult, if not impossible, to obtain any influence in these firms. *It also mentions the now familiar fact that when blue collar workers of firm X and firm Y are promoted and put on monthly salary they are usually lost to the unions at once.* In those firms monthly salaries do not apply only to the customary white collar jobs, but also to skilled labor, previously ranked as hourly wage jobs.[1]

The union leader commented that this development is of the utmost significance to trade unionism in general. His opinion was widely shared, and the consultation he asked for has since led to a thorough study of this question by his union's central federation. It is symptomatic, however, that no definite solution was reached.

Although this transition from blue to white collar work can undoubtedly have unfavorable effects for the trade union it is still the general impression—and owing to the lack of statistical material it must remain an impression—that at the lower level far more employees are organized than at the two higher levels. The reasons for this are varied: *materially*, lower white collar workers feel their position or promotion often threatened (*a*) by the influx of female employees, (*b*) by the widespread custom of dismissing older salesmen, and (*c*) by the automation of office work.[2] Reorganization resulting from automation, for example, gives the unions new and useful work at this level.[3] The fact that lower white collar employees often have been manual workers themselves or have been brought up in blue collar families is a *social* factor encouraging union membership. This is true even of the border area between lower and

---

[1] D. van Loen, Secretary of the Dutch Union 'ABC', in a letter to the Dutch Federation of Trade Unions (NVV), 6 July 1960.

[2] 'Wherever office work is rationalized, most features of job status undergo a complete change, especially those which largely used to account for the prestige and ambiguous position of a social group *otherwise subjected to the same subordinate status as the other workers*.' 'The division between managerial duties reserved to top and middle management, and the tasks performed by the employees is becoming constantly sharper. Whereas the employee could formerly hope to rise gradually in the hierarchy through a number of intermediate stages, he now finds himself confined to the role of mere operator, which not only fails to prepare him for more highly qualified posts but makes it more and more difficult for him to adjust to situations requiring initiative. Hence ... *possibilities decrease for the employee's self-improvement and promotion* ... *etc.*' C. Marenco, 'Psycho-sociological incidences of office work rationalization on employee status', *Trade Union Information*, no. 35 (Organization for Economic Cooperation and Development), pp. 10–11.

[3] C. T. Plant, 'Some sociological problems raised by the introduction of electronic computers in offices', *Trade Union Information*, No. 35, pp. 26–9.

intermediate white collar groups, as shown by a study of young technicians and office workers in a large European electro-technical concern: the union members among them came significantly more often from a blue collar background than did the nonmembers, and the majority (70 per cent) came from families in which the father was a union member.[1] The presence of a *psychological* factor is indicated by Dahrendorf when he states that, in his own sphere of employment, the lower office worker has virtually the same position as the manual worker elsewhere: 'These posts are in fact largely operative, and within the tertiary sector they are often the real blue collar jobs.'[2] The absence of manual workers makes it unnecessary for them to demonstrate their higher status by adherence to middle-class symbols, thus removing a psychological barrier for joining the union.

Intermediate level and trade union
The greater chance of *individual* advance at this level is one of the reasons members of this category of the new middle class tend to improve their lot individually rather than collectively. The leveling tendencies already described, however, lead to increasing social awareness and to the recognition that one's position can be improved not only through one's personal efforts but also through an organization. This is illustrated by our survey of electrotechnical young white collar workers, who identified themselves predominantly with the intermediate level. When asked about the advantages and drawbacks of their 'white collar collective contract', they showed considerable skepticism and ignorance. Nevertheless:

(*a*) the number of advantages named by each person was greater than the number of drawbacks;

(*b*) the number who declared that the contract had no disadvantages was greater than the number who felt it brought no advantages;

(*c*) the number who thought the contract's advantages outweighed its disadvantages was greater than the number who believed the opposite.[3]

Despite the prevailing doubt and ambivalence, therefore, white collar workers with firsthand experience of collective arrangements are more often for them than against them. Interestingly, the employees in favor of the contract were not a group of malcontents, or unable to keep their positions in any other way. On the contrary, it was found that the ones who were most satisfied and inclined to recommend their company as an employer, also took the most favorable view of the collective agreement.

To look after one's interests collectively, however, is a broader thing

[1] M. van de Vall and J. Roelands, *De jonge Philipsbeambte, zijn cao en de vakbond* (report) (Utrecht, 1959), Chs. 3 and 4.   [2] R. Dahrendorf, *Class and Class Conflict*, p. 53.
[3] M. van de Vall and J. Roelands, *De jonge Philipsbeambte*.

than joining a union, and appreciation of the former does not necessarily imply that the employee will view the latter favorably: only 11 per cent of the white collar workers interviewed belonged to a union and only 10 per cent more replied that they would join if asked. Such figures show that social awareness at this level does not automatically lead to membership in a trade union.

When union leaders, as they are often inclined to do, explain this rejection of unionism solely in terms of the white collar worker's misplaced status feelings, they tend to ignore two facts. The first is that Western industry generally is sharply opposed to employees at the intermediate and senior level joining a trade union. Such action sometimes conflicts so sharply with the management's ideology that it probably robs the employee of any chance of reaching the top.[1]

The second fact is that the white collar worker's economic lot often becomes inextricably tied to the one company for which he works. At the intermediate and higher level, his value depends largely on his clerical, social, technical, or commercial expertise in *internal* company problems. At this level, there is less horizontal mobility—social ascent by moving from one company to another—than vertical mobility—ascent within the hierarchy of his own firm. That part of his interests which he shares with others, outside the firm, is, therefore, relatively small; and, consequently, so is his interest in a union.

The unaccommodating, and sometimes hostile, attitude of management toward the unions, together with the employee's economic dependence on this same management, cause many white collar workers to remain, for safety's sake, outside the trade union movement. As a result, the degree of organization of middle-level office workers, in terms of membership in industrial unions, shows little increase.[2]

Higher level and trade union

Although it is among the higher ranks of the white collar workers that the equalization of incomes is most marked, they show few signs of collective efforts to look after their interests. These employees, most of whom have academic training, identify themselves closely with management, while

---

[1] '... the management of G(eneral) M(otors) regards trade unions as a source of disruptive influence. Union leaders habitually invade managerial prerogatives, make fantastic demands which ignore the "economic facts of life", and the whole range of union activities tends to harm employees' relations "by further separating the manager from the workers"... In view of this estimate spokesmen for GM state it as management's task to deal with the trade union at arm's length and in strictly legal terms...' R. Bendix, *Work and Authority in Industry* (New York, Harper & Row, 1963), p. 329. It is easy to imagine that a white collar worker who belongs to a union stands little chance of being appointed to management staff.

[2] A. L. den Broeder, *De Ontwikkeling van het Ledental der ANMB* (report to the Dutch Metal Workers' Union, The Hague, 1961), p. 5.

senior government officials feel union organization is not in keeping with their status and prestige. The very suggestion of collective action infringes their code of ethics, as illustrated by the professors who objected to the mere question from the vice-chancellor of an old European university: 'Of course we are too respectable to strike.'[1]

The types of organization at this level are (*a*) the scholarly organization, (*b*) the professional organization, and (*c*) very rarely, the trade union. The scholarly organization originated in the learned societies of the seventeenth century, in which experts and laymen joined to make contributions to their subject. These are still found today in many fields: biology, astronomy, geology, archaeology; and, more recently, sociologists and economists have formed national societies in which interested laymen, as well as university teachers, researchers, and executives may delve into their particular branches of knowledge.

As the utilization of learning gradually developed into various occupations, professional organizations grew out of these societies or were founded alongside them. It is characteristic of the professional organization that membership is usually restricted to a select group, such as full-time graduate practitioners, and that it performs other functions for its members besides the purely scholarly one. By furnishing advice on academic training, publishing a professional journal, setting up study groups, and keeping unqualified persons out of the profession, it raises professional standards. By formulating a code of ethics (in medicine, psychology and sociology), it imposes rules of professional conduct and sees to it that they are observed. Its congresses, sometimes attended by thousands, stimulate the individual member, recognize his contribution to knowledge and strengthen his identification with the profession; at the same time, they enable him to become acquainted with latest advances in his subject and to survey the labor market in his field.[2]

Although it seems a small step from professional organization to trade union, the step is rarely taken. One practical difficulty is that employers can join a professional organization—and they often do—but can hardly belong to a trade union. A more important factor, however, is that the members tend to regard collective bargaining and trade unions as socially inferior, as negative status symbols that would lower them to the level of the office worker. Another factor is that, in the eyes of the senior official, 'management thinking'—as contrasted with the 'labor thinking' of the trade unions—goes with his status (whether real or imagined).

[1] S. Groenman, *Correspondentieblad der Centrale van Hogere Rijksambtenaren*, No. 346, p. 116.
[2] W. Kornhauser, *Scientists in Industry: Conflict and Accommodation* (Berkeley, University of California Press, 1962), p. 86.

In the rare cases when a professional organization institutes collective bargaining, its demands differ sharply from those of a union. Kornhauser states that it will often claim special status for its members, above that of other employees, or demand an increase in the highest income levels of the profession rather than the lowest. The American Society of Civil Engineers and the American Chemical Society are known to have started collective bargaining *temporarily*, to forestall the incursion of trade unions into their occupational groups.[1]

For these reasons, the number of senior officials belonging to traditional unions rarely exceeds a few hundred, and when they do join, it is generally as a matter of principle. Some trade unions are planning to grant them a special (and higher) status in their organizations, but it is doubtful that this will alter the situation.

The blurring of class boundaries, the changing social stratification in which occupation competes with property as a yardstick, the explosive expansion of the white collar group, all these processes have drastically altered the environment of trade unionism. The social conditions which, a century ago, led manual workers to join the trade unions seem for the modern white collar worker to be absent, or less powerful, or counteracted by opposing forces.

The conclusion of the previous section, therefore, that there are pronounced economic differences between nineteenth-century society and the union's present environment, applies equally well in the sociological area.

PSYCHOLOGICAL ASPECTS

Mentality and the trade union

A third difference between the class society and the welfare state is psychological, that is, there has taken place a massive change in mentality. Such changes are not new in the history of labor and have been of great importance to trade unionism. For the movement owes its origin not only to the actual 'pauperization' of the working proletariat[2] but also to the nascent consciousness that this situation could be changed by collective action.

At the beginning of the nineteenth century, unmitigated poverty had

---

[1] W. Kornhauser, *Scientists in Industry*, pp. 105–6.

[2] 'Families tried in every way possible to achieve a reasonable income so as to keep extreme poverty at bay. Whole families would sit round the table shelling peas for a ridiculously small wage. Life was made still more difficult by the use of gin as a temporary narcotic and to relieve the ever-present pangs of hunger.' W. van de Vall, 'Een paar losse herinneringen aan de arbeidersbeweging in Groningen bij de eeuwwisseling', *Cultureel Maandblad*, III, No. 8 (October 1962), p. 169.

led to widespread apathy and resignation. 'If we consider the worker's personality,' writes Brugmans, 'we see someone who resigns himself listlessly to his miserable existence; who lacks the physical and mental strength to get any higher; and who is so uneducated that the possibility of improving his lot never even crosses his mind.'[1] Subservience and dread of the master had become traditional. 'It was this tradition more than anything else', Hudig declares, 'that hampered the growth of the unions: the masses had no nerve.'[2]

The change in attitude of the working classes, about the middle of the last century, was rooted primarily in the new perspective that by banding together they could improve their lot. Henriette Roland Holst describes how the workers became aware of their strength, and how 'throngs of thousands of human beings, singing resounding battle songs or in solemn silence, flowing in endless waves through streets and squares' gave this realization concrete form. From its own display of strength,' she declares, 'the proletariat imbibed hope and courage.'[3] The new prospect of economic security had increased the need for it; and this led to the formation of trade unions as we know them today.

Just as in the last century Marx and Engels observed that changes in society were accompanied by changes in the ideas and desires of the working population,[4] so nowadays we are faced with the question of whether or not the affluent society and the welfare state are accompanied by another change in the mentality of the working masses. Theoretically, this is possible. According to modern social psychology, changes in the sociocultural situation are often accompanied by shifts of emphasis in the individual's need structure.[5] Sociological data confirm this: investigators report that the basic personality[6] of the European worker is changing, that characteristics formerly in the background of his personality structure are becoming more accentuated, while others are gradually growing weaker. Some call it the Americanization of the European worker.

---

[1] I. J. Brugmans, *De arbeidende klasse in Nederland in de 19e eeuw* (The Hague, 1929), p. 181.
[2] D. Hudig, J., *De vakbeweging in Nederland 1866–1878* (Amsterdam, 1904), p. 24.
[3] H. Roland Holst-van der Schalk, *Revolutionnaire Massa Aktie* (Rotterdam, 1918), p. 93.
[4] K. Marx, *Communist Manifesto*, pp. 51–2.
[5] 'The membership of any significant group must necessarily reflect itself in various changes in the individual's psychological field and therefore in his need structure.' D. Krech and R. S Crutchfield, *Social Psychology, Theory and Problems* (New York, McGraw-Hill, 1943), p. 384.
[6] On this concept: 'The cultures of mankind vary widely among themselves, but each one has the effect of producing a certain similarity in personality among the individuals who practice the culture. These similarities among members of a social group have been called by such names as "basic personality structure".' John Gillin, 'Personality Formation from the Comparative Cultural Point of View', *Personality in Nature, Society and Culture*, ed. C. Kluckholn and H. A. Murray (New York, A. A. Knopf, 1949), p. 165.

The new mentality

Social research in a number of countries indicates that changes are taking place among the younger generations of West European workers: that they depend less upon collective action to improve their condition and tend to concentrate more on individual problems.

As for the first aspect of change, the turning away from collective ideals and organizations, Kluth finds, in Germany, that 'the young man today no longer views his destiny as a collective destiny',[1] while Lohmar describes a decline in the young worker's desire to belong to a social group and to advance with that group.[2] French researchers have noticed an abstention from trade union and political problems and a general 'dépolitisation du monde ouvrier'.[3] In Britain, Zweig quotes the comment: 'The more the industry becomes socialist, the less socialist the men become.'[4] In a later publication, he examines the modern British worker's tendency to unite less with his fellows, whether in organizations, in informal groups, or in his spare time. Unlike the worker of the past, he rarely sees his workmates outside working hours; there are no more united wage campaigns, and little mutual aid is asked or given. He sees the trade unions for what they are: they are efficient at their jobs and should get on with it.[5] Similar observations are made in Holland,[6] where the new generations consist of level-headed young people who, businesslike and practical, avoid existing idealistic organizations.[7]

The second aspect of this psychological change, the heightened concentration on one's own personal affairs, is an extension of the first, and once again the reports from different countries are similar in tone.

The situation in Austria is aptly described by Bednarik, who after intensive observation reaches the conclusion that the outlook of the older worker was determined by a social utopia, whereas the young worker is influenced by dreams of personal affluence and advance.[8] Lohmar talks

[1] H. Kluth, in H. Schelsky, *Arbeiterjugend, gestern und heute* (Heidelberg, 1955), p. 216.
[2] D. Lohmar, in H. Schelsky, *Arbeiterjugend*, p. 138.
[3] See, for instance, *Le Populaire Dimanche* (17 June 1951); also Marcel David, 'Le Monde Ouvrier' in Georges Vedel, éd., *La Dépolitisation, Mythe ou Réalité?* (Paris, Libr. Armand Collin, 1962), pp. 213–49.
[4] F. Zweig, *The British Worker* (London, Pelican, 1960), p. 191.
[5] F. Zweig, 'The New Factory Worker', *The Twentieth Century*, June 1960.
[6] For example, the following remark by a young employee: 'Things are very different now from when my father was young. If I had been living then, I too would have fought for better social provisions and holidays. But this is not necessary any longer, and *now I honestly wouldn't know what to fight for*. Anyway, the government does an awful lot.' (Interview No. 219, in the Survey of Appendix A (2)).
[7] M. Tjebbes and H. A. Wigbold, 'Wordt de P.v.d.A. de partij van de Dreestrekkers?' *Vrij Nederland* (15 November 1958), p. 4.
[8] K. Bednarik, *Der junge Arbeiter von heute—ein neuer Typ* (Stuttgart, 1953), p. 55.

of 'an inclination to confine oneself to the private sector',[1] a tendency described by Lockwood in Britain as the 'privatization of the worker'.[2]

Zweig concludes that the modern British worker is directing more of his attention to family life, tending to loosen his ties with the working community, and concentrating more on himself as an individual. 'Home-centredness and personalization, together with the decline in gregariousness, mean a greater individualization of the worker' is his final summing-up.[3]

In Holland, Goudsblom has discovered that what he terms the 'new adults' set their hopes for the future lower than their parents did and have more modest and more personal ideals;[4] Ruitenberg believed that young people today have a different outlook than in 1912 or 1919 and that their own personal responsibilities weigh too heavily for them to carry 'the whole world' as well.[5]

These trends also are seen in modern literature. In the writers of the 'beat generation', we find this same alienation from society and from the ideals of the older generation. This generation feels no concern with the world of its fathers and so does not even oppose it.[6] Its attitude is of disaffiliation from, rather than transformation of, society.[7]

The 'basic personality' of the nineteenth-century working population with its *class*-awareness was the psychological condition for the rise of the trade unions. In the affluent welfare state, however, organized labor is faced with a new personality type in which *self*-awareness has grown. Whether this is a temporary or a permanent condition depends partly on the underlying causes.

Causes of 'individualization'

With regard to the first condition, absence of collective ideals, sociologists agree that a generation can hardly feel emotionally involved in things that have become so much a part of everyday life as trade unions, social

---

[1] D. Lohmar, in H. Schelsky, *Arbeiterjugend*, p. 121.

[2] D. Lockwood, 'The New Working Class', *Archives Européennes de Sociologie*, No. 2 (1960), p. 254. [3] F. Zweig, 'The New Factory Worker'.

[4] J. Goudsblom, *De nieuwe volwassenen, een enquête onder jongeren van 18 tot 30 jaar* (Amsterdam, 1959), p. 56.

[5] L. H. Ruitenberg, 'De Klassieke Jeugdbeweging', *Wending*, XI (1956-7), p. 255.

[6] In 'A Being of Distances', A. Trocchi writes about the main character: 'Sometimes he watched men or women or traffic in the streets, but always from the outside and with the same feelings with which he would have listened to a story which had no point; and yet there they were, everything, everyone, each under his umbrella, each under his own lie of significance.' *The Outsiders* (New York, Signet Books, 1961), pp. 122-3.

[7] These observations seem at variance with the increased militancy among college students in Europe and the United States. Although research has found these militants to be a small minority whose political means and goals are denounced by the majority of their fellows, the possibility of this action indicating a reversal of the trend toward self-absorption cannot be discounted. One thing however appears to be certain: the new militancy shows little inclination toward identification with the 'established' union movement.

insurance, and an income which offers them durable consumer goods. Raised in a society with public welfare provisions and trade union services, the younger generation accepts them as the products of technological progress, without a sense of gratitude or victory.[1] Part of the reason they feel no involvement in the welfare state is that they did not watch it develop. Laserre, describing the same reaction in the cooperative movement, terms this 'the problem of the second generation':[2] the contemporary form of conflict between successive generations.

The causes of the second condition, growing self-awareness, lie chiefly in the increased opportunities for social advancement, both from one generation to another (intergenerative) and within the same generation (intragenerative). As for intergenerative advance, the growth of the new middle class increased the number of white collar jobs and ranks, giving the working man's son greater scope to ascend to an office job. Although in time more of these posts will be filled from the new middle class itself,[3] such factors as urbanization, the lower birth rate among the upper strata of society, and a democratic educational system still leave the ambitious blue collar child enough opportunity to work his way up. As a result, more people have risen socially than have fallen in the welfare state. A sample of 400 employees in a Dutch city showed subjective social ascendance, in comparison with the male parent, to outweigh social decline among both blue collar and white collar workers.[4] In the category of the white collar workers, the ascents even outnumbered the descents by two to one. It is safe to assume, since this tendency has been confirmed by both European and United States investigators,[5] that it is common to

[1] H. Schelsky, *Die skeptische Generation* (Düsseldorf, 1958), p. 468.
[2] G. Laserre, 'Le Fonctionnement de la démocratie coöpérative', *Revue des études coöpératives*, XXIX (April–June 1957), p. 73.
[3] In the random sample survey (n = 473), representative for all young office workers at Philips, Eindhoven, 44 per cent were found to come from 'new middle class' families and 28 per cent from blue collar and farm backgrounds. Sons of manual workers were rarest on the sales staff (15 per cent) and most common among scientific researchers (38 per cent). See van de Vall, 'Jonge beambten bij de N.V. Philips' Gloeilampenfabrieken', p. 13; see also App. A(5) below.
[4] Based on the semi-structured questions: 'What is/was your father's occupation?' 'What is your occupation?' 'Compared with your father's occupation, do you think your position is now equal to his?' 'Why?' With younger workers, future expectations were taken into account. The survey was carried out in Utrecht, under the author's supervision, by the Sociological Institute of Utrecht University. See also App. A (2) and (3).
[5] '. . . in each succeeding decade a larger percentage of employed persons is to be found in occupational classifications (such as professional, nonfarm managers and officials, etc.) that require a relatively high level of educational attainment, pay high wages and have a high socio-economic status.' M. W. Reder, *Labor in a Growing Economy* (New York, John Wiley & Sons, 1957), p. 22.
    'It has been frequently observed that there appears to be more occupational ascent than descent.' T. Caplow, *The Sociology of Work* (Minneapolis, University of Minnesota Press, 1954), p. 621.

advanced industrial society. Consequently, 'ascent' is spreading as the social norm and also applies to the *blue* collar worker.

Independent of its external causes, this process may be expected to develop its own impetus. For the widespread occurrence of social ascent, in turn, stimulates the urge to advance: 'In such an indefinite social structure', writes Schelsky, 'the desire to advance becomes the essential trait of social consciousness.'[1] The conclusion is that the desire for individual advance will take a more and more prominent place among the needs of the working population.

Similar tendencies occur in respect of intragenerative advance, i.e. within one's individual career. For one psychological effect of the labor shortage is that the worker is stimulated to improve his position by changing his job. Another effect is that he becomes more aware of his value to the company, which bolsters his self respect and increases his individualism. Golden and Ruttenberg report a similar individualization among workers in the 1920s, when there was a shortage on the United States labor market.[2] There is an accompanying tendency, viz. to reject the trade unions because the opportunity for individual advance has weakened the interest in collective action.

In addition to such macrosocial causes as urbanization, democratic education, increase in white collar work, and a tight labor market, there are also microsocial factors at work, i.e. within the firm. In big industry, the conception of labor as a free commodity, negotiable at short notice, is gradually being replaced by a more humane view which allows for greater job satisfaction and loyalty to the firm.[3] As a result, changes in the industrial structure gradually take into account the blue collar worker's desire to advance. Foote reports that the United States steel industry is extending its blue collar hierarchy to increase upward mobility.[4] This trend, called the 'movement from jobs to careers' covers—as in the white collar sphere—an ascending scale of ranks and jobs up which the worker can climb in the course of his career. German sociologists call this the 'Etatisierung' of manual labor,[5] while Dahrendorf talks of a 'new

[1] H. Schelsky, *Wandlungen der deutschen Familie in der Gegenwart*, p. 228, quoted in J. Idenburg, *Op het keerpunt der onderwijs-geschiedenis* (Groningen, Wolters, 1957), p. 69.
[2] 'The individualism of the workers, so evident in the twenties, when union membership reached a low point, grew out of this relative freedom of action.' C. S. Golden and J. J. Ruttenberg, *The Dynamics of Industrial Democracy* (New York, Harper & Brothers, 1942), pp. 3–4.
[3] R. A. Lester, *As Unions Mature* (Princeton, N.J., Princeton University Press, 1958), p. 37.
[4] N. N. Foote, 'The Movement from Jobs to Careers', *Transactions of the Third World Congress of Sociology* (Amsterdam, I.S.A., 1956), p. 1.
[5] 'In respect of white collar workers Fritz Marbach has already referred to a "Veretatisierung" of the modern company, i.e. a transition to conditions like those enjoyed by civil servants; *to an increasing extent the same will apply to blue collar workers.*' H. Kluth, in H. Schelsky, *Arbeiterjugend*, p. 132, my italics. Later, Kluth goes more deeply into the young German worker's increased need to advance individually.

qualification structure' in blue collar work in which promotion depends on personal qualities (sense of responsibility, adaptability, grasp of job, intelligence) as well as on technical skills.[1] The introduction of the 'expert' rank at the Philips works in Holland is probably symptomatic. While the lower and intermediate ranks of office workers enjoyed more fringe benefits (e.g. better working hours; greater chances of promotion; less strict disciplinary measures in respect of fines, punching-in, and permission to smoke; longer holidays; no loss of pay in case of sickness or accident), the new arrangement also grants these privileges to the blue collar 'expert'.[2] There are signs that the labor shortage causes firms to enlarge the career perspective of even *unskilled* workers.[3]

A related factor is what in United States industry is called the 'professionalization of labor'.[4] This is also being copied on the European scene: it is the policy by which company loyalty is obtained—not only by increased chances of promotion but also by titles granted to skilled workers, such as 'instrument maker first class' or 'turner second class'.[5] Kluth has observed that factory workers granted the title 'Chemiebetriebswerker' (chemical operatives) showed more keenness in their work and greater loyalty to their company, and he attributes this to their belief that they have escaped from the general and anonymous category of 'workers'. The policy, followed at Krupp in West Germany, is one which seems to meet the workers' need for individualization.[6]

Various researchers point out that the younger blue collar workers are especially sensitive to this change in the industrial structure. Kluth reports that of the young factory workers he interviewed no less than 83 per cent believed they had prospects of promotion within their firm and only 5 per cent emphatically denied it.[7] In the same vein is the observation, in a study of Dutch youth, that even among younger unskilled workers opportunities for advancement increase company loyalty.[8] The appreciation of the many avenues to the higher ranks in big industry is also reflected in the young workers' widespread preference for this type of firm.[9]

[1] R. Dahrendorf, *Class and Class Conflict*, p. 47.
[2] 'Statusgroeperingen', een studie over de ontwikkeling van de sociale status en rechtspositie van handarbeiders en lagere beambten bij de N.V. Philips' (report) (Eindhoven, 1955), p. 27.
[3] Illustrated by an advertisement for personnel by General Tyre in Amsterdam, which expressly offered opportunities for training and promotion to *unskilled* workers.
[4] N. N. Foote, 'The Professionalization of Labor in Detroit', *American Journal of Sociology*, LVIII, No. 4 (January 1953), p. 371.
[5] H. D. Zeelenberg, 'Sociale waardering voor hoofd- en handarbeid', *Mens en Onderneming*, IV (1950).
[6] H. Kluth, in H. Schelsky, *Arbeiterjugend*, p. 138.   [7] *Ibid.* p. 138.
[8] *Moderne jeugd op weg naar volwassenheid* (The Hague, Staatsuitg., 1953), p. 108 f.
[9] H. Schelsky, *Arbeiterjugend*, p. 252.

Trade unions and the new mentality

This new mentality is of particular importance to the unions in connection with the structural changes in industry which integrate the employee more closely into the company, both objectively and subjectively. According to Mallet, *objective* integration is proceeding in three ways:

(*a*) In *income*, as employees' wages become more closely linked with the economic growth of the company or industry as a whole. Regardless of individual achievement, the firm's economic prospects are gaining a much greater influence in collective labor agreements and wages, and the rapid spread of profit sharing plans tends to reinforce this.

(*b*) In *dependence*, since even the skilled craftsman's job is being limited to a small number of machines, often built especially for the company, and this reduces his mobility on the labor market.

(*c*) In future *prospects*, as a continuing labor shortage causes employers to counteract the labor turnover by means of long-service bonuses and career prospects.[1] In the United States, trade union-enforced seniority rules have a similar effect. In this way, the future of employer and employed are becoming more integrated.

Subjective integration results from the fact that industry is gradually moving towards the independent, self-financed corporation, in which the 'external' shareholders are losing power and influence to the 'internal' management. Some managers will have risen from the ranks of ordinary employees and, thus, will more easily identify themselves with the latter. A more humane attitude toward labor and working morale may, to some extent, be a result of this. If, on their part, the employees become more closely involved with the company, it is conceivable that their economic as well as their psychological needs will eventually converge with the aims of industry, as viewed by the modern manager.

This raises the question of whether or not such an integrated industrial community would still have room for an external power group like the union. On the employers' side this question is already being answered: one authoritative view is that 'the trade union becomes superfluous and even harmful if, in representing the firm's employees, it disrupts the working community by suggesting a conflict of interest'.[2] Since this problem is central to the unions' position in modern industry, we will discuss it in more detail in Chapter 2. Here we may conclude, however, that the affluent society and the welfare state represent a new environment for organized labor, not only economically and sociologically, but also psychologically.

---

[1] S. Mallet, *La Nouvelle Classe Ouvrière* (Paris, Editions du Seuil, 1963), pp. 54–7.

[2] A. M. Kuylaars, 'Onderneming en Vakvereniging', *Mens en Onderneming*, IV (1950). (Dr Kuylaars is a director of a large mining company.)

POLITICAL ASPECTS

Politics and the unions

As with many other social movements which originated in the nineteenth century, moral, religious, and political ideals have played a major part in European trade unionism. Some countries at first had nonpolitical trade unions, but in the long run none of the major European unions has preserved its political neutrality.[1] Conversely, attempts to replace political labels by the term 'general' have seldom fully succeeded.[2]

This situation has changed so little that a United States observer still warns anyone who wants to understand European trade unionism neither to neglect its political background nor to forget that in Europe 'politics' is a positive factor, with an ideological, philosophical, and even mystical content.[3] Of the various political movements behind organized labor, socialism is undoubtedly the oldest. Many European unions were founded by socialists or became connected after some time with the socialist movement.

Although the importance of the Catholic and Protestant unions in some West European countries is considerable, they are not as important internationally. In many cases, they are a result of the rise of socialism or a reaction against it. The reason for this may be that Christianity gives first priority to neighborly love, represented by charity toward fellow men in need, whereas socialism aims for a society from which such need is banished. It was not until the end of the nineteenth century that, influenced by socialist ideas, Christian circles gradually adopted this latter attitude and put it into practice by founding trade unions. This might explain why most of the denominational unions are of a later date and are internationally less widespread.

As for the historical relationship between unionism and socialism, this gradually weakened after World War II. However, in most European countries where trade union and socialist party have dissolved their formal ties, a sociological bond has remained. Many union officials will belong to the socialist party, union and party members will sit on each other's committees, union leaders (often in consultation with their central committees) will hold socialist seats in parliament, and the programs of both organizations may coincide on a number of points.[4] Sturmthal's view is therefore correct: anyone wishing to understand trade

[1] W. H. Vliegen, *Die onze kracht ontwaken deed* (Amsterdam, Arbeiderspers), p. 275.
[2] *Ibid.* p. 59.
[3] A. Sturmthal, *Unity and Diversity in European Labor*, p. 39.
[4] See the constitution and rules of the Dutch Federation of Trade Unions, given royal assent on 11 December 1959, and the basic program of the Dutch Labor Party.

unionism in the European welfare state must get to know contemporary socialism.

After an analysis of the factors which have recently influenced socialism, some of the changes in its ideals will be indicated. Finally, we shall try to find out whether or not any trend within postwar socialism might again link it to the trade unions.

Welfare state as socialism

The relationship of the welfare state to socialism is aptly described by Crossman, when he calls the welfare state the successful adaptation of capitalism to the demands of modern trade unions.[1] This definition states the two major elements in their relationship: (*a*) although a social system like the welfare state partly meets the requirements of socialist ideals, (*b*) it cannot be called socialist, since it has essentially maintained the capitalist economic structure. To show how this 'welfare-capitalism' influences socialism as a trade union ideal, i.e. as a complex of ideals appealing to the majority of workers, we shall review some of its characteristics.

The power structure

In the nineteenth century, economic power rested chiefly with the owners of the means of production. The government restricted itself to the exercise of military and civil control and there were only first signs of the formation of power among the workers. It was not until about the turn of the century that the integration of government into society began which so far has had its climax in the welfare state.

As a result of this integration of state and society, governmental economic power has long since overtaken that of private business. A similar integration into society has taken place with the third power group: the trade unions and employers' associations, which are now thoroughly involved in the nation's economic and social policy. Consequently, the welfare society has a 'plural' power structure, where policy is hammered out by the three sectors of society together: industry, government, and the large politico-economic organizations.

Another consequence is that important socialist ideals have been realized incidentally. Myrdal's view that European industry has undergone a silent process of socialization in the welfare state is supported by such facts as the double taxation of company profits, both as revenue and as dividend, by governmental supervision of industrial agreements, by the control of personnel (particularly dismissals) and wage policy, and by restrictions on investment and on relocation of industries.

[1] R. H. S. Crossman, 'Towards a Philosophy of Socialism', *New Fabian Essays* (London, Turnstile Press, 1953), p. 6.

At about the same time as Europe's socialist parties are giving up the idea of nationalization, Myrdal concludes, European industry is being subjected to gradual nationalization.[1] In this way, the power structure of the welfare state, to some extent, approaches socialist ideals.

The authority structure

Within the company, shifts in authority are taking place because the bulk of internal power is gradually being transferred from ownership to management. As ownership becomes spread among a large number of anonymous shareholders, the authority in the company is gravitating more and more toward its administrative and technical directors. Industrial sociologists have pointed out that, from the point of view of labor and contrary to Burnham's pessimistic predictions,[2] this development is not necessarily unfavorable. With the disappearance of the old-style 'capitalist' and the advent of expert managers, many of whom have risen within the firm, the chances of more democratic industrial relations may even be increasing.[3] There are signs that these expectations are not unfounded; one such sign is the tendency, confirmed by union officials, toward a gradual decline in industry's resistance to organized labor and a greater willingness, particularly in the employers' federations, to accept the unions as equal partners. This change in the direction of a more democratic structure of industrial authority is another step toward the realization of socialist aims.

The social structure

With the arrival of the affluent society and the welfare state, fundamental social relationships of the last century have finally been consigned to the past. During the past fifty years, the dichotomy between proletariat and bourgeoisie has made way for a more differentiated social structure in which occupational, power, property, interest, and status categories are constantly shifting, both internally and with respect to each other.

The only positions which remain comparatively static, in König's view, are the two extremes of 'Lumpenproletariat' and 'Grossbourgeoisie'.[4] In between these poles, however—and here König is backed by the French sociologist Aron—a process of differentiation is taking place in which class loyalty is giving way to identification with occupational, cultural, or

---

[1] G. Myrdal, *Beyond the Welfare State, Economic Planning in the Welfare States and Its International Implications* ('Store Lectures') (New Haven, Conn., Yale University Press, 1958). It goes without saying that these two processes of nationalization are not identical.

[2] J. Burnham, *The Managerial Revolution* (London, Penguin Books, 1954).

[3] F. van Heek, 'Klassen- en Standenstructuur als Sociologische Begrippen' (Speech given in Leiden, 1948), p. 20.

[4] R. König, *Soziologie Heute* (Zürich, 1949), p. 68.

interest groups.[1] The static class boundaries of the past, determined largely by hereditary wealth, are being replaced by a more dynamic structure, more opportunity for social mobility, and, as a result, greater individual freedom. The 'ascribed' status derived from factors outside the individual's control (inherited wealth, a noble title, parental environment, etc.) is losing ground to the 'achieved' status based upon individual ability and achievement.[2] This suggests that social justice is increasing and, hence, that modern society is realizing another socialist ideal.

The security culture

In relation to the economic and social situation before World War II, with its cycles of unemployment, the welfare state differs mainly in the way the government guards full employment. As a result, economic security has undoubtedly increased.

Security has also increased at another level, viz. in the expansion of social legislation. The hand-to-mouth existence of the old-style blue collar worker, of whom Kautsky once wrote 'Capitalism has brought them insecurity, misery, oppression, servitude, humiliation, exploitation',[3] is virtually a thing of the past. Indeed, it is not unlikely that the contemporary wage earner enjoys greater social security than many a nineteenth-century employer. Friis reports that the Western welfare states devote between 10 and 15 per cent of their net national incomes to social welfare.[4] This trend probably reaches its peak when, as in Britain and Sweden, socialized medicine is extended over all income levels and the last vestiges of class have disappeared from the social security system. It scarcely needs mentioning that this security culture is in conformity with socialist desires.[5]

Ideological implications

It was to be expected that these social reforms would not be without effect politically, particularly on socialism. We have already encountered some of the major consequences of the fact that many of socialism's aims have been realized in the welfare state. Despite the resulting satisfaction in labor circles, at the same time it cannot be denied that these aims have

[1] 'Au lieu d'une prolétarisation, c'est-à-dire, de la confusion des millions des travailleurs dans la condition ouvrière, des différenciations croissantes et parmi les travailleurs d'industrie et parmi les professions extérieures à l'industrie, au sens étroit du terme.' Aron, 'Remarques sur les particularités de l'évolution sociale', p. 44.

[2] R. Linton, *The Study of Man* (New York, 1936), p. 115.

[3] K. Kautsky, *Die proletarische Revolution*, p. 53.

[4] H. Friis, 'The application of sociology to social welfare planning and administration', *Transactions of the Fourth World Congress of Sociology* (Milan-Stresa), II (London, International Sociological Association, 1959), p. 63.

[5] G. Myrdal, *Beyond the Welfare State*, p. 72.

ceased to act as guides. 'The very successes of the labor movement destroy the foundations of its idealism', writes Schelsky, while in Fance, Spinelli concludes that in the welfare state socialism has lost its ideological content and that its unions and parties are faced with the historic task of self annihilation.[1] In Germany, Kaiser considers the chances of new and vigorous trade union ideals negligible,[2] and similar opinions are heard in Britain and the United States.[3] Apart from the question of whether it would be advisable or not, it seems highly unlikely that the socialist unions will follow Spinelli's advice. For history shows that a reorientation of ideals is quite possible: the transition from Marxism to Revisionism is one example that socialism can adapt itself to changing conditions. As yet, it is impossible to say whether or not the labor movement will achieve an ideology of the welfare state. Nevertheless, we can try to discover which branch of socialism might lend itself best to this kind of reorientation.

The socialist ideologies

With regard to its goal-setting role for the trade unions, postwar socialism can be divided into four branches; some exist explicitly as active movements, others are implicit in articles, attitudes, etc. They are: (*a*) orthodox socialism as formulated by Marxism and later by Revisionism, (*b*) utopianism, found primarily in theoretical writings, (*c*) the pragmatism prevalent among the labor movement's leadership, and (*d*) personalism, found in Protestant and humanist circles.

Orthodoxy

During the last century, the doctrine of Marx and Engels, later revised by Bernstein, brought thousands of workers into the ranks of the socialist trade unions. Psychologically, it gave their cheerless existence an eschatological outlook. Today, however, the days of socialist orthodoxy as a political stimulus are virtually past. For history has not realized its leading doctrines, which predicted the fall of capitalism, its replacement by collective ownership of the means of production, the transition from class struggle to classlessness, and the decline of national identities and

---

[1] A. Spinelli, 'Le Socialisme, ideé et mouvement', *Preuves*, No. 106 (December 1959), p. 41.

[2] J. N. Kaiser, *Die Repräsentation organisierter Interessen* (Berlin, 1956).

[3] In Britain: 'The welfare state, which is neither capitalism nor socialism, has been created. This was a development which no theory had bargained for. But whereas capitalists may find it expedient to accept the new status quo, even to acclaim it as their own invention, socialists are now divided and confused. The very success of their achievements seems to threaten the ground beneath their feet.' *Twentieth Century Socialism, the Economy of Tomorrow* (London, Socialist Union, 1956), pp. 15–17.

In the United States: 'We have been successful. That's why it is so difficult to change.' 'When it fails, it seems that nothing fails like success.' E. Kassalow, quoted by T. B. Morgan, 'Is Labor on the Skids?' *Look* (11 September 1962).

the assimilation of the middle class by the proletariat. According to Burnham, if the gap between reality and a political ideal becomes too wide, it will lose its grip on the masses.[1] It is, indeed, a fact that the widening gulf between the Marxist view of society and the reality of the welfare state has been accompanied by a weakening of the 'pull' of its doctrine. Nowhere is this more sharply felt than among Marxists themselves, who no longer cherish illusions about the inspiration emanating from their ideals. Symptomatic is the complaint of one of the movement's most militant leaders; 'Young socialists(!) hardly know me and to the postwar generation I am a stranger.'[2]

This trend is hastened by the small prospect that even in the future such orthodox socialist aims as a fully planned economy, classlessness, and complete nationalization will ever become real in Western Europe and the United States. In this respect, the British experiences with nationalized industries have had a sobering effect: it did not make for a more equal distribution of wealth, the employee gained no more freedom, and the industrial structure did not become more democratic.[3] The unfavorable reactions of the British workers were a major factor in leading the European socialist parties to drop the principle of nationalization. Orthodox socialist ideals have for the present lost their value to the trade union movement and are nowadays adhered to only by a mixed minority of intellectuals and unskilled blue collar workers.

Utopianism

A reaction to orthodoxy is the desire for more viable socialist ideals. Unlike orthodoxy, the utopian school of thought rejects the concept of the class war, but neither does it accept the 'exercise in social engineering' of contemporary European socialist parties. The former it considers not convincing, the latter not sufficiently inspiring.[4] Even before World War II, this school expressed a desire for a new and systematic theory of socialist society, looking to future generations to provide it.[5] After the war, this wish was repeated by theoretical as well as by practical politicians: 'Without the creative force of a new and magnificent vision of the future,' writes Ruygers, 'socialism will not hold its grip on the great

[1] J. Burnham, *The Managerial Revolution*, p. 52.
[2] S. de Wolf, *Voor het land van belofte, een terugblik op mijn leven* (Bussum, 1954), p. 294.
[3] B. Russell, 'Pitfalls in Socialism', *Political Ideals* (London, Allen & Unwin, 1963), Ch. 3.
[4] I. Murdoch writes under the heading, 'A House of Theory', 'Our socialist ancestors had ideas but no techniques. We are often amazed at their naivety. We have the techniques: these we can explain clearly. But we can give only a rather brief and denuded explanation of our ideas. We have reached a stage where the amount of theory is decreasing while the social need for it increases.' *Conviction* (London, MacGibbon and Kee, 1958), p. 277.
[5] H. Verwey-Jonker, 'Vijfentwintig jaar socialistische theorie', *Ir. J. W. Albarda, een kwart eeuw parlementaire werkzaamheid* (Amsterdam, Arbeiderspers, 1938), p. 330.

majority,'[1] Another element of this socialist utopianism is the vision of a 'socialist culture', which so far has elicited little response.

The need for socialist ideals confirms the supposition, so far as the great majority of trade union members are concerned, that socialism in the welfare state is losing its power of inspiration. In this connection, there is sociological value in Polak's assertion: 'We must state clearly not only *what* socialism is nowadays, but above all *where* it is trying to lead us.'[2] The problem, however, is to describe this 'where' in such a way as to exert a powerful stimulus on the organized workers.[3]

Pragmatism

Socialist pragmatism is almost the direct opposite of socialist utopianism. It is based on the view that the welfare state is not unacceptable and that, so long as European socialism has no practicable alternative, it can hardly do better than try to improve it. Among the trade union leadership, this is the attitude which has the greatest number of supporters. Its disadvantage, however, is that as labor's integration in national policy proceeds, its leaders easily come to accept the status quo and reject more progressive ideals.

An example of this conservatism is the following quotation from one of socialism's younger theorists:

The view that it is the task of socialist theory to give the labor movement a view of the society of the future has proved both correct and incorrect. By its rejection of all idealism, the present, silent generation makes a valuable contribution. Performing the daily duties without believing in a Socialist Utopia; finding satisfaction in the small tasks: this offers more prospect of a proper development of our society and of the socialist movement's role within it than any utopia. The absence of theoretical speculations proves that the need for them has become so much less. The most urgent problem facing the labor movement is how to rid itself of the many theories and utopias that stand in the way of real reforms.[4]

Naturally, there are many leaders of public bodies, political parties, trade unions, and private companies who find deep satisfaction in their daily tasks, regardless of whether or not they consist of social reforms. Chapter 5 will show how 'responsible participation' is an answer to

[1] G. Ruygers, 'Socialistische Bezinning', *De Grondslagen van het Socialisme*, ed. Dr Wiardi Beckman Stichting, Research Bureau, Dutch Socialist Party (Amsterdam, Arbeiderspers, 1947), p. 27.

[2] F. L. Polak, 'Gedachten over het Socialisme van de toekomst', *Socialisme en Demokratie* (1959), No. 9 and No. 10.

[3] On Britain: 'Trade unions today have all the power they need to fight the battle for an enlargement of workers' rights and responsibilities. What they lack is the purpose.' Socialist Union, *Twentieth Century Socialism* (London, Penguin Books, 1956), pp. 113–14.

[4] J. M. den Uyl, 'Theorie en Beweging', *Socialisme en Demokratie* (1956), p. 145 f.

widespread, deep-seated psychological needs. But the very fact that such participation is confined to the small elite whose work allows for self-expression and responsibility, implies that this privilege is withheld from the many who are *not* in leadership positions.

Nevertheless, this very pragmatism could offer trade unionism an idealistic perspective. If socialism in the welfare state would endeavor to release the sense of purpose which is inherent in participation, if its ideal were to see that this 'deep satisfaction in the performance of a meaningful task' could be shared by the majority of workers, it would probably gain in inspirational power. But despite the views of the pragmatists, this will not be possible without new theoretical reflection. One requirement would be, for example, to replace the conception of democracy as 'delegated power', a popular concept among trade union leaders, by Laski's conception of democracy as 'participation'.[1]

Personalism

Personalist thinking, found among Christian and humanist socialists, is concerned with a view of the individual rather than a view of society. Not man's social conditions, but his spiritual and intellectual development and its underlying principles, are its central point. In an open letter to a disillusioned trade unionist (!) one of its leaders writes that personalist socialists are fully aware of the crisis socialism is facing in the welfare state, but that they welcome it as a long-awaited opportunity to re-evaluate the movement's moral tenets.[2]

In the efforts of this group to spiritualize socialism, the twentieth-century problem of 'mass society' holds the same place as did 'class society' in the nineteenth century. Its attitudes towards Marxist ideals are negative, as a statement about 'the poverty of the proletarian ideology, which at the cultural level has never revealed any creative power' illustrates.[3]

Personalists seek to replace that ideology by ethical elements which hitherto have remained in the background of socialist thought: basic human equality, respect for one's fellowmen, social justice, solidarity and civic spirit, educating to responsibility, and 'planning for freedom'. Its political aspect is the effort to achieve a social structure in which a truly democratic personality can develop.

[1] H. J. Laski, *Trade Unions in the New Society* (New York, Viking Press, 1949), p. 170.
[2] W. Banning, 'Desillusie of Verdieping?', *Tijd en Taak*, No. 43 (1 November 1950). See also: Norman Thomas, 'Humanistic Socialism and the Future', *Socialist Humanism, an International Symposium*, ed. Erich Fromm (New York, Doubleday, 1965), pp. 319–27.
[3] W. Banning, quoted by A. van Biemen in *Samen op Weg* (Amsterdam, Arbeiderspers, 1958), p. 116.

It is far from certain whether personalist thinking can serve as an idealistic basis for trade unionism. So far, the climate has been hardly favorable: the primacy of economics is strong in the unions, and there is little thought there about the moral implications of industrial relations and human labor. There is something to be said for the view that personalism, as it seeks to remove collectivism and politics from our lives, does not lend itself to mass movements. According to Spinelli, this can only be a task for 'reformers and moral and religious innovators'.[1] Indeed Socialism's personalistic branch cannot claim a large following, although the presence of denominational unions in Europe indicates that the gap between religion and labor may be less wide than Spinelli thinks. As for its following, we have seen that the youngest generation shows a trend toward 'individualization' and of increasing involvement with personal problems. If labor's ideals should undergo a parallel 'personalization', they might be able to respond to psychological needs among the new generation of the welfare state.

A new trade union ideology?

It is, of course, premature to conclude that none of the above ideologies has a chance of survival in the welfare state. Indeed, it is not inconceivable that the marriage of pragmatism, with its ethos of democratic participation, and personalism, with its ethics of democratic man, may provide a real basis for a new idealism in the unions. We shall now have to see whether and where this view finds support.

Such support can be found in *Britain*, where the union's democratic functions have always been more pronounced than in any Western nation.[2] There are historical reasons for this. Lindsay has described how, after the industrial revolution had destroyed the democratic forms of rural life, the trade unions took their place as champions of democracy.[3] In the eyes of many Laborites, they are still the democratic force in industrialism.

According to Crossman, labor has made the error of expecting that material progress would automatically lead to greater equality and freedom. Although the welfare state has by and largely achieved the economic elevation of the working masses, political and economic power is still concentrated in a small ruling elite. Crossman sees it as labor's task to prevent the responsibility for decision-making from becoming a social

---

[1] Spinelli, 'Le Socialisme', p. 44.

[2] 'The merit of having first grasped the fact that trade unions are indispensable organs of democracy and not only passing coalitions, belongs to a group of English writers (Rogers, the Webbs).' Bernstein, *Evolutionary Socialism*, p. 140.

[3] A. D. Lindsay, *The Modern Democratic State*, I (London, Oxford University Press, 1947), 190 f.

privilege. This would mean spreading participation in the policy-making of government, industry, party, and trade union over a large number of people, even at the expense of efficiency.[1]

Similar support is found in *Germany*. Briefs, for instance, grafts on to trade unionism the ideology of the Neo-Fabians, which he calls a 'critical humanism in action'. Against the dehumanization taking place in industrial organization, this 'personalism based on solidarity' defends the value and the dignity of the individual; against leadership for the privileged and the growth of bureaucracy in society, it lays down standards of freedom and equality in social relations. Whether or not this is 'socialism' is irrelevant to Briefs in view of the new moral horizons it gives to trade unionism.[2] While Crossman wants primarily to make participation more widespread, Briefs wants a more personalistic content.

In *France*, André Philip redirects this personalism toward a socialist goal when he maintains that the autonomy of the individual can only be saved by democratic reforms of the economy, industry, public welfare, and politics. He sees a twofold task for organized labor: to rethink its own democratic values and to use socialism as a means of realizing them.[3]

Gunnar Myrdal in *Sweden* is more specific. Beyond the welfare state, he visualizes a society in which increasing numbers of citizens participate in the decision-making of local, regional, and national administrations, voluntary pressure groups or lobbies, cooperatives and democratic industrial organizations. In this 'democratic democracy' parliament would be the framework within which the other structures transfer decision-making from the political leadership to the population. Thus, to the elements of democracy and personalism, Myrdall adds a third, a utopian element. Utopian but not unrealistic: 'this utopia,' he writes, 'in my belief, is a real goal.'[4]

There is little to add to this review of socialist ideals. A social system in which the individual has a truly democratic relationship to the power structures of industry and government would avoid both the restrictions upon individual freedom inherent in Communism and the threat to individual security which seems inherent in Capitalism. If the trade unions would work toward an advanced industrial society, in which individual freedom and social security have reached an optimal synthesis, they would live up to their highest traditions.

---

[1] R. H. S. Crossman, 'Towards a Philosophy of Socialism', p. 29.

[2] G. Briefs, *Das Gewerkschaftsproblem*, pp. 84–5.

[3] A. Philip, 'La Pensée Politique des Partis Ouvriers', *Les nouveaux comportements politiques de la classe ouvrière* under the direction of L. Hamon (Paris, Presses Universitaires de France, 1962), p. 211.

[4] G. Myrdal, *Beyond the Welfare State*, p. 131.

3

CONCLUSION

Since the concepts of 'affluent society' and 'welfare state' cover many economic, sociological, psychological and political phenomena, four aspects which are particularly relevant to trade unions have been singled out. These are (1) the increasing prosperity and changing distribution of the national income as compared with the 'Verelendung' of the last century; (2) the changing social structure, especially the rise of the white collar labor force; (3) changes in the basic personality of the manual workers; (4) changes in socialist theory as a basis for trade union ideals.

The conclusion is that, on each of these points, contemporary society differs radically from the social system to which the labor movement owes its existence. Economic changes have gradually removed the chief reason for its creation, i.e. the impoverishment of the working classes. Sociological changes are turning the category which it traditionally looked after, the working proletariat, into a minority. Psychologically, the worker's mentality has shifted from collective idealism to individual realism. And, finally, political changes are leading to a reorientation of trade union ideals. Before analyzing the implications of these changes for the trade union's relationship to its members, Chapter 2 will present a survey of the functions which the unions are fulfilling or have ceased to fulfill in this new environment.

2. The trade unions

'The union problem is a complex of economic, legal, ethical and social problems which can be understood only by knowing the viewpoint of organized labor in all its riches, diversity, contradictions and shifting character.' HOXIE

INTRODUCTION

Trade unions are not easy to define. A description used in recent studies is a case in point: 'Trade unions are associations of workers who by means of collective bargaining endeavour to improve their working conditions, and economic and social position.'[1]

One can raise several objections to this description. It is, for example, hardly complete. In addition to fighting for higher wages, advanced unions have taken on such new tasks as advisory and executive functions in government committees on education, recreation, social welfare, public health, and national defense. Hoxie's list of problems can, therefore, be considerably extended.

Secondly, the definition limits the unions' goals to the group of organized workers. In many advanced industrial countries, however, agreements between labor and management are binding for *all* workers in an industry, members and nonmembers. With union members often a minority of the labor force, much of a contract's benefits extends outside their ranks.

Thirdly, the definition assumes the members' interests to be the union's sole source of motivation. But unions have widened their concerns sometimes even to the extent of supporting the needs of the national economy against the demands of their members. Modern trade unions are multipurpose organizations whose goals for society increasingly take precedence over goals for the union membership.

These discrepancies between definition and reality indicate that the rise of the affluent society and the welfare state is accompanied by changes in the structure and functions of labor organizations. As a result, the traditional conception of the trade union is becoming outdated. In an attempt to analyze the union's present role, in advanced industrial society, we shall use the following classification:

Macrosocial functions: in behalf of society
in behalf of industry
in behalf of all workers.
Microsocial functions: in behalf of the members.

[1] W. Hirsch-Weber, *Gewerkschaften in der Politik, von der Massenstreikdebatte zum Kampf um das Mitbestimmungsrecht* (Cologne, Westdeutscher Verlag, 1959), p. 13.

Using this broad outline, our analysis will not be exhaustive. Such industrial societies as the United States, Great Britain and the Netherlands can count 184, 657, and 142 national unions, respectively[1] and a classification covering all their functions would be either too vague or too detailed. We shall aim, instead, for an heuristic model from which each union will differ in its own way.

MACROSOCIAL FUNCTIONS

In behalf of society

Historically, the ideals of the labor movement have always extended the horizons of its membership.[2] Replacing capitalism by a better socioeconomic structure, for example, was for many labor leaders no less important than the direct goal of raising the workers' wages. Political action in the class war has always provided the unions with *latent* macrosocial functions.[3]

Sociologists are not certain whether our present socioeconomic system is still ruled by a war between two classes. Of the many conflict theories, one is sufficiently empirical to provide a reliable answer. It is Dahrendorf's theory of the 'institutional isolation of the social conflict', which holds that the formerly nationwide conflict has become isolated within one social institution, e.g. within industry:

Increasingly, the social relations of industry, including industrial conflict, do not dominate the whole of society but remain confined in their patterns and problems to the sphere of industry. Industry and industrial conflict are, in post-capitalist society, institutionally isolated, i.e. confined within the orders of their proper realm and robbed of their influence on other spheres of society.[4]

In the welfare state, with its full employment, social security, and mass education, the macrosocial class war has gradually lost its vigor. Within

---

[1] United States: Bureau of Labor Statistics, *Directory of National and International Labor Unions in the United States, 1961*, Bulletin No. 1320 (Washington, D.C., U.S. Dept. of Labor, 1962).

Great Britain: C. Cyriax and R. Oakeshot, *The Bargainers, A Survey of Modern British Trade Unionism* (New York, Praeger, 1961). Out of these 657 unions, 291 have more than 1,000 members.

The Netherlands: Omvang der Vakbeweging, CBS, 1967.

[2] There were exceptions, of course; examples are Gomper's AFL in the United States, and the Socialistenbond in the Netherlands. Both tried to keep the struggle for the workers' lot strictly within the boundaries of 'trade action', i.e. refrained from political action. This idea of the 'business union' is still stronger in the United States than in Europe.

[3] Viewed in this way, the unions were only one element in a much broader socialist community, which also had room for the political party, the consumer association, workers' educational institutions and all kinds of cultural societies. But this community is now rapidly disappearing even in Europe.

[4] R. Dahrendorf, *Class and Class Conflict in Industrial Society* (Stanford, Stanford University Press, 1963), p. 268.

the social system of industry, however, relatively little has changed. The result is that the societal class conflict has been reduced to a merely industrial, or microsocial, conflict.

Moreover, not only the scope but also the character of the dissension has sometimes changed. Labor relations in West Germany provide an illustration. The spread of workers' councils, labor directors on executive boards, and union–management supervisory councils indicates such a degree of labor–management cooperation that the term 'class *war*' would be outright misleading.[1] Even in the capitalist United States' labor and management have moved toward a system of 'conflict within cooperation', where the legitimacy of each other's existence is accepted. The war between two industrial classes has gradually been succeeded by a system of labor–management accommodation.[2]

As a side-effect of industry's continuing isolation, trade union action has gradually become less 'political'. Winning a strike is less often identified with a step toward a socialist society, the goals of the unions and of the socialist parties have become separated, and their connections have weakened or become a matter of tradition.[3] All this has diminished the unions' *latent* macrosocial functions.

During the same time, however, some *manifest* macrosocial functions have expanded. The unions became officially involved in the national economy and deeply concerned with education, social welfare, housing, recreation, and many areas of modern government. Their alienation from socialism opened the way to an intensive integration in the control of society. Indications of this societal integration are found in many countries.

In *Britain*, union politics differed considerably in the two World Wars. While mainly restricting themselves to moderation in wage demands in World War I, British trade unions participated actively in winning World War II. Leaders of national unions took part in the Joint Advisory Council, the Joint Consultative Committee, and the Central Production Advisory Committee; and labor leader Ernest Bevin was in charge of the Ministry of Labour and National Service. 'There was hardly a facet of the war effort', according to MacDonald, 'with which the unions were not directly associated.'[4] Today, British trade unions are accepted in the full

---

[1] On the other hand, the term 'peace' is hardly valid for a system that between 1951 and 1958 experienced more than nine thousand open labor disputes. See F. J. Furtwängler, *Die Gewerkschaften, ihre Geschichte und Internationale Auswirkung* (Hamburg, Rowohlt, 1956), p. 97.

[2] For use in this context of the term 'accommodation', see: Clark Kerr, *Labor and Management in Industrial Society* (New York, Doubleday Anchor, 1964), p. 15 and John K. Galbraith, *Economics and the Art of Controversy* (Boston, Beacon Press, 1965), pp. 31–2.

[3] R. Dahrendorf, *Class and Class Conflict*, p. 275.

[4] D. F. MacDonald, *The State and the Trade Unions* (London, Macmillan, 1960), Ch. 9.

sense of the word. TUC representatives participate in royal commissions, departmental committees, and ministerial advisory bodies. Governments, whether Labour or Conservative, treat them with respect and consult them on a wide range of problems. According to Churchill, the trade unions have grown into 'a fourth state of the realm'.[1]

In *West Germany* after World War II, the trade unions being among the few organizations still intact were in part concerned with the national food supply. In the interest of the national economy, they resisted the planned dismantling of German heavy industry.[2] This sense of national responsibility has since remained in the German labor unions. It is reflected, for example, in the number of trade union members in the West German parliament, now close to two hundred.[3]

In *the Netherlands*, the labor movement has also devoted its attention to the entire national economy since 1945.[4] It participated actively in the postwar reconstruction, in industrialization, in anti-inflationary policies, and in supporting Dutch industry in international competition. With the unions' cooperation, Dutch wages stayed below those of neighboring countries, a decisive factor in the industrialization of the Netherlands.[5] Contemporary Dutch trade unionism has become an integral element of the national welfare state.[6]

In the *United States*, the postwar, or 'mature', unions have also broadened their activities and responsibilities with regard to society.[7] Union leaders are increasingly participating in community activities and industrial, educational, and governmental policies. The national unions issue statements not only on the position of their industry, but also on the national economy, foreign policy, federal programs, and national legislation. According to Ornati, labor will soon be represented in most of the federal and state regulatory commissions, as well as in other agencies concerned with social and economic problems in the United States.[8]

All of this indicates that the unions of advanced industrial society are becoming deeply involved in issues of national scope. They differ only in

---

[1] 'Trade Unions in a Changing World', *The Political Quarterly*, XXVII, No. 1 (1956), p. 1.
[2] W. Hirsch-Weber, *Gewerkschaften in der Politik*, II, Ch. 1.
[3] 'As against 172 in the third post-war German parliament, the newly elected fourth parliament contains 183 members of trade unions affiliated to the German Trade Union Federation. 167 of them belong to the Socialist Party, 15 to the Christian Democrats and Christian Socialists, and one is a Free Democrat.' *DGB Auslandsdienst*, No. XII (November 1961), 11.
[4] F. de Jong, *Om de Plaats van de Arbeid* (Amsterdam, De Arbeiderspers, 1956), p. 303.
[5] W. Albeda, *De Rol van de Vakbeweging in de moderne Maatschappij* (Hoorn, Edecea, 1957), pp. 195–6.
[6] F. de Jong, *Om de Plaats van de Arbeid*, p. 123.
[7] A. Lester, *As Unions Mature* (Princeton, N.J., Princeton University Press, 1958), pp. 27–8.
[8] Oscar Ornati, 'Fewer Strikes, Smaller Wage Hikes', *Challenge*, November 1960, pp. 18–20.

method of integration. While unions in the United States use mainly informal means of participation in government, European unions use such formal vehicles as national councils of economic consultation.[1]

Many factors account for the unions' integration in the welfare state society. Underlying is the 'principium medium of increasing social interdependence', i.e. that actions in the economic, political, cultural, and other areas of complex social systems become intertwined to the extent that they operate as one indivisible whole.[2] The rise of nationwide bargaining, for example, involves the unions in issues of productivity, income distribution, inflation, corporate structure, consumer interests and taxation.

A second factor is the increase of socio-political activities in trade union action. This occurs in two directions: besides the expansion of existing macrosocial tasks, *new* functions also add to the union's integration. While the national labor federation (AFL–CIO, TUC, DGB, NVV, LO) is consulted on cabinet level, leaders of individual unions participate in problems of legislation, education, social welfare, public transport, and low rent housing.[3]

This brings us to a third factor of societal integration. With bargaining widely transferred to central executive bodies, a growing functional hiatus in the union local is now being filled with activities in fringe areas.[4] Here is an illustration of how a European union, in defiance of its constitution, encourages functional expansion at the local level:

Our union locals get almost daily into contact with various forms of leisure. Despite the restrictions in our constitution(!), they should, we think, develop activities in the area of leisure. Local unionists should co-operate with other groups. If they are not invited, they should offer the services of the local union. Let it be known that your local is seriously interested in leisure activities.[5]

This trend is also apparent in the United States. Illustrative is McKee's description of a local CIO branch in Lorain where, after transfer of bargaining to the central executive in Pittsburgh, the union leadership

[1] *Collaboration between Public Authorities and Employers' and Workers' Organizations at the Industrial and National Levels* (Geneva, ILO, 1958), *passim*.
[2] K. Mannheim, *Man and Society in an Age of Reconstruction* (London, Routledge & Kegan Paul Ltd., 1940), p. 44.
[3] The manifest character of this integration becomes clear when contrasted with the following example of latent social integration at the local level: 'Although the unions have taken on many features of the large modern organization, local branches have very much the character of social clubs. They run their own licensed bars (with skittle alleys) and organize sports and games.' J. G. Leibbrand, unpublished report of a survey of Luxembourg trade unionism (1957), p. 11.
[4] 'Wages remaining one of the unions' major fields of activity, it is regrettable that the more important wage decisions are moving to such a high organizational level that the individual member's influence becomes largely illusory.' W. Albeda, *De Rol van de Vakbeweging*, p. 205.
[5] *Plaats en Taak van de Bestuurdersbonden* (Amsterdam, NVV, n.d.), p. 13.

became more active in local politics and civic affairs.[1] More than 60,000 unionists in the United States are now participating in various areas of the public life of their communities.[2] Local and national integration of the union in extra-industrial areas has become a general trend.

This integration with other social institutions is not without dangers for the unions. Experiences of European unions indicate that responsibility for the national economy, for example, may very well come into conflict with the demands of the members.

In their responsibility for the postwar reconstruction, unions in Holland would withhold wage demands if inflationary or harmful for industry's export position.[3] These voluntary restrictions were highly beneficial for the economy of the nation.[4] The workers, however, became increasingly dissatisfied: many became attracted by higher wages in West Germany and after a Swedish shipowner paid Amsterdam dockworkers 10 per cent over their union wage,[5] a wave of wildcat strikes swept through the country. Within weeks, wages in Holland had risen to the level of other nations. This having been achieved against the policy of the unions, thousands left their ranks. The result was that the unions' position in the national economy was seriously endangered.

Whether to serve the workers in a direct way, by means of wage demands, or more indirectly, by protecting the benefits of the welfare state, is one of the basic dilemmas of the integrated union. Any pressure group which becomes integrated into society runs the risk of substituting the common good for its special interest. Trade unions have the additional problem of whether or not a movement which arose out of the workers' protest against the industrial order can, without losing its identity, support that same industrial order.

[1] 'In Lorain, the local labor leaders have only a minor part in the process of collective bargaining, which takes place in Pittsburgh. And, as in Windsor, the CIO in Lorain has also extended the scope of its activities to include the community. Active in politics and civic affairs, they have become a new and important power in the community.' J. B. McKee, 'Status and Power in the Industrial Community: A Comment on Drucker's thesis', *American Journal of Sociology* LXI, No. 6 (1956).   [2] A. Lester, *As Unions Mature*, p. 45.

[3] 'In the first 15 years after the liberation [the Dutch] succeeded in maintaining a wage level lower than that of other countries. The difference in wage level and social charges, not taking into account productivity, between Belgium, Western Germany and France on the one hand and Holland on the other, amounted roughly to 25 per cent in 1959.' J. Pen, 'The Strange Adventures of the Dutch Wage Policy', *British Journal of Industrial Relations*, 1, No. 3 (1963), p. 329.

[4] 'The low wage level certainly was one of the causes of the rapid growth of Dutch exports, which account for half of the national income, and so of the satisfactory expansion of the Dutch economy.' J. Pen, *ibid.*, p. 329.

[5] This led to curious legal consequencies. After this shipyard (the Amsterdam Dry Dock Company) had raised its workers' wage by ten cents an hour, it was taken to court by the National Employers' Federation, of which it was a member, for infringing the national collective contract concluded by that organization. Advocates of centralized bargaining usually tend to overlook its legal implications as related to a company's autonomy.

In behalf of industry

Contemporary unions are increasingly willing to view their demands within the larger context of industry's economic position.[1] It is not unusual for example, to see modern union leaders and managements acting together in behalf of 'their' industry:

The U.S. teamsters' union together with the trucking firms competed against the combined railwaymen's union and railroad companies in an endeavor to influence the Federal Administration in Washington. In the same way the mineworkers' union and mining companies lobbied against the St. Lawrence Seaway in order to protect the coal-using railroads, and are now jointly fighting the increased competition of the oil industry. The use of union labels on company products and the joint support of tariffs cutting foreign competition are also examples of labor–management co-operation.[2]

These cases indicate the existence of a large area in the affluent society where the interests of labor and management are converging. We saw the same to be true for Europe, where unions have maintained industrial peace in order to provide industry with good economic conditions. This was an important factor in the various 'economic miracles' in Western European recovery.[3]

Adjustment to industry's structure is indicated by the reorganization of the older craft unions into industrial unions, embracing all workers in an industry. This strengthens the union's bargaining position, but weakens its leaders' resolution in conflicts. Before presenting his claims to the employer, the union official now has first to mediate between the manual workers, professionals—such as engineers—and office workers within the union's ranks, apart from the fact that the young workers' demands for higher wages will conflict with the older workers' demands for seniority. Observers in West Germany have noticed that union leaders find it harder to start a conflict for this type of compromise.[4]

Another gain for industry is that in the industrial union the members' demands are often mitigated by the leaders' awareness of such intervening variables as unemployment in the industry, elasticity of demand for the products,[5] the system of individual and group incentives, or the

---

[1] In his 1964 report on UAW wage policy, Mr Reuther makes it very clear that UAW members can only obtain optimal wages when the United States automobile industry prospers. *Report of President Walter P. Reuther to the 19th UAW Constitutional Convention, Part Two : Economic Conditions* (Atlantic City, N.J., 20–7 March 1964).

[2] E. J. Burtt, Jr., *Labor Markets, Unions and Government Policies* (New York, St. Martin's Press, 1963), p. 361.

[3] Since World War II, peaceful industrial relations have drawn over four hundred foreign firms to the Netherlands to establish branches. About half of these (46 per cent) were from the United States.

[4] L. Heyde, 'Der Arbeitskampf', in *Handwörterbuch der Sozialwissenschaften*, Pt. 5, p. 298.

[5] J. T. Dunlop, *Wage Determination under Trade Unions* (New York, Augustus M. Kelley Inc., 1950), p. 226.

structure of the industrial organization.[1] Consequently, the industrial union's claims are better adjusted to management's problems than are those formulated by a craft union.

Finally, there is the question of the unions' influence on productivity. Observers in the United States are less optimistic about this than in Europe.[2] Only one out of four major labor agreements (450 out of 1,773 contracts) in the United States contain provisions for union–management cooperation; even fewer (345) center on in-plant production.

TABLE 5. *Content of formal statements of union–management cooperation in the United States, 1963–1964*[3]

	Pledges	Joint committees	Pledges and joint committees	Total*
Production problems	301	37	7	345
Technological change	44	20	—	64
Industrial welfare and sales promotion	136	42	2	180
Legislative and tariff matters	5	4	—	9

* Total >450 because pledges and joint committees in more than one area have been allocated to each area.

In the overwhelming number of cases (301 out of 345) where union and management cooperated on productivity, no formal machinery was established to implement those clauses. Both the low number and the informal structure of the provisions justify Kerr's conclusion that the unions' net effect on productivity in the United States is on the negative side.[4] In Europe, the unions seem to have a greater impact upon production. Their motivation is that a raise of wages evokes less resistance when paid out of increased productivity than out of a reduction of corporate profits or the managerial payroll.

[1] P. F. Drucker, *The Concept of a Corporation* (New York, Mentor, 1964), pp. 167–8.

[2] 'The British Trade Union Movement is playing a strong and decisive role in helping to raise efficiency and productivity in industry.' R. Harle, 'The Role of Trade Unions in Raising Productivity', *The Political Quarterly*, xxvii, No. 1, 93. Also: *Trade Unions and Productivity*, London, British Trades Union Congress, n.d., *passim*. For similar observations in the Netherlands, see W. F. van Tilburg in *Tijdschr. v. Efficientie en Documentatie*, xxxii, No. 13 (November 1962).

[3] T. L. Ellis, 'Cooperation Provisions in Major Agreements', *Monthly Labor Review*, lxxxix, No. 3 (1966), p. 283.

[4] C. Kerr, 'Productivity and Labor Relations', in *Labor and Management in Industrial Society* (New York, Doubleday-Anchor Books, 1964), p. 272. For two exceptions on this trend (and a more optimistic view) see: George W. Taylor, 'Collective Bargaining' in *Automation and Technological Change*, ed. John T. Dunlop (Englewood Cliffs, N.J., Prentice Hall, 1965), p. 89.

The above figures highlight another difference between intraplant labor relations in Europe and the United States. While only 6 per cent of the United States labor agreements (112 out of 1,773 contracts) provide for joint union–management committees, joint consultation has become almost universal in European industry. It is hardly possible to understand the most fundamental difference between the labor relations of the two continents without insight into joint consultation.

Joint consultation[1]

Although its underlying ideals are more than a century old, joint consultation in industry is still a rather young institution. Despite fifteen decades of theory and experimentation, workers' councils did not become widespread in Europe until after World War II. They have made the structure of European industry different from both the underdeveloped industries of Asia and Africa and the industrial corporations in the United States.

Weber has described how the system of capitalism is not purely of economic origin;[2] joint consultation is even less so. Its history is predominantly rooted in political, ethical, and religious thought.

In France in 1829, utopian socialists favored the delegation of entrepreneurial tasks to the workers.[3] In Germany in 1853, workers' participation in decision-making was defended by the liberal philosopher Von Mohl.[4] In Britain around 1900, the guild socialists considered joint control over the workshop an effective counterpoise to capitalist rule.[5] At the turn of the century, Bernstein introduced the idea in the social-democratic parties of the Continent. Councils of codetermination did, for a short time, exist in the German Republic of Weimar.[6]

Since the class war has been replaced by the affluent society and the welfare state, the movements of utopianism, guild socialism, and revisionism have lost most of their strength. But whatever the differences from the past, in one respect little has changed: at present, the origins of joint consultation still lie largely outside the enterprise, i.e. in the socialist, Protestant, and Catholic movement. This explains partly why in the

---

[1] This section is partly based upon M. van de Vall, 'The Workers' Councils in Western Europe: Aims and Results', in *Procceedings of the Seventeenth Annual Meeting, Industrial Relations Research Association*, ed. G. G. Somers (Chicago, 1965), pp. 280–91.

[2] M. Weber, *The Protestant Ethic and the Spirit of Capitalism* (New York, Charles Scribner's Sons, 1958), *passim*.

[3] C. Fourier, *Le Nouveau Monde Industriel et Sociétaire* (Paris, 1929), pp. 73–8.

[4] H. J. Teuteberg, *Geschichte der Industriellen Mitbestimmung in Deutschland* (Tübingen, Mohr, 1961), p. 24.

[5] G. D. H. Cole, *Self Government in Industry* (London, 1919), pp. 94–100.

[6] M. Beck, *Wirtschaftsdemokratie* (Zürich, Polygrafischer Verlag, 1962), p. 25.

United States, where socialism and the political branches of Protestantism and Catholicism never have flourished, joint consultation has not become popular. The trade union participation that exists in United States industry is based mainly upon economic motivations.[1]

Socialist theory

Politically, socialist theory views the simultaneous existence of political democracy and industrial autocracy as a source of social and individual strain. The welfare state, it is argued, has sharpened the workers' awareness of a disharmony between democracy in their political life and benevolent autocracy in their work.[2] Joint consultation is viewed as a safeguard against authority over individuals who lack the means to control it. Socialist theory does not favor political democracy in the industrial structure; its goal is to give the workers, like the stockholders, some formal means of control over management.[3]

Economically, socialist theory stresses the widening rifts between labor, ownership, and management. While the division between workers and employer is longstanding, the one between management and stockholders is relatively new. The spread of stock to millions of investors has, according to socialist thinkers, weakened the owners' control, while management's power has correspondingly increased. The result is a hiatus in the legitimation of managerial authority in advanced industry. Socialists want to fill this hiatus by giving labor partial control over the enterprise.[4]

Socialist theory holds that only basic changes in the industrial power structure will enhance the workers' sense of freedom.[5] The introduction of workers' councils is viewed as one of these structural innovations.

Catholic and Protestant theory

Religious thinkers devote relatively more attention to the *ethical* arguments concerning workers' participation than do the socialists. They consider the right to be heard in the process of decision-making in industry a right given by God and, as such, basically equal to the rarely contested property right.[6]

Comparing them, the ethical arguments in religious and socialist theories are quite similar: in both, joint consultation is viewed as enabling

[1] M. Derber, W. E. Chalmers and M. E. Edelman, 'Union Participation in Plant Decision-Making', *Industrial and Labor Relations Review*, xv, p. 95.

[2] R. N. McMurry, 'The Case for Benevolent Autocracy', in *Human Relations in Management*, ed. I. L. Heckman, Jr., and S. G. Huneryager (Chicago, South-Western Publishing Co., 1960), pp. 96–112.

[3] A. Christmann and O. Kunze, *Wirtschaftliche Mitbestimmung im Meinungsstreit* (Köln, Bund-Verlag, 1964), Pt. I, p. 282.

[4] *Ibid.*, Pt I, p. 322.   [5] *Ibid.*, Pt I, p. 283.

[6] 'Entschliesungen der Bochumer Katholickentages, 1949', *ibid.*, Pt. II, p. 106.

the individual, in the course of his work, to satisfy deeply rooted needs of self-esteem and self-actualization.[1]

Over the last few years, however, attention has gradually been shifting from the workers' council to changes in the higher levels of industrial organizations, e.g. the introduction of labor directors and labor representatives on the board of directors. The main reason is that the workers' councils seem rarely successful in contributing to or controlling management.

The unions' theory

With collective bargaining as their major function, leaders of the European unions have given much thought to its relationship to joint consultation. Out of a wealth of publications, two different points of view emerge, i.e. the cooperation theory and the conflict theory of joint consultation.[2]

The *cooperation* theory stresses the common goals of management and labor. It holds that in addition to opposing interests, e.g. wages and fringe benefits, management and labor also have common interests, e.g. productivity, safety, quality of production, workers' morale, and organization.[3] Each of these two problem areas should be served by a different institution: the conflicting aspects by collective bargaining, the common aspects by the workers' council. This conception of the workers' council as a complement to union bargaining is found in British nationalized industry.[4]

The *conflict* theory holds that even in the welfare state, or in nationalized industry, labor and management have no common goals. Although the issues between them may have changed partly into inequalities of authority and power, a basic value-conflict still exists.[5] While the major parts of this conflict should be handled by bargaining, some aspects, especially those extending over time or involving continuous control, might be channeled into a permanent body, i.e. the workers' council. These aspects are:

(*a*) control over the application of the union contract in matters of individual hiring, firing, promotion, replacement, and gratification;

[1] M. Beck, *Wirtschaftsdemokratie*, pp. 55–62.

[2] In West Germany alone, between 1945 and 1961, no less than 7,000 publications about joint consultation and codetermination have appeared. See *Bibliographie Zur Mitbestimmung und Betriebsverfassung* (Köln, Deutsches Industrie Institut, 1963).

[3] In the United States, the cooperative aspect of industrial relations is often emphasized in nonunionized companies, as part of a larger syndrome that includes profit-sharing and company-recreation.

[4] From discussions of the author with Mr D. Delay of the TUC, Mr M. Skinner of the Electricity Council, and Mr Kessler of the National Union of Mineworkers, in England.

[5] R. Dahrendorf, *Class and Class Conflict*, p. 268.

(*b*) solution of minor conflicts and checks on nonfunctional, irrelevant, and, therefore, unjustified authority;

(*c*) facilitating the adjustment to technical change, organizational innovation, and changes in the production process;

(*d*) advice and assistance in long-term planning of unavoidable closures (e.g. coal mines) or curtailments (e.g. because of automation) so as to minimize their harm to the workers;

(*e*) Supervision and partial administration of the company's social-security plans and welfare provisions.[1]

With the exception of the last, these are all aspects of the conflict of interests between workers and management. The idea of the workers' council as an extension of the social conflict is found among West German labor theoreticians.[2]

It should be clear that neither the cooperation theory nor the conflict theory views the council as a substitute for bargaining or as eliminating labor conflicts. The 'cooperative' council takes care of interests which are neglected by bargaining and the 'conflict' council takes care of continuing matters of negotiation. The problem, therefore, is not whether there should be consultation *or* bargaining,[3] but whether consultation should be a complement or an extension of the union contract.

Still, the workers' council does not leave the social conflict entirely unchanged. In some cases, the regular discussions in the council lead to a situation in which, as one observer put it, 'opponents are no longer bargaining, but associates are managing'.[4] It would be wrong, however, to view this as the development of a harmonious 'community of work'. This type of labor–management consultation usually means a compromise between different values rather than a merger of goals.[5]

The structure of joint consultation

Although the system differs in various countries, there is usually a council in which representatives of blue collar workers, white collar workers, and

---

[1] A. Christmann, 'Mitbestimmung und sozialer Konflikt, löst die Mitbestimmung die sozialen Gegensätze?' in *Das Mitbestimmungsgespräch*, 9. Jahrgang, Nos. 5/63 and 6/63.

[2] From discussions of the author with Dr G. Leminski of the Wirtschaftswissenschaftliches Institut der Gewerkschaften (WWI), Dr W. Höhnen (WWI), and Dr H. Seidel of the Hanns Böckler Gesellschaft, Düsseldorf, West Germany.

[3] The theme of Session VIII of the seventeenth Annual Conference of the Industrial Relations Research Association (IRRA), 28–9 January 1964, at Chicago was: 'Does modern enterprise organization require trade union participation in management decision making, or only consultation, or bargaining?'

[4] W. M. van Putten, *De Menselijke Achtergronden van de Ondernemingsraad* (Bussum, 1955), p. 35. This is even stronger with the 'labor director' in the West German iron and steel industry. See H. Kairat, 'Die Soziale Rolle des Arbeitsdirektors', *Soziale Welt*, No. 1 (1966), p. 48.

[5] M. Derber *et al.*, 'Union Participation', p. 102.

management discuss the problems of the company. The members of the first two groups, not necessarily unionists, are in most cases elected, while those of management are usually appointed. Either workers and management have equal status in the council—Denmark, Norway, Britain, and Sweden—or the director of the company is, *qualitate qua*, the council's chairman—France, Belgium, the Netherlands, and Spain.[1] In West Germany and Italy, management has no representative on the council.

The various systems differ according to three criteria: legal basis, hierarchical level, and responsibilities of the council.

The *legal basis* is voluntary when the system has been created in private bargaining between labor and management and compulsory when created by legislation. Surprisingly, the legal basis is of little consequence for the operation of the system: councils are voluntary in Denmark, Italy, Norway, Britain, Switzerland, and Sweden and compulsory in West Germany, Belgium, the Netherlands, and Spain, but there is no difference between the operation of the two groups.

With regard to *hierarchical level*, consultation exists at various places in the economy. Workers' councils are found in the local company or, one step higher, in the industrial corporation. At an intermediate level, for the entire steel or mining industry, we sometimes find a consultative board of unions and managements. At the highest level is the national economic council, such as the Conseil Économique in France, where leaders of management and labor, together with specialists representing the public interest, advise the government on economic policy. Such national economic councils now exist in France, Belgium, the Netherlands, Italy, and Sweden. In the United States, national consultation is most closely approached through the institution of 'Public Hearings' by Congress and Administration.

The *degree of responsibility* of the workers' council, ranging from advice on fringe benefits to full managerial power, is the most fundamental difference in the systems of joint consultation. In France, the councils are responsible only for the welfare plans in the company; in the coal and steel industry of West Germany, union representatives (labor directors) are part of management; in Yugoslav industry, the workers' council exerts full managerial functions, e.g. personnel, sales, and production policies.[2]

Usually, the council advises management on day-to-day social problems in the plant: working conditions, personnel issues, holidays,

[1] ILO, *Consultation and Cooperation between Employers and Workers at the Level of the Enterprise* ('Labour-Management Series', No. 13) (Geneva, 1962), pp. 17–23.
[2] S. Kavčič, *Self-Government in Yugoslavia* (Beograd, 1961), *passim.*

vacations, and methods of payment, as is the case in Holland, Belgium, Scandinavia, and Britain. This type of council is less an instrument of control than a shortcut in the communication between management and the workers.[1]

At present, workers' councils are found in 30 per cent (Holland) to 75 per cent (France) of West European industry, with the highest number in the larger industries. After the first rapid spread, their growth has now slowed down or has even been reversed. Sturmthal has observed that of all institutions in industrial relations created after World War II, none has been less successful than the workers' council.[2]

Management's views of the workers' council

Ultimately, management will determine the success or failure of joint consultation. Observers in Belgium stress its crucial role in the council's operation,[3] and in Britain, a positive attitude of management is found to be fundamental for the council's success.[4]

There are two different points of view about the council among leaders of European industry. At the *lower* ranks of the managerial world, among local managers, the feelings are predominantly negative. The reason is that local managements are often afraid that the council will lead to restrictions of their power in the plant. They view the council as a threat to a strong and decisive leadership in the company and are fearful that, in the long run, it will have damaging effects for the organization.[5] Besides, while the cost of bargaining can be passed on to stockholders and consumers, loss of power is entirely borne by management. In this situation, the workers' council is easily conceived as a union-inspired endeavor to undermine management's authority in the plant. This resistance is usually stronger at each *lower* supervisory level, culminating at the level of the foreman.

At *higher* managerial levels, in the national employers' organizations, there is a more sophisticated image of the council. Here joint consultation is viewed within the framework of general changes in modern labor relations. It is expected that the 'human relations' approach will change the enterprise into a 'Gemeinschaft', i.e. a community-of-work, whose

---

[1] 'Ce sont, en définitive, beaucoup plus des organismes de contact que des organismes de contrôle et d'action.' C. Leger, *La Démocratie Industrielle et les Comités d'Entreprise en Suède* (Paris, Librarie Armand Collin, 1950), p. 209.

[2] A. Sturmthal, *Workers' Councils* (Cambridge, Mass., Harvard University Press, 1964), p. 36.

[3] *De Informatiefunctie van de Ondernemingsraad* (report), (Antwerp, Centrale voor Productiviteits-bevordering, 1964).

[4] ILO, *Consultation and Cooperation between Employers and Workers*, p. 67.

[5] L. J. M. Herold, 'Psychologische Beschouwingen over de Wet op de Ondernemingsraden', *Mens en Onderneming*, IV (1950), p. 10.

members share the same economic values and where the ethos of co-operation replaces the doctrine of conflict. In this new type of enterprise, the workers' council will represent the interests of all parties in the plant. According to this view, an enlightened managerialism will within a few decades, replace the unions in industrial relations.[1] The workers council is here defined as a 'progressive' substitute for the 'conservative' labor union.[2]

While local managements view the workers' council as a weapon in the hands of the unions against the manager's power in the plant, the national leaders of industry are inclined to view it as a weapon in the hands of management against the power of the unions. The simultaneity of these opposite views suggests that divergences between leaders and rank and file exist not only in unions but also in employers' associations.[3]

Management may use various tactics to counteract the unions' use of the council as an instrument of industrial control. 'Chloroformage', i.e. rendering the council harmless by keeping it dormant,[4] is popular. More successful and inconspicuous is the gradual conversion of the council into an instrument of 'human relations'. How opposed this is to the council's goals becomes clear when we compare the principles of joint consultation with those of human relations:

(1) The principles of *joint consultation* are basically those of economic democracy. Both, joint consultation and codetermination aim at a re-organization of the industrial structure, with the ultimate purpose of increasing labor's control over management. By curbing management's autonomy in decision-making, it is the unions' hope to widen labor's power in the enterprise. The workers' council is one means to achieve this goal.

(2) The *human relations* approach seeks to innovate industrial authority without fundamentally changing its structure. Delegating minor decisions to subordinate levels increases the workers' readiness to accept change and their responsiveness to management's major decisions.[5] The

---

[1] A. M. Kuylaars, 'Medezeggenschap in de Onderneming', in *Mens en Onderneming*, IV (1950).

[2] The president of the German Federation of Employers' Associations, Raymond, in a speech at Kiel, 26 June 1952, quoted in G. Triesch, *Die Macht der Funktionäre* (Düsseldorf, Karl Rauch Verlag, 1956), p. 415.

[3] We quote from a speech by the President of the Dutch Central Federation of Employers (CSWV): 'In view of the situation in the Federation, one might expect that a strong link between our leadership and our members has been met. However, this problem is still very unsatisfactorily solved.' *Het Handelsblad*, 9 May 1956. For a similar observation in the United States, see A. M. Ross and P. T. Hartman, *Changing Patterns of Industrial Conflict* (New York, John Wiley & Sons, 1960), p. 48.

[4] G. Laserre, *Les Expériences Françaises de Participation des Travailleurs* (report) (Vienna, 1958), p. 9.

[5] R. Tannenbaum and F. Massarik, 'Participation by Subordinates in the Managerial Decision-Making Process', *The Canadian Journal of Economics and Political Science*, XVI (August 1950), pp. 412–13.

latent effect of this policy is an increase of managerial power. That the principles of human relations are not inherently democratic is illustrated by the German national socialists, who had never heard of Hawthorne and applied them as 'Menschenführung im Betriebe'.[1]

The council's conversion into an instrument of human relations in industry often passes through several stages. First, management will prevent the council from exerting control by withholding data, by transmitting data too late, or by presenting them in an inaccessible form.[2] Second, management will move the council's attention away from financial and economic problems to peripheral issues of safety and social welfare.[3] In the last stage, continuous cooperation with executives will have created such a spirit of company-mindedness in the council that its members may feel closer to management than to the union.[4]

On the whole, the attitude of European management toward the council is predominantly negative: for France, it is reported that no more than five per cent of the managers really want them to succeed,[5] and in the Netherlands[6] and West Germany,[7] it is not much different. Characteristically, Swedish employers regard the workers' council as a safeguard against more radical reforms.[8]

The unions' view of the workers' council

The European unions favor joint consultation not only out of idealism, but also for more pragmatic reasons. Workers' councils can assist in the day-to-day execution of the collective contract, introduce minor social improvements, facilitate adjustment to change, and may help in settling grievances.

During the closure of obsolete British and West German coal mines, the councils gave valuable assistance in the long-term planning of the relocation of miners. In large corporations they provide a shortcut in line-communication. Further, they offer a useful training ground for voluntary union leaders and, in the case of weaker unions, may open roads toward more effective intraplant action.

---

[1] E. Potthoff, 'Zur Geschichte der Mitbestimmung', in E. Potthoff, O. Blume, und H. Duvernell, *Zwischenbilanz der Mitbestimmung* (Tübingen, 1962), p. 15. See also W. Chamberlain, *Industrial Relations in Germany, 1914–1939* (Stanford, Stanford University Press, 1942), *passim.*

[2] G. Ventejol, *Le Conseil d'Entreprise et les Problèmes Économiques de l'Entreprise* (Paris, OECD, 1956), pp. 5–6.

[3] G. Laserre, *Les Expériences Françaises de Participation.*

[4] *De Informatiefunctie van de Ondernemingsraad*, Antwerp Centrale voor Productiviteitsbevordering.   [5] G. Laserre, *Les Expériences Françaises de Participation*, p. 9.

[6] L. J. M. Herold, 'Psychologische Beschouwingen', p. 94.

[7] M. Beck, *Wirtschaftsdemokratie*, p. 53.

[8] ICFTU, *Workers' Participation in Industry* (study guide) (Brussels, August 1954), p. 48.

Probably most important from the point of view of the unions is that joint consultation legitimizes the workers' right to be heard in non-wage problems.[1] With the European unions being often less oriented towards the single company than towards an entire industry, the workers' council fills a functional hiatus in the relationship between union and company.

Still, there is little doubt that European labor has an '*Unbehagen an der Mitbestimmung*', a vague sense of disillusion about joint consultation.[2] The reasons are many. One is that the workers' council will sometimes try to take part in collective bargaining. This is strongly resented by the unions. 'The council shall under no condition negotiate about wages or fringe benefits,' they protest, 'bargaining is solely a task of the unions.'[3]

A second problem, already mentioned, is management's policy of handling workers' grievances through the workers' council in order to avoid union intervention. The trade unions, afraid that the council may develop into a European version of the United States company union, are strongly opposed to this trend.[4]

A third problem is that workers' councils have not been effective in curbing management's authority. Forced into the enterprise by law or by trade union pressure, without any economic power, with the intellectual level of its members below that of management, the council seldom succeeds in influencing the flow of command. The socialists once welcomed it as a step towards industrial democracy; now they realize that it lacks the power and ability to influence management in crucial decisions. That a council may assist in the workers' adjustment to a shutdown cannot conceal, for example, that it had no voice in the decision to close.

A fourth and major problem lies in the workers' evaluation of the

---

[1] The right of the workers to be heard on nonwage issues has been lacking in clearcut legitimacy. Gouldner's description of this omission is illustrative: 'For example, workers were angry that no one had told them anything about the new machinery, and that management did not seem to be interested in their feelings concerning it. But they were not in the least certain that it was their business; they doubted that they had the right to complain about it. "Management feels the machines are none of our business", said a mill worker, "and maybe it is not." Doubting their legitimacy, workers could not readily make an issue of these complaints.' A. W. Gouldner, *Wildcat Strike* (New York, Harper Torchbooks, 1965), p. 35.
   While the so-called 'human relationists' in industry try to introduce workers' participation in these matters along *informal* lines, the crucial function of the workers' council and of joint consultation in general is that it establishes the *legitimacy* of the workers' right to hear and be heard. Not only, as happens in collective bargaining, about wages, but also about important nonwage issues. Gouldner's analysis illustrates the importance of this right for the workers and, for that matter, for industry.
[2] Christmann, 'Mitbestimmung und sozialer Konflikt', *Des Mitbestimmungsgesprach*, No. 5/63.
[3] *Rapport van de Commissie Ondernemingsraden van het NVV* (Amsterdam, n.d.), p. 15.
[4] 'Trop d'employeurs se sont efforcés de constituer des Comités d'entreprise "maison", c'est à dire sans les syndicalistes. Nous condamnons formellement de tels précèdes qui, outre l'éviction du syndicalisme, favorisent un corporatisme d'entreprise ou se perd la notion même d'interest général.' G. Ventejol, *Les Conseil d'Entreprise*, p. 9.

council, indicating that it is unable to satisfy psychological needs which have been frustrated in the process of production. In Belgium, the workers seldom pay attention to the council[1] and the general attitude of the French workers has changed from optimism in the first postwar years to widespread disillusion.[2] Researchers in West German industry find that the idea of codetermination has very little reality among the labor force.[3] Significant is that similar reactions come from workers who do participate in the councils and who, accordingly, should know their psychological benefits best. A survey of council members in the Netherlands discovered that the majority (60 per cent) are not satisfied with their council and that even more (64 per cent) would prefer to be replaced.[4] From these observations we may conclude that the Catholic, Protestant, and Socialist goals behind joint consultation are not met by the workers' councils. Worse, one must even count with the probability that a workers' council which fails to realize the workers' high expectations has a greater demoralizing effect than no council at all.

International and national surveys reveal doubts about the councils' role in industry in many European unions.[5] A sample of these reactions is given below.

Swedish trade unions are using various devices to prevent the workers' councils from harming the union's position in the company. Direct devices forbid the council to deal with wage issues or union contracts; indirect devices grant participation in the council only to members of the Swedish Labor Federation. Nevertheless, observers still report that the councils threaten to undermine the solidarity of the workers.[6]

West German unions are concerned about management's policy of using the workers' council as a means to achieve company unionism. They

[1] *De Informatiefunctie, van de Ondernemingsraad,* Antwerp Centrale voor Productiviteitsbevordering.

[2] G. Laserre, *Les Expériences Françaises de Participation.*

[3] R. Dahrendorf, *Das Mitbestimmungsproblem in der deutschen Sozialforschung, Eine Kritik* (Tübingen, 1956). More data are given by Hans Kairat, 'Die Soziale Rolle des Arbeitsdirektors', p. 52.

[4] J. J. de Bruin, *Het Funktioneren van de Ondernemingsraden* (report) (Amsterdam, 1962).

[5] In addition to the examples given, see the doubts about the workers' councils in the labor movements of *Austria* in *Survey of the Participation of Trade Unions in the Determination of Economic and Social Policies in Their Countries,* International Confederation of Free Trade Unions, Executive Board, Brussels, 2–5 December 1963, Agenda Item 9 (hereinafter referred to as ICFTU); *Finland,* ICFTU, p. 3; *France,* G. Ventejol, *Le Conseil d'Entreprise;* G. Laserre, *Les Expériences Françaises de Participation,* pp. 14–16; A. Sturmthal, *Workers' Councils,* p. 36; *Greece,* ICFTU, p. 6; *the Netherlands,* G. Ventejol, *Le Conseil d'Entreprise,* p. 8; and *Italy,* ILO, *Consultation and Cooperation between Employers and Workers,* p. 62.

[6] 'Les comités présentent de plus un incontestable danger de desagrégation de l'unité ouvrière, parce qu'ils émoussent la conscience de classe.' C. Leger, *La Démocratie Industrielle,* p. 212. See also Heiki Waris, 'Workers' Participation in Management in Scandinavian Industry', in *Transactions of the Fourth World Congress of Sociology* (London, ISA, 1961), Vol. III.

view settlements of labor issues through the council as a threat to the union's position in the company.[1] Some labor leaders denounce the 'community of work' as a form of neofeudalism which is fundamentally discordant with modern democracy.[2] This explains why the German steelworkers union (IGM) has recently introduced 'groups of trusted members' in the industry. Each of the trusted members is responsible for twenty other union members in the plant. The aim of these groups is to strengthen the union's ties with the rank and file in the work situation. Management's reaction is that the 'trusted members' are supposed to bring the workers' council under tighter union control.[3] The official functions of these groups are:

(*a*) to take care of human relations at work;

(*b*) to represent the unions at company meetings;

(*c*) to aid and advise individual union members;

(*d*) to keep union members informed on wages, piecework, and the union contract;

(*e*) to watch over safety controls in the plant.[4]

Thus, it is not very likely that the West German unions are trying to control the workers' councils. It seems much more probable that by means of the trusted members they are trying to push the councils aside.

The attitude of the *British* unions with regard to the council is influenced by the role which management allows the council to play.[5] Originally, the unions were one hundred per cent in favor of the councils, but lately some wariness seems to have set in. In a study of six hundred councils, the authors criticize the unions' policy of getting the councils under their control. British trade unions are gradually realizing that workers' councils can serve not only to strengthen but also to weaken their position in industry.[6]

Trade unions in *Belgium* have followed the policy of putting up groups of trusted 'union delegates' besides the workers' activities in the workers'

[1] Fürtwangler, *Die Gewerkschaften*, p. 104.
[2] 'In allen demokratischen Ländern, vor allen Dingen in den Vereinigten Staaten, kennt man diese Werksgemeinschaft, kennt man feudalistische Systeme dieser Art nicht.' V. Agarz, *Landesbezirkskonferenz des DGB Bayern* (Rede) (München, 16 January 1956), in G. Triesch, *Die Macht der Funktionäre*, p. 419.
[3] G. Triesch, *Die Macht der Funktionäre*, p. 419.
[4] *Richtlinien für die Vertrauenskörper in der Industriegewerkschaft Metall für die Bundesrepublik Deutschland* (Frankfurt am Main, 1958), pp. 12–15.
[5] 'In general we found that the attitude to systems of joint consultation of outside union officials, branch secretaries, district organizers, etc., was largely determined by the degree of trade-union recognition and the quality of management-union relations.' *Joint Consultation in British Industry* (London, National Institute of Industrial Psychology, 1952), p. 89.
[6] W. Robson-Brown and N. A. Howell-Everson, *Industrial Democracy at Work, A Factual Survey* (London, Pitman, 1950), p. 79.

council. Observers report that the union members feel a greater affinity with these groups of union delegates than with the workers' council.[1]

The data suggests that the unions' policies toward the workers' councils is partly determined by management's views of the structure of the enterprise. Where management tries to transform the council into a device of 'human relations', the union reacts with the introduction of 'groups of trusted members'.[2] But where management accepts that even the best labor–management relationship embodies a latent conflict in which the parties' position is determined by their power, the unions cooperate fully in the council.

Joint consultation in the United States

At first sight, labor relations in the United States have little in common with labor relations in Western Europe. United States trade unions have few ideological ties to political or religious movements, and workers' councils are virtually absent in United States industry.[3] It seems that the *value structure* of industrial relations in the United States is not directly favorable toward joint consultation.

Other differences are more superficial. Continuous cooperation between labor and management, for example, is not unknown in the United States. Derber *et al.* found in no less than 75 per cent of the companies they studied a situation of 'moderate joint participation' with such traits as: (*a*) a disposition of union and management to work together on a continuing basis; (*b*) union influence limited to jobs, work conditions, wages and fringe benefits; (*c*) bargaining and grievance settling with little inclination to strike; and (*d*) a moderate degree of joint problem solving.[4]

These facts suggest that the *functional structure* of labor–management relations on the two continents is not dissimilar, or, in other words, that a basic condition for a more formal institutionalization of joint participation exists in the United States. This is confirmed by the fact that unions and management in this country indeed are experimenting with several devices of joint consultation in bargaining.[5]

This leads to the question whether the unions will extend their influence beyond the area of jobs and wages, and move toward establishing

[1] C. H. Marx and E. H. de Waal, *De Toekomst van de Ondernemingsraad* (Alphen a/d Rijn, Samson NV, 1960), p. 10.

[2] Committees of workers' representatives, apart from the council, are found in Belgium, France, the Netherlands, and West Germany.

[3] M. Derber, 'The Idea of Industrial Democracy in America, 1898–1915', *Labor History*, No. 3 (Fall, 1966), 269, VII.

[4] M. Derber, W. E. Chalmers, and M. T. Edelman, *Plant Union–Management Relations: from Practice to Theory* (Urbana, Ill., Institute of Labor and Industrial Relations, 1965), pp. 42–3.

[5] 'Joint Consultation Devices in Collective Bargaining', *Monthly Labor Review*, LXXXVIII, No. 2 (1965), p. 173.

union-appointed labor directors and workers' representatives on the executive boards of large United States corporations.[1] The answer to this question depends for a great deal upon a third factor, viz. the division of power in United States industry. And in this regard, the prospect is less clear. The reason is that over the last ten years, according to observers, the balance of power outside[2] and inside the plant[3] in the United States has shifted to the side of management. The implication is that the *power structure* of United States industrial relations is not favorable to codetermination unless the unions will succeed in reversing this trend.

In behalf of all workers

Trade union wage policy

The labor market, government policy, union demands, and employers' resistances all influence wages. The wage structure is the result of these and other forces; to isolate the unions' role in their interplay becomes increasingly difficult.[4]

When labor is scarce, for example, and profits are high, wages will show a tendency to climb independently of the demands of organized labor. The unions will then mainly seek to diminish wage differences between the various economic sectors. In the reverse situation, with rising unemployment, the unions will be slow in raising wage demands, but will put pressure upon government to maintain full employment. This means that *indirectly* they are still keeping wages high. It shows that the integration of the unions into the economic process has not rendered them less effective; it has only made their action less visible, i.e. harder to detect.

Other factors add to this obscuration. One is that higher wages do not result solely from a victory of the union over the employer, but result no less from increasing productivity. Another is the rapid spread of industry-wide bargaining, which eliminates the costs of labor from competition between firms within one industrial sector. Both trends have changed the spectacular 'war over wages' into highly technical negotiations, in which statistics loom larger than strikes or close-outs.

[1] Some observers of the United States labor scene believe that the United Automobile Workers (UAW) is definitely aiming for codetermination in the United States automobile industry. See Victor Riesel, 'Reuther Held Aiming for Seats on Firm Boards', *Courier Express* (Buffalo, 13 September, 1967), p. 12. Riesel's syndicated column appears in 200 newspapers in the United States.

[2] Martin Meadows, 'A Managerial Theory of Unionism', in *The American Journal of Economics and Sociology*, xxv (1966), p. 126.

[3] George Strauss, 'The Shifting Power Balance in the Plant', *Industrial Relations*, i (1962), p. 65.

[4] '... those who have examined statistics on wage movements cannot agree on whether, up to this date, unions have had any significant effects on wage rates.' R. A. Dahl and Charles E. Lindblom, *Politics, Economics and Welfare: Planning and Processes* (New York, Harper Torch-books, 1953), p. 144.

The expanding role of government in the determination of wages is also complicating. In the United States, it is confined to the establishment of minimum wages, as a protection for the lowest paid workers.[1] In some European countries, the government determines basic increases in wages for the entire labor force.

As for the unions' impact upon wage determination, the best we can say is that it results from a continually changing interplay of stimulating and restricting social, political and economic forces. The most important of these will be discussed below.

Stimulating factors

A most favorable environment for trade union action is when there is a growing discrepancy between the volume of output per manhour and the compensation per hour of the worker. If, for example, the business share of national production has been increasing while the wage-earners' share has been going down, the unions have a strong case for wage demands.[2]

Other factors lie more within the unions themselves. Founded to relieve the workers' plight, they have always been active in matters of profits and wages; their thousands of voluntary workers and specialized staffs daily deal with wages, prices, inflation, and income distribution. This makes the unions the oldest and best equipped institution in the area of wage determination.

Their expertise would carry little weight, however, if it were not based upon strength. Numerically, unions are the largest organizations in the area of work, with memberships ranging from 33 to 95 per cent of the labor force. The solidarity among their members is stronger than in most organizations, and their strike funds amount to many millions.[3] Their hold over their sector of the electorate can boost or damage a political career. One can hardly overestimate the weight this diversified power lends to the unions' voice in wages and profits.

This influence has been acknowledged by management, government, and the public; it is one of the reasons that in those sectors of the labor force where no unions exist, new organizations are still being formed.[4]

---

[1] E. J. Burtt, Jr., *Labor Markets, Unions, and Government Policies* (New York, St. Martin's Press, 1963), pp. 371–8.

[2] 'The Profits Explosion and Inflation', *AFL–CIO American Federationist*, LXXIII, No. 9 (1966), p. 1.

[3] B. Gleitze, *Wirtschafts und sozialstatistisches Handbuch* (Köln, Bund-Verlag, 1960).

[4] 'The advent of employee organizations and collective bargaining in the public sector is the most significant development in the industrial relations field of the last 30 years.' J. Stieber, 'Collective Bargaining in the Public Sector', in *Challenges to Collective Bargaining*, ed. Lloyd Ulman (Englewood Cliffs, N.J., Prentice Hall, Inc., 1967), p. 87.

Restricting factors

The factors limiting the unions' influence over wages are essentially the same: the economic environment, the employers, the government, the workers, and possibly the unions themselves.

The *environmental* factors are size of firm, skill ratio, labor supply, and the community. In small firms, for example, union power is usually low; in plants with a low skill ratio, many stay out of the union; if labor is plentiful, the unions have less influence over wages; in areas with little union tradition, such as the Southern United States, unions have a hard time achieving recognition.[1]

The *employers* are the unions' oldest and strongest opponents. Observers consider organized management usually to be more powerful than organized labor.[2] Even in European welfare states with a labor party in government, employers are still the dominant pressure group.[3]

Employers resist the unions directly at the bargaining table, either by simply fighting its demands or, as increasingly happens, by means of their own proposals. One way to indirectly oppose the union is to pay wages above union scales. This 'wage drift' occurs with rising employment and is known in Scandinavia, in the Low Countries, and in the United States building trades.[4] It tends to undermine the workers' confidence in their organization.[5] The introduction of profit-sharing plans, which often exclude union members, is another form of indirect and increasingly successful opposition.[6] Industry also wields great political power,[7] and a third form of indirect managerial opposition to union wage

[1] M. Derber, W. E. Chalmers, and M. T. Edelman, *Plant Union-Management Relations*, pp. 52–68.

[2] In the United States, this is substantiated by the fact that between 1956 and 1963 productivity in industry rose 24·4 per cent, against a rise in the real wages for the highly unionized factory workers of 16·8 per cent. See *Report of President Walter P. Reuther to the 19th UAW Constitutional Convention*, pp. 53–4.

[3] C. de Galan, *De Invloed van de Vakbeweging op de Loonshoogte en Werkgelegenheid* (Leiden, Stenfert Kroese, 1957), pp. 148–9.

[4] A. Rees, *The Economics of Trade Unions* (Chicago, University of Chicago Press, 1963), pp. 57–8.

[5] In the Netherlands in 1963, wage drift raised the ratio of trade union to wildcat strikes to 1 : 57, according to data received by the author from the Central Bureau of Statistics, in The Hague, the Netherlands.

[6] Of the profit-sharing companies participating in a Dun & Bradstreet December 1961–January 1962 survey, 60·8 per cent did not employ unionized production/operating workers; 21·2 per cent employed unionized production/operating workers, but this group was *ineligible* for profit sharing. A minority of 18·0 per cent employed unionized production/operating workers who were eligible for profit sharing. The survey covered only companies with fewer than 500 employees; over 99 per cent of the 4·7 million companies in the United States are of that size. See B. L. Metzger, *Profit Sharing in Perspective* (Evanston, Ill., Profit Sharing Research Foundation, 1964), pp. 17 and 109.

[7] E. J. Hughes gives a fascinating account of how, at a given moment, the interests of the United States electronics industry clashed with the foreign policy of President Eisenhower and his Cabinet—and triumphed. See E. J. Hughes, *The Ordeal of Power* (New York, Dell, 1963), pp. 122–5.

policy is through pressure on government, with the argument that cutting labor costs will strengthen industry's international position and so the national economy.

Among the groups of *workers* who undermine the unions' role in the determination of wages are: (1) the nonunionized workers, who, by their existence, disprove the union's claim of representing the entire labor force; (2) the organized white collar workers, whose professional unions fight only for limited group interests; (3) the members of communist organizations either because they infiltrate the unions' voluntary leadership or because of their tactical timing of wildcat actions.

Union action against the first group will proceed either by such restrictive means as the closed shop and, increasingly, the union shop, or as in European unions, by upgrading the advantages of union membership. White collar organizations are often invited to join the larger movement; some professional unions, e.g. of teachers, have been quite responsive to such invitations. As for communist influence, it is almost nonexistent in the United States and is, with the exception of France and Italy, in most European countries mainly confined to unskilled workers, a gradually vanishing group.

We saw that the influence of *government* upon the process of wage determination has been expanding. With wages a decisive factor in a nation's export, investment, inflation, and taxation, the government is automatically involved in the wage disputes of the country's basic industries. It has also a direct stake in wages and prices: in some sectors the government is either the largest employer (services) or the only consumer (arms, space-craft). Finally, it is the government's duty to guard the public against wage-price settlements at the consumers' expense and against work stoppages that cripple the country. This leads increasingly to government intervention.

An intervening government will often lean toward the interests of management rather than toward the demands of labor. Anti-inflationary measures, for example, turn more easily into curbs on wages than on prices or profits. This often makes managements surprisingly cooperative toward welfare-state governments.[1]

Trade unions, being multipurpose organizations, sometimes turn themselves into restraining factors on wages. This occurs when labor leaders subordinate wage goals to a macrosocial goal, e.g. curbing inflation or protecting a national industry. In underdeveloped countries, unions sometimes sacrifice the workers' demands to the need for savings and investment.[2] Unions in advanced industrial societies may protect 'their'

---

[1] P. Thoenes, *The Elite and the Welfare State* (London, Faber & Faber, 1964), p. 181.
[2] C. Kerr, J. T. Dunlop, F. Harbison, and C. A. Myers, *Industrialism and Industrial Man* (New York, Oxford University Press, 1964), p. 202.

welfare state by a strike-stop and so create a prolonged period of industrial harmony. Kerr found nearly as many examples of the unions restraining wages over the past decade as examples of spurring them on.[1]
The explanation is that in that decade the unions' macrosocial responsibilities have expanded.

Changes in collective bargaining

This interplay of forces is also complicated by the process of collective
bargaining itself. We saw already that even insiders are at variance about
its impact upon the income distribution. While some view it as a union
device to control jobs and curb employers, others view it as a managerial
instrument to protect dividends and investment. According to the first
view bargaining has a leveling effect, according to the second view it
tends to widen the income distribution.

From conflict to accommodation. No less confusing is the fact that collective bargaining is changing. From a historical war between Capital and
Labor, it has developed into a threefold process of accommodation:
between groups of workers (unskilled versus skilled, blue collar versus
white collar, young versus old, females versus males); between management and stockholders, and between management and the union.[2] As a
result bargaining has turned into a lubricating factor in the mechanism of
advanced industrial society. Its technical nature is illustrated by the fact
that even in economic systems where the workers 'own' the means of
production, some forms of bargaining are still utilized.[3]

Diversity and centralization. European and United States' unions are
presently moving in reverse directions on a scale between local and national negotiations. While the European unions expand the role of local
branches, the American unions are moving to coordinated bargaining.
The reason for this latter trend is that corporative mergers and product
diversification rapidly augment the disadvantages of local bargaining.
It is relatively easy for a conglomerate concern, when dealing with
separate contracts and different expiration dates, first to conquer some
weaker unions and then subdue the stronger ones.[4] In this way, mergers
have a double benefit: while product diversification diminishes the risks

[1] C. Kerr, *Labor and Management in Industrial Society* (New York, Doubleday-Anchor Books, 1964), p. 264.
[2] J. T. Dunlop, 'The Social Utility of Collective Bargaining', in *Challenges to Collective Bargaining*, ed. L. Ulman, pp. 162–3.
[3] *Gesetzbuch der Arbeit* (Berlin, Staatsverlag der Deutschen Demokratischen Republik, 1963), p. 325.
[4] David Lasser, 'Coordinated Bargaining, a Union Point of View', *Proceedings of the 1968 Annual Spring Meeting of the Industrial Relations Research Association* (Columbus, Ohio, 1968), p. 512.

in the product market, diversified bargaining will diminish risks in the labor market.[1] This enabled one corporation for years to negotiate wage increases not much higher than the rising cost of living.[2] How large these benefits can be is indicated by the fact that to prevent coordinate bargaining the Union Carbide Corporation in its fight with the unions was willing to sacrifice no less than 35 million dollars.[3] Which seems a high price to protect the union members against their leaders' 'aggrandizement of power . . .'[4] A more convincing argument is that coordinated contracts run against the contemporary managerial policy of delegating greater autonomy to the various 'profit centers' in the modern corporation.[5]

A negative element in coordinated bargaining is that it tends to support professionalization. The greater variety of workers, the differentiated hospital insurance and pension plans, the management techniques and intricate legal regulations require highly trained negotiation specialists.

This has led to the disappearance not only of the rank and file member from the bargaining table but also of the self-made, charismatic union boss. The latter, risen from the ranks in a period of conflict, with strong psychological appeal to the membership, has been widely succeeded by university educated economists. This has diminished the number of conflicts in modern bargaining, but it has also moved its dramatics away from the workers' world.

Another negative effect is that breakdowns in coordinated bargaining will cause greater economic damage. A prolonged strike in a nationwide industry—prolonged because of the parties' greater strength—does more harm to the national economy than a conflict in a local company. This is one reason why the national interest, represented by the government, has become increasingly incorporated in the private interests engaged in collective bargaining.

With the majority of contracts in single plants,[6] bargaining in the

[1] George H. Hildebrand, 'Coordinated Bargaining, An Economist's Point of View', *Proceedings of the 1968 Annual Spring Meeting of the Industrial Relations Research Association*, p. 526.
[2] David Lasser, 'Coordinated Bargaining', p. 513.
[3] Earl L. Engle, 'Coordinated Bargaining, A Snare—and a Delusion', *Proceedings of the 1968 Annual Spring Meeting of the Industrial Relations Research Association*, p. 523.
[4] *Ibid.* p. 520.
[5] Edward L. Cushman, 'Management Objectives in Collective Bargaining', in Arnold R. Weber, *The Structure of Collective Bargaining* (Glencoe, Ill., The Free Press, 1961), pp. 62–3. Also: Peter F. Drucker, *The Concept of the Corporation* (New York, The New American Library, 1964), pp. 46–69.
[6] Neil W. Chamberlain, 'Collective Bargaining in the United States', in *Contemporary Collective Bargaining in Seven Countries*, ed. Adolf Sturmthal (New York State School of Industrial and Labor Relations, Cornell University, Ithaca, N.Y., 1957), p. 259. This author mentions that 68 per cent of the collective contracts in the United States is in single plant units.

United States is still less centralized than in Western Europe. But there is little doubt that with the spread of bargaining between national unions and conglomerate corporations,[1] and with increased government intervention, Western Europe and the United States are gradually moving toward the same 'collectivist' system of industrial relations.[2]

Bargaining in the public sector. Although more or less completed in Western Europe, the unionization of public employees is still in process in the United States. Between 1956 and 1962, the number of unionized government employees rose in that country with 33 per cent to 1,225,000. This increase was mainly responsible for the slight recovery of union membership from its low in 1961.[3]

In this sector the deficiencies of bargaining have caused greatest public criticism. Such employees as garbage collectors, welfare employees, firemen, hospital attendants, teachers, airport employees and policemen serve entire sections of the population, with the result that a breakdown of bargaining in these areas can endanger the health and safety of society.

Conflicts between the new 'professional' unions and the older 'traditional' unions over the representation of these public employees, sometimes resulting in strikes, tend to increase this public criticism.

In order to prevent strikes of public employees, such punitive measures as fines against the union, jailing of union officers or anti-union legislation have proved rather ineffective. For this purpose more positive measures, for example compulsory arbitration, would probably have a greater effect.

Conclusion. Few will deny that, at least in the United States, collective bargaining is in a crisis. Apart from its almost incurable inflationary effects, the social and economic impact of breakdowns in the negotiations has become increasingly alarming.

One reason for these breakdowns is that the bargaining process has moved away from the rank and file, with the result that they feel less involved and less hesitant to reject a negotiated contract. In the United States, in cases where a negotiator was actively involved, such rejections

---

[1] A. H. Raskin, 'Collective Bargaining and the Public Interest', in *Challenges to Collective Bargaining*, ed. L. Ulman, pp. 162–3.

[2] B. C. Roberts, *Unions in America, A British View* (Industrial Relations Section, Princeton University) (Princeton, 1959), p. 79.

[3] Allan Weisenfeld, 'Collective Bargaining by Public Employees in the U.S.,' in *Collective Bargaining in the Public Service*, Proceedings of the Annual Spring Meeting, IRRA (Milwaukee, Wis., 1966), pp. 1–2.

have increased since 1962. For the period 1964–7 they show the following trend:[1]

Year	Total joint meeting cases	Rejection percentage
1964	7,221	8·7
1965	7,445	10·0
1966	7,836	11·7
1967	7,193	14·2

With these figures reflecting a growing alienation between officers and the union membership, the question arises how to increase the latter's responsibility and involvement. The European unions with their history of centralized contracts have generally taken recourse to systems of joint consultation. It is expected that in the workers' councils the members will get a better understanding of the motives and functions of management and of the company's economic situation. This will make them less inclined to surprise the negotiating parties with unexpected or unreasonable demands.

This convergence of stimulating and restricting forces, each expanding at its own rate and complicated by various changes in the bargaining process itself, obscure our perception of the union's influence upon the workers' share of the national income. The effects of this obscuration upon the membership will be dealt with in Chapters 5 and 6.

MICROSOCIAL FUNCTIONS

In behalf of the members

The viability of a voluntary organization will depend on the presence of deeply felt needs among its members and their conviction that nothing will satisfy these better than the organization. If social change prevents the organization from satisfying these needs, if the needs are being served at lower cost by another institution, or if the members do not any more perceive this as a function of the organization, its membership will decline.[2]

Social change, either in society or in the organization, entails the risk of endangering this very process of need-satisfaction upon which voluntary membership is based.[3] The relevance of this for the unions of the advanced welfare state is indicated by the following observation:

[1] William E. Simkin, *Refusals to Ratify Contracts*, address before the Graduate School of Business, The University of Chicago (Chicago, Ill., 17 November 1968), p. 7.
[2] See Ch. 6.
[3] A. Etzioni, *Modern Organizations* (Englewood Cliffs, N.J., Prentice Hall, 1964), p. 41.

Every worker needs food, clothing and a home—which means that he needs a job. To defend his job and his wages is one reason for forming or joining a trade union.

A worker needs help to meet the consequences of accidents at work, financial assistance when sick or in case of a death in the family, support when out of work, and money to live on when too old or ill to work any longer. To meet these needs is another reason for the trade unions. *In some countries these needs are now met very largely by State schemes for accident insurance, sickness benefits, unemployment insurance, old-age pensions, and so on.*[1]

The last sentence refers to a growing problem in the relationship between the modern trade union and its members. In the last twenty years many union ideals have reached the status of basic human rights; the care for these rights is one of the tasks of the welfare state. Both the realization of ideals and the transference of social care to other institutions, have made inroads upon the unions' usefulness in the eyes of the rank and file.

United States unions, less idealistic and with a preference for 'industrial' over 'state' welfare, are to a lesser extent threatened by these developments than their European counterparts.[2] The latter have shown little sociological awareness. This is illustrated by their policy with regard to unemployment insurance, traditionally one of the union's most valuabie internal functions.

In the *Netherlands* in 1930 17 per cent of the labor force was insured against unemployment, with the unions paying fl. 12,000,000 in unemployment benefits.[3] Although the Dutch government subsidized these funds with 100 to 200 per cent, this function was in the hands of the unions. After World War II unemployment insurance was transferred to the state, with the unions only paying some additional benefits.

Scandinavian data suggest a close correlation between unemployment insurance as trade union function and union appeal upon the workers. In Sweden and Denmark, where the unemployment insurance is in union hands, their membership amounted in 1953 to respectively 60 and 50 per cent of the labor force. In Norway unemployment insurance has been taken over by the state agency of public health; union membership there amounted to 45 per cent of the labor force. In Finland, where the unions never engaged in unemployment insurance, only 33 per cent of the labor force was unionized.[4]

---

[1] J. Price, *Functions of Trade Unionism in Relation to Welfare Policy* (The Hague, Van Keulen, 1958), p. 1 (my italics).   [2] A. Lester, *As Unions Mature*, p. 42.

[3] C. Lammers, *De Vakbeweging en haar problemen* (Amsterdam, Arbeiderspers, 1951), p. 59.

[4] *Freedom and Welfare, Social Patterns in the Northern Countries of Europe*, ed. G. R. Nelson (sponsored by the Ministries of Social Affairs of Denmark, Finland, Iceland, Norway and Sweden) (Denmark, 1953), pp. 105 and 412.

The Scandinavian data support the hypothesis that further transference of union tasks to welfare state agencies will lead to a loss of membership allegiance. Data from social research sustain this in a more explicit way. Ex-members in the Netherlands who were asked their motivations for breaking with the labor organization (App. C) answered, for example:

'Since the Unemployment Insurance Act there is not much work left for the Union. Remains only that they may help you with legal aid, in case you get fired.'

'The unions don't even pay unemployment benefits anymore. All that they're needed for now is if you are treated unfairly.'

In Chapter 4 we shall find that the union's internal functions, i.e. in behalf of the members, are what largely attracts its membership. The transference of such functions to other institutions is in the eyes of Scandinavian, Dutch, and British workers a loss for the union.[1]

Of the remaining internal functions, 'individual assistance in the work situation' is evidently the most highly appreciated. This is supported by the fact that Dutch workers who continued their membership had profited from the union's individual assistance to a much greater extent than ex-members.

TABLE 6.   *Union assistance received by members and by recent ex-members**

I have received personally for my union dues:	Members %	Ex-members %
1. *Individual Assistance*		
Legal support in conflicts with employer	35	10
Financial aid in case of accident or illness	7	3
Employment service or aid when unemployed	6	3
Advice or aid in case of family problems, etc.	5	
Information on problems on the job	5	1
Miscellaneous forms of individual assistance	4	5
Total	62	22
2. *Collective forms of assistance*	26	7
3. *No assistance at all, or no known assistance*	18	71
	(100% = 200)	(100% = 200)

* See Appendices A, B, and C; Total of percentages > 100 due to multiple answers.

While 62 per cent of the members had received individual assistance,

[1] For England: 'The trade unions were deprived of the main justification they had for acting as benefit societies and were forced to concentrate on a narrower field, or find new activities. Conversely, the workers lost much of their interest in the trade unions as benefit societies and looked to State agencies to provide them with the social insurances they needed.' D. F. MacDonald, *The State and the Trade Unions*, p. 141.

less than one-quarter (22 per cent) of those who left the organization had. Only 18 per cent of the members had never received any union aid, as against 71 per cent of the ex-members. With the average period of membership in both groups being equal, this suggests a positive correlation between individual assistance received and the member's loyalty to the union.

When confronted with a drain on their internal functions, United States unions and European unions tend to react in opposite ways. Unions in the United States show a preference for security provisions, such as closed shop and union shop, which serve as a check on membership rotation. This has resulted in a rapid increase of security agreements in United States labor relations since World War II:

TABLE 7. *Union security provisions in major collective-bargaining agreements in the United States*[1]

	1946 %	1949–50 %	1954 %	1958–9 %
Closed shop	33	—	—	—
Union shop	17	49	64	74
	50			

The percentages are computed over all workers and under all agreements covering 1,000 or more workers in the United States, exclusive of those relating to railroads and airlines.

Union security is usually viewed as a defense against management's anti-union policies.[2] This implies however, that it is also a weapon against the workers' reluctance to join.[3] In the long history of the unions, workers who were convinced of the union's value have always been willing to maintain their membership, whether the boss was pro- or anti-union. The spread of closed and union shops is partly a symptom of their growing hesitation.

European unions often have political or religious affiliations, and to

[1] R. Theodore, 'Union Security Provisions in Major Union Contracts', *Monthly Labor Review*, LXXXII, No. 12 (1959), 1349.
[2] G. W. Brooks, 'The Security of Worker Institutions', *Monthly Labor Review*, LXXXVI, No. 6 (1963), p. 655.
[3] In the United States textile industry, for example, where only one third of the workers are organized in the Textile Workers' Union, the other two thirds can be fairly certain of receiving union wage rates or better. Drucker reports to have heard repeatedly from workers in the industry that under these conditions they see no reason for joining a union. It is this attitude, apart from management's anti-union policy, that makes union security a necessity. P. F. Drucker, 'Labor in Industrial Society', *The Annals of the American Academy of Political and Social Science*, Vol. 274 (March 1951), p. 145.

4

enforce these upon the workers interferes with freedom of association.[1] Confronted with even stronger functional drainage than in the United States, they seek their solution in expanded services and preferential treatment of members. One means is to renounce the principle of equality of union members and nonmembers in the collective agreement; nation-wide contracts in Belgium are already granting some fringe benefits only to union members.[2] However, the agency shop, in which nonmembers are required to pay a sum equal to the union dues, is a more rapidly spreading device in European labor relations.[3]

An example of expanded union services is attention given to the workers as consumers. European unions are now getting involved in low-rent housing programs, consumer credit plans, automobile financing, cultural and educational programs,[4] travel agencies, consumer cooperatives, dis-count houses, and mutual funds. If it is true that the workers in advanced societies increasingly conceive of themselves as consumers,[5] these new union functions may have a basis of new and real needs.

CONCLUSION

Often outlawed in the nineteenth century, labor unions became gradually tolerated at the beginning of the twentieth century. Between the two world wars they were generally accepted as negotiating partners and, at present, they are deeply integrated in the welfare state. This integration proceeds against two opposite trends, among the workers and within the unions themselves.

As for the workers, we saw in Chapter 1 that their macrosocial values of solidarity and idealism are replaced by a deeper concern with personal needs. This trend, partly conditioned by the welfare state, was described as the 'individualization' of the workers.

The trade unions are undergoing changes in the opposite direction.

---

[1] H. Brickman, 'Freedom of Association in Eight European Countries', *Monthly Labor Review*, LXXXVI, No. 9 (1963), pp. 1020–5. See also M. Dudra, 'Approaches to Union Security in Switzer-land, Canada and Colombia', *Monthly Labor Review*, LXXXVI, No. 2 (1963), pp. 136–7.

[2] R. Blanpain, *De Syndikale Vrijheid in Belgie* (Antwerp, 1963), p. 82.

[3] The introduction of agency shop devices in the Dutch building trades led to serious riots in Amsterdam in 1966.

[4] K. Braun, 'Cultural Activities of West European Organized Labor', *Monthly Labor Review*, LXXXVI, No. 4 (1963), 370–7. For an in-depth study of trade union sociocivic education in a European labor movement, see G. Wuthe, *Gewerkschaften und politische Bildung* (Hanover, Verlag f. Literatur u. Zeitgeschehen, 1962). Additional information in Alice H. Cook and Agnes M. Douty, *Labor Education Outside the Unions, a Review of Postwar Programs in Western Europe and the United States* (School of Industrial and Labor Relations, Cornell University, Ithaca, N.Y., 1958), p. 148.

[5] R. Dubin, 'Behavioral Science Analysis and Collective Bargaining Research', *Proceedings of the 1965 IRRA Spring Meeting* (Buffalo, N.Y., 3–4 May 1965), p. 505. (Reprinted from the *Labor Law Journal*, August 1965.)

While their micro-functions, in behalf of the individual member, are being transferred to other institutions, their macro-functions, in behalf of industry and nation, are expanding.

Both trends undermine the unions' value in the eyes of the workers. But unions have learned to adjust themselves to changes in their environment. In the nineteenth-century class society primarily 'strike insurance' they switched in the crisis of the 1930s to the role of 'unemployment insurance'. Whether their new role of 'individual problem insurance' will also meet with success, will possibly depend upon their ability to encounter another threat the labor force is facing, viz. the adverse effects of automation. Before analyzing this among new and former members we shall first examine what problems arise from the reverse trends in workers' needs and union functions.

3. The leaders and the members

From the beginning, labor has coped with a problem called 'masse et militants', 'Führer und Massen', or 'trade union apathy'. So, the problem appears to be inherent and not a consequence of the welfare state. The earliest observations were made by the Webbs, as far back as 1894:

Nor must it be supposed that the great majority of the million and a half Trade Unionists render, even as privates, any active service in the Trade Union forces. *Only in the crisis of some great dispute do we find the branch meetings crowded*, or the votes at all commensurate with the total number of the members. At other times the Trade Union appears to the bulk of its members either as a political organization which dictates they are ready to obey at Parliamentary and other elections, or as *a mere benefit club in the management of which they do not desire to take part*.[1]

Observations from other countries show how widespread this problem was. In Germany, before World War I, Robert Michels quoted with approval the words of Ströbel, then editor of *Vorwärts*:

The neutrality the trade unions have been preserving for years has caused the majority of their members to become indifferent to politics and *judge the unions only in terms of the most trivial occupational and short-term interest*.[2]

In Holland, where the development of the unions lagged half a century behind, this indifference was no less marked; as early as 1918, Roland Holst denounced the general apathy in the Dutch trade unions:

The habit of having their leaders think and act for them had weakened the members' initiative. The form of conflict which turned a comparatively small number of prominent figures into real actors in the drama of the class struggle *consolidated the former passivity of the masses* and their lack of faith in their own power.[3]

Such historical data suggest that nonparticipation has long been widespread in trade unionism and that, statistically, the problem is normal. For this reason, some United States and European sociologists doubt that the apathy within the movement has ever increased.[4] Others go even

---

[1] S. and B. Webb, *History of Trade Unionism*, p. 384, quoted by J. Goldstein, *The Government of British Trade Unions* (London, Allen and Unwin, 1952), p. 60 (my italics).

[2] R. Michels, *Zur Soziologie des Parteiwesens in der modernen Demokratie* (Leipzig, 1911), p. 139 (my italics).

[3] H. Roland Holst-van der Schalk, *Revolutionaire Massa-Aktie* (Rotterdam, 1918), p. 191 (my italics).

[4] S. M. Lipset, M. A. Trow, and J. S. Coleman, *Union Democracy* (Glencoe, Ill., Free Press, 1956), p. 11; and W. Banning, 'Non-participatie in de tegenwoordige Westerse samenleving', *Sociologisch Jaarboek*, XIII (Amsterdam, 1959), p. 96.

further, regarding all statements of a gap between leaders and members as untrue, and a sign of ignorance or malevolence.[1] This, however, provides no answer to the question why the *interest* in trade union apathy has sharply increased since World War II. From 1948 on, a growing number of publications have dealt with this problem, conventions have discussed it, and funds have been available for research. No less important is that the investigators, whether Tagliacozzo in the United States, Klenner in Austria, or de Jong in Holland, consider the interaction between leaders and members postwar trade unionism's biggest problem.

In *Britain*, one of the first postwar studies contained the observation that only 20 per cent of union members were meeting-minded and that 50 per cent went to no meetings at all. The importance of this was expressed as followed: 'The greatest of all dangers facing the organization of the trade union movement today is the development between the center and the men on the job of a gap in outlook and activity, sufficiently wide to hamper the working of the unions.'[2] Some years later, a stir was caused by Goldstein, who demonstrated membership apathy to be one of the major conditions for Communist infiltration of British trade unions.[3] Labor circles regard trade union apathy as a serious problem, particularly now that efforts are being made to make the workers sufficiently interested and knowledgeable to participate in joint consultations.[4]

From *Scandinavia* come similar reports. In *Denmark*, also, organizational apathy is a condition of Communist infiltration into the unions[5]; in *Sweden*, we were informed by trade union leaders that the apathy of a majority of the members seriously impedes the education and training of the younger generation; in *Norway*, Holter observed that young members take little interest in their unions and that organizational apathy is seriously damaging the organizations.[6]

In *Germany*, where sociological studies of trade unions are relatively scarce, Mausolff makes similar observations[7] and Triesch, a fierce opponent of the DGB, speaks of 'the lack of interest of the members'.[8] In

---

[1] C. Lammers, *De vakbeweging en haar problemen* (Amsterdam, Arbeiderspers, 1951), p. 189.

[2] Political and Economic Planning, *British Trade Unionism* (London, 1948), p. 170.

[3] J. Goldstein, *The Government of British Trade Unions*. This work is subtitled *A Study of Apathy and the Democratic Process in the Transport and General Workers Union*. At the time of publication, the book received wide press coverage.

[4] I. Mikardo, 'Trade Unions in a Full-employment Economy', *New Fabian Essays*, ed. R. H. S. Crossman (London, F. A. Praeger, 1953).

[5] 'Onrust in Denemarken', *Nieuwe Rotterdamsche Courant* (26 April 1956), p. 3.

[6] H. Holter, 'Disputes and Tensions in Industry', *Scandinavian Democracy*, ed. J. A. Lauwerijs (Copenhagen, 1956), p. 219.

[7] A. Mausolff, *Gewerkschaft und Betriebsrat im Urteil der Arbeitnehmer* (Darmstadt, 1952) pp. 101–4.

[8] G. Triesch, *Die Macht der Funktionäre* (Düsseldorf, Karl Rauch Verlag, 1956), p. 59.

Austria, in 1953, two studies pointed to widespread trade union apathy, especially among the younger workers. There, Bednarik's field obervations[1] were confirmed in the standard work by Klenner, from which we quote: 'It is an absolute imperative for the democratic development of our political and economic life that confidence and close contacts be established again between the leaders of politics, industry and labor and the blue and white collar workers.'[2] In Klenner's view, nonparticipation is threatening the further development of economic democracy.

In *France*, the problem of 'masse et militants' is described as follows by Guy Thorel: 'Visit the factories, walk round building sites, chat in the offices, attend meetings with large or small audiences. Listen to the "militants" and watch the "masse". You will be struck by the fact that there is rarely a dialogue between them. The militants conduct a monologue while the "masse" remains passive.'[3] This picture is supported by Lefranc, the historian of French trade unionism.[4] Labor leaders in France are also concerned: in a series of articles in *Le Figaro*, they argue in favor of a trade union policy which will restimulate the members.[5]

In the *Netherlands*, the problem has also received much attention. The secretariat of the national federation of trade unions has prepared a training course to fight it, and its historian writes that membership apathy 'constitutes *the* problem of postwar trade unionism'.[6] It is interesting that the same is true for the Dutch denominational unions: an anniversary issue of the Catholic trade union monthly devoted most of its space to the matter,[7] while Kuiper's analysis of organizational apathy is based on data from the Protestant labor movement.[8]

In the *United States*, interest in union apathy is great, particularly in academic circles. Since 1945, hundreds of scholarly publications have, in one way or another, touched upon this problem. In her review of a part of this vast literature, Tagliacozzo concludes that: 'The issue of democracy versus bureaucracy in labor unions has moved into the foreground of

---

[1] K. Bednarik, *Der junge Arbeiter, ein neuer Typ* (Stuttgart, 1953), *passim*.

[2] F. Klenner, *Die Oesterreichischen Gewerkschaften, Vergangenheit und Gegenwartprobleme*, III (Vienna, 1953), 1785 f.

[3] G. Thorel, 'Masse et Militants', *Esprit*, XIX, Nos. 180–1 (July–August 1951), p. 170.

[4] 'It is only a minority who still attend meetings: their only function is to ratify decisions taken at a higher level.' G. Lefranc, *Les expériences syndicales en France de 1939 à 1950* (Paris, 1950), pp. 9, 359–60.

[5] M. P. Hamelet, 'Le syndicalisme au carrefour', *Le Figaro* (August–September 1958).

[6] F. de Jong, *Om de Plaats van de Arbeid*, p. 336.

[7] *Lering en Leiding*, XXVII, Nos. 8, 9, 10.

[8] G. Kuiper, 'Terreinverkenning voor het sociografisch onderzoek naar de sociale afstand tussen leiding en leden' (speech given in Amsterdam, 1954).

attention.'[1] And not only of the theorists: in 1959 Congress enacted Part IV of the Labor–Management Basic Rights, Ethical Standards and Disclosure Act, which aims at insuring organizational democracy through the regulation and supervision of union elections'.[2]

These empirical observations contrast sharply with the doubts and denials, mentioned above, that trade union apathy has been increasing. A possible explanation for this apparent contradiction can be found by comparing the postwar observations with those of earlier investigators. In that case three points of difference become evident.

The Webbs, Michels, and Roland Holst have in common that none is a union official. Quite the reverse, they all dissociate themselves from the movement's leadership and accuse it of welcoming rather than combating nonparticipation. Michels, for instance, describes how union leaders govern democratic organizations according to oligarchic principles, by sealing off any opportunity for opposition.[3] Contrary to this, many post-war observations are made by union leaders themselves or by intellectuals connected with the trade union movement. In Holland, the unions financed research on apathy,[4] and our discussions with Swedish and German union officials have revealed that they, too, consider it an urgent problem.[5] A first point of difference, therefore, is that, around 1900, trade union apathy was only studied by theoreticians as a *sociological* problem, whereas today labor leaders increasingly consider it a *social* problem, to be solved by sociologists.[6]

A second point of difference lies in the definition of the problem. The Webbs, Michels, and Roland Holst were primarily concerned with the question of whether or not the membership controlled and corrected the leaders' decisions, i.e. they were primarily concerned with *upward* control.

---

[1] L. Tagliacozzo, 'Trade-union Government, Its Nature and Its Problems, A Bibliographical Review, 1945–1955', *American Journal of Sociology*, LXI, No. 6 (May 1956), p. 336. Also, Arnold S. Tannenbaum, 'Unions', in *Handbook of Organizations*, ed. James G. March (Chicago, Rand McNally, 1965), p. 743.

[2] Howard Jenkins Jr., 'Trade Union Elections', in *Regulating Union Government*, ed. Marten S. Estey, Philip Taft and Martin Wagner (New York, Harper & Row, 1964), p. 154.

[3] R. Michels, *Zur Soziologie des Parteiwesens*, p. 139.

[4] For the Protestant federation, see Kuiper, 'Terreinverkenning voor het sociografisch onderzoek', p. 14. For a similar investigation in the Catholic unions, see *Het Centrum*, 19 January 1957. The writer has conducted three investigations for the socialist federation.

[5] Discussions with officials of the Industrie-Gewerkschaft Metall (IGM) in Frankfurt (January 1961), at Schliersee (March 1961), and at Utrecht (November 1962): and with officials of the Swedish Metal Workers Union (LO) at Malmö, July 1961.

[6] One reason is the claim by opponents of trade unionism that the rift between leaders and members has now become so great that the latter need to be 'protected'. When the Taft–Hartley Act, which severely injured the American trade unions, was approved by Congress in 1947, this was the official justification. See *The Trade Union Situation in the United States* (Geneva, ILO, 1960), p. 27. There are indications, however, that this internal concern about union apathy is still stronger in Europe than in the United States. See Albert Rees, *The Economics of Trade Unions* (Chicago, Chicago University Press, 1962), p. 180.

Contemporary researchers, however, define the problem differently, since they are chiefly concerned with the influence of the leaders over the members, i.e. with *downward* control. An illustration of this is provided by a report of the Dutch Building Workers Union on the problem of 'Leaders and Members'. The union's executive committee complains that 'in some situations the leaders have too little *grip on the members*' and that 'in times of tension the members lack the necessary *trust in their leaders*'.[1] It is also illustrated by Thorel's description of the strain on union leaders: 'The trade-union leader's real tragedy is not that he may fail to obtain an improvement of working conditions or a rise in wages, *but his failure to make himself understood by the members*.'[2] According to this view, the modern trade union leader's problem is not the struggle for material improvements, but the problem of how to influence and hold his union's members. We shall return to this problem on p. 102 below.

The third point of difference is the most basic one. Primarily interested in trade union democracy, the Webbs, Michels, and Roland Holst concerned themselves almost exclusively with nonattendance at branch meetings. But for contemporary researchers the problem is broader, covering two other forms of nonparticipation as well. One is membership turnover, i.e. the fact that against the thousands who join the unions there are nearly as many who leave; the other is the unofficial strike in which workers (including union members) by-pass the union official and follow nonunion leaders in a walkout. Sociologically, these phenomena are closely related, not only because, from the union viewpoint, they are all forms of nonparticipation but also because the same group of members is often involved in all three. Those members who never attend meetings often show a membership turnover and also have a lower resistance to the wildcat strike.[3] The causal relationship between these trends is that low attendance at the meetings probably precedes the other two: an organization with a low proportion of active members lacks the social cohesion that curbs turnover and prevents undisciplined action. All of this is most obvious in Western Europe, where union membership is more on a voluntary basis than in the United States. There are several indications, however, that similar trends exist in the United States, as will become evident when each of these problems is discussed in detail.

MEMBERSHIP TURNOVER: THE PROBLEM OF LOYALTY

Just as political democracy assumes that a responsible citizen will join a political party, so the labor movement assumes it to be every worker's

[1] Alg. Ned Bouwbedrijfsbond, *Rapport Commissie Leiding en Leden* (Utrecht), pp. 4, 11.
[2] G. Thorel, 'Masse et Militants', p. 173.
[3] See Ch. 6, p. 185. See also: Political and Economic Planning, *British Trade Unionism*, p. 32.

moral duty to join a trade union. It is only the democratic right of free-dom of association that keeps European trade unions from insisting that this should become a legal duty as well.[1]

This voluntary character distinguishes organized labor from other economic and political institutions, such as industry and government. For although not every member joins his union of his own free will,[2] he still has more freedom with regard to the union than the worker has with regard to his company or the citizen has with regard to his national government. We saw that the advantages of this freedom for the trade unions themselves are smaller and more difficult to assess than the draw-backs.[3] It explains why trade unions make frequent use of systems that restrict the worker's organizational freedom.

The best known of these forms of union security are: (*a*) the closed shop, where the employer agrees to hire only union members; (*b*) the union shop, where the employer dismisses all nonunion workers within a given period; (*c*) the preferential shop, where an employer faced with comparable candidates gives preference to union members in hiring; (*d*) the maintenance of membership clauses, which forces union members in the company to remain in the union; (*e*) the check-off clause, under which union dues are deducted from wages and made over to the union; (*f*) the employment card which insures that only those workers are hired who have received union-recommended training; (*g*) the special collective contract, which provides special benefits to union members; (*h*) the provision for preferential treatment of union members in the event of promotion or layoff; and (*i*) the agency shop, where all workers pay dues to the union although there is no obligation to join.[4]

One of the advantages of voluntary membership is that it strengthens the organization's claims to democratic legitimacy. Before the public forum, its voluntary character serves as the basis of trade unionism's 'inner justification', which, according to Max Weber is a requirement of any exercise of power.[5] But, although the voluntary system may support

[1] *Rapport van de Commissie ter bestudering van het vraagstuk van het verplichte lidmaatschap van de financiele lasten van de vakbeweging*, 8 February 1949.

[2] Systems like the closed shop are (for example, in the printing trades) also known in Europe, though to a lesser extent than in the United States. See W. E. J. McCarthy, *The Closed Shop in Britain* (Berkeley, University of California Press, 1964). We shall see in Ch. 4 what types of moral pressure are used to make the worker join the union.

[3] Working on the basis of an average union subscription of Fl. 30 a year (which is on the low side), the fact that not all employed persons in Holland are union members means an annual loss of income for the movement as a whole of Fl. 60 million.

[4] See R. Blanplain, *De syndikale vrijheid in Belgie* (Antwerp and Amsterdam, 1963), pp. 76 f. and H. G. Heneman, Jr. and Dale Yoder, *Labor Economics* (Cincinatti, South-Western Publishing Co., 1965), pp. 227-8. It needs to be stressed that our list is by no means complete.

[5] M. Weber, 'Politik als Beruf', *Gesammelte Politische Schriften* (Munich, Drei Masken Verlag, 1921), p. 398.

the union's legitimacy as a democratic institution, there is little doubt that at the same time it undermines its numerical strength. For the labor movement can only claim to represent *all* workers if the percentage of non-members in the labor force remains reasonably low. This implies a basic contradiction between the legitimate and the numerical basis of trade union representation, as is illustrated when the unions claim to speak for the *entire* working population even though they have relatively little strength among white collar workers.

The fact that membership is voluntary has not been without its effect on the level of union membership among the European labor force. Figure 5,[1] shows how membership in the three federations of Dutch trade unions has developed over the last forty years.

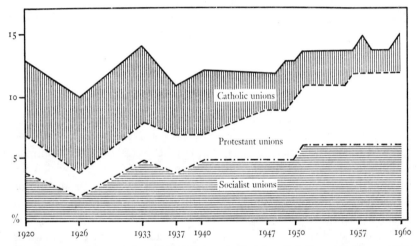

FIGURE 5. Percentages of the Dutch labor force in Socialist, Catholic and Protestant labor unions between 1920 and 1960.

These statistics permit the following conclusions:

1. In each of the federations, membership fluctuated more between the wars than it did after 1950, when the welfare state had become established. Prior to 1940, the drops in membership coincided with economic slumps, and observers contend that they must be explained in terms of these crises.[2] This correlation between economic depression and falling union membership has also been observed in the United States,[3] and seems to have been general. Conversely, we see that in an

[1] *Zestig jaren statistiek in tijdreeksen* (Zeist, De Haan, 1959), and *Omvang der vakbeweging in Nederland op 1 January 1961* (CBS) (Zeist, 1962).

[2] C. Lammers, *De vakbeweging en haar problemen*, p. 46.

[3] See M. W. Reder, *Labor in a Growing Economy* (New York, John Wiley and Sons, 1957), pp. 31–6.

expanding economy membership increased. Thus, *before* World War II prosperity correlated positively with trade union growth.

2. During the entire period, membership figures for the socialist and the denominational federations follow the same pattern. All three were sensitive to prewar economic trends and all show some loss of dynamic impetus since 1950. This indicates that religion plays a secondary role among the factors influencing trade union membership. The worker's religious affiliation determines not *whether* he joins a union but *which* union he joins. Also, the power of the Catholic and Protestant organizations to attract and hold members proves to be no greater than that of the Socialist trade unions.

3. Since World War II, and since 1950 in particular, the percentage of workers in each federation has been comparatively stable. But, despite the considerable postwar rise in prosperity (see Chapter 1), the level of membership shows *no* increase. This deviation from the prewar correlation is not only new, it is also comparatively widespread. We saw that in the United States' unions a rise in prosperity always led to an increase in membership. But there, too, the correlation reversed after World War II; and since 1956 the proportion of union members of the labor force has actually decreased.[1] These parallel trends in both the European and the American labor movement lead to the conclusion that the correlation between prosperity and trade unionism has been reversed.

The implication is that the welfare state, although propagated and defended by the labor movement,[2] is not particularly conducive to union membership. Thus it is difficult to escape the impression that, barring drastic social change, the unions have reached the peak of their numerical strength.

[1] Union membership in 1956 was 24·8 per cent of the total United States labor force; till 1964, there was a consistent decline, to 21·9 per cent. In the U.S. non-agricultural labor force the decline was from 33·4 per cent to 28·9 per cent. Source: U.S. Department of Labor, Bureau of Labor Statistics, April 1966. Kassalow goes so far as to say that a definite frontier has been reached: 'Though this decrease was only a minor one, there is other evidence which suggests that in recent years American unions have reached a membership frontier', *Harvard Business Review*, Vol. XL, January–February 1962, p. 41. Bernstein, on the other hand, takes the view that this setback is temporary, not structural: J. Bernstein, 'The Growth of American Unionism 1945–1960', in *Labour History* Vol. 2, No. 1 (1961). Which is the correct view, time will tell.

[2] An American illustration of how trade unionism propagates the welfare state is AFL–CIO vice-president Walter P. Reuther's statement before the Joint Congressional Economic Committee, 9 February 1959. It stressed the need for : federal assistance to depressed areas; an improved unemployment insurance system; federal funds for education, health, recreation, etc. to local communities; the elimination of poverty by raising the minimum wage level; improved social-security benefits, including medical care; government supervision of automation; atomic and solar energy; a reduced standard workweek, national programs for housing, hospitals, highways, and conservation; federal control of the stock market; and stricter taxation of unearned income. See W. P. Reuther, *Selected Papers*, ed. H. M. Christman (New York, Pyramid Books, 1964), pp. 227–32.

Analyzing the structure of this comparatively static membership, it becomes clear that we are confronted with an extreme form of non-participation. Figure 6, with the Dutch Federation of Trade Unions' enrollment and discontinuance figures for the period 1953–61, indicates that the cause of the standstill in membership is not so much the inability to *attract* workers as the inability to *hold* them in the organization:[1]

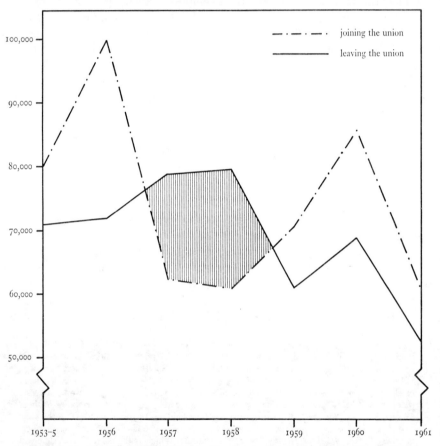

FIGURE 6. Number of members joining and leaving the Dutch Federation of Trade Unions between 1953 and 1961.

This graph illustrates how a European labor movement annually attracts tens of thousands of members and how, in the same period, almost as many cut their union ties. As a result, its growth is slight or halting. Table 8 shows that a similar trend is found in other countries.

[1] *Tweeëntwintigste Verslag van de werkzaamheden van het Nederlands Verbond van Vakvereningen*, 1959–61 (Amsterdam, 1962), p. 22.

TABLE 8. *Membership turnover*[1]

Trade union	Membership	Joining %	Leaving %
Transport and General Workers Union, England, 1947	1,317,842	34·4	36·6
Industrie-Gewerkschaft Metall, West Germany, 1954–55	1,522,000	41·5	28·9
Gewerkschaft Textil, West Germany, 1953–4	431,343	25·0	35·4

The causes of membership turnover, particularly the motives for joining and, sometimes only a few months later, resigning, are studied in detail in Chapters 4 and 6.[2] At this stage, we can only conclude that turnover is one aspect of the wider problem of nonparticipation in the trade unions.

WILDCAT STRIKES: THE PROBLEM OF DISCIPLINE

As an expression of strain between labor and management, the strike is related to other, less articulate forms of economic dissension, such as absenteeism, working-to-rule, slowdown, restriction-of-output, job turnover, and sabotage.[3]

At one time the strike, requiring more sacrifices from the workers than other forms of dissension, was predominantly an economic conflict; low morale, for example, was rarely thought to justify a walkout. There are signs, however, that this has been changing since World War II. United States and British observers have noticed that, as a cause of strikes, sociopsychological tensions such as dissatisfaction about human relations, about working conditions compared with those of other workers, and reactions against strict regulations or against changes in production methods, are becoming relatively more important.[4]

[1] The British statistics are taken from J. Goldstein, *The Government of British Trade Unions*, p. 74; the German figures from G. Triesch, *Die Macht der Funktionäre*, p. 52.

[2] It has been pointed out to the author that the high turnover, or lack of power to hold members, is not limited to the welfare state. Dr Werner Thönessen, on the staff of I. G. Metal, writes: 'My researches of fluctuations in membership in the largest German metalworkers' union, the DMV up to 1933 and IG Metal since 1945, have revealed that high turnover is by no means a monopoly of the latter period but is consistently encountered in prewar times as well ... I cannot help feeling that here we have missed one of the few criteria enabling us to draw a quantitative comparison between the present and the past.' In a letter, dated 1 February 1961.

[3] J. A. C. Brown, *The Social Psychology of Industry* (London, Penguin Books, 1954), p. 256.

[4] 'While wage questions still appear the most important issue, their importance is diminishing and that of what may be called frictional issues is increasing', K. H. G. C. Knowles, 'Strike-proneness and its Determinants', *American Journal of Sociology*, 1954, p. 214. Also Arthur M. Ross and Paul T. Hartman, *Changing Patterns of Industrial Conflict* (New York, Wiley and Sons, 1960), p. 6, and *Britain, an Official Handbook* (London, Central Office of Information, 1964), p. 475.

There is some basis for the contention, however, that this change has not affected all forms of labor stoppage, but only the more spontaneous wildcat strike. With the social conflict gradually being institutionalized in bargaining and arbitration, the unions are less in a position to use the strike as a tactical weapon.[1] At present, it is only resorted to in the rare situation that all communication has broken down. Because the union's members seldom know the details of the confidential negotiations, the result is that, when a strike is called, they are rarely moved by bitter resentment.[2] The spontaneous wildcat strike, on the other hand, has retained its function as an outlet for psychological tensions.[3] This is not altered by the fact that wildcat strikers will often demand higher wages.[4]

From the point of view of the trade unions, the wildcat conflict, originating, as it does, outside the union, is mainly symptomatic of a lack of confidence or discipline among its members. It may even be a symptom of rebellion, since in the welfare state this type of strike is often directed against the union's leaders. But, before examining this hypothesis, we shall see whether or not strike-proneness has changed in the welfare state.

A comparison of the frequency of work stoppages before and after World War II in two countries as different as the United States and the Netherlands reveals some contrasting trends. As the absolute strike figures in the two countries show considerable disparity, an index has been used in which the number of strikes in 1939 = 100. Graphically, this leads to the results given in Figure 7.[5]

---

[1] In their admirable comparative analysis of trade union strikes, Ross and Hartman find the following factors leading to abstention from strikes by the unions: (*a*) workers' satisfaction moving from economic to personal, sexual and other non-economic problems; (*b*) the decline of class antagonisms; (*c*) the increasing proportion of white collar workers in trade unions; (*d*) the employers' gradual accommodation to unionism and bargaining; (*e*) the intervening role of the state; (*f*) the generally unfavorable outcome of strikes for the unions; (*g*) loss of union membership due to strikes; (*h*) the high cost of strikes for union and workers; (*i*) labor political action paving the way to renunciation of the strike. As Ross and Hartman devote little attention to the wildcat strike, we shall mainly go into the latter. A. M. Ross and P. T. Hartman, *Changing Patterns of Industrial Conflict*, pp. 54–60.

[2] Holter, in Scandinavia, finds that many members under such circumstances go so far as to complain because the union leader, as an expert negotiator, has not managed to reach a peaceful settlement. H. Holter, 'Disputes and Tensions in Industry', p. 219.

[3] 'In such cases, the frustration persists and intensifies; and eventually, consequences of the less adaptive sort occur. These consequences of less adaptive sort frequently take the form of strikes.' D. Krech and R. S. Crutchfield, *Theory and Problems of Social Psychology* (New York, McGraw–Hill, 1948), p. 551.

[4] 'These unofficial strikes are . . . symptoms of a breakdown in relations between management and the workers at the place of work itself.' *Britain, An Official Handbook* (London, Central Office of Information, 1964), p. 475.

[5] United States figures were taken from *Work Stoppages in Fifty States and the District of Columbia*, 1927–62, BLS Report, No. 256 (Washington, D.C., 1964). The Dutch figures were made available by the Central Statistics Office (CBS). Since there are no Dutch figures for the war years, this period has not been included.

Until the middle of the 1930s the index of work stoppages in the United States climbs consistently *up* to the 1939 level, while the Netherlands reveal the inverse trend, i.e. from 1927 to 1939 the Dutch strike figures climb *down* to that level. These inverse trends continue after World War II until 1953, with the strike figures for the United States remaining above the index-year and the Dutch figures, after the peak of the postwar accommodation, remaining below that level. If the strike can be taken as a symptom of social conflict, the conclusion is that in Holland such conflict was fiercer before the war, but that we find the opposite in the United States.

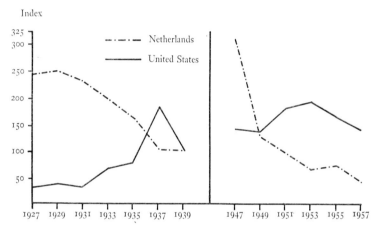

FIGURE 7. Index of the annual number of work stoppages in the United States and the Netherlands before and after World War II (1939 = 100).

This means that there is no fixed relationship between strike-proneness on the one hand and welfare state and affluent society on the other. In the United States, union strikes have increased, and even in a European welfare state with highly integrated unions they have—although decreasing —not entirely disappeared. From the fact that social conflict has not died in the Netherlands it should not be inferred, however, that the structure of the conflict has not changed either. In Figure 8, the data are broken down into official strikes and wildcat strikes (United States and other European statistics do not allow for this) and this breakdown shows that the present labor conflicts differ from the prewar conflicts both in frequency and in kind.[1]

There is a contrast in the relationship between the two types of labor conflict in the periods before the stabilization of this European welfare state and afterward. Up to 1940, trade union strikes were always more

[1] Based on data collected by the CBS at the author's request.

frequent than wildcat strikes, although showing a decrease from 1925 onward. This decline continued after the war to such an extent that the number of union strikes since 1951 has been negligible.[1] Considering that labor unions were originally 'strike associations',[2] this illustrates how much their function over that period has changed. In comparison, the Dutch wildcat strikes present a contrast in several respects. Far less frequent between the wars than union strikes, they have invariably out-numbered them since 1945. Equally important is that they have been more numerous after World War II than before. Hence, when the social conflict in this welfare state is waged by means of open labor disputes, this tends to occur *outside* the trade union movement.

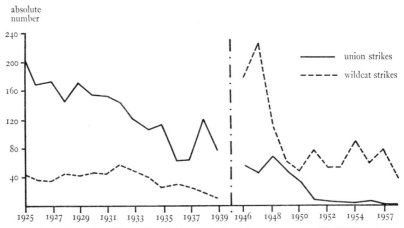

FIGURE 8. Union and wildcat strikes in the Netherlands before and after World War II.

It goes too far, however, to explain the occurrence of wildcat strikes solely in terms of the unions' position within the welfare state.[3] This view neglects their historical background. For as long ago as 1901, Bernstein de-scribed two wildcat conflicts in the steel industry, one in the German Ruhr, the other in Yorkshire.[4] An article by Max Weber in the *Frankfurter Zeitung* suggests that wildcat strikes were a serious economic problem in 1919. We quote:

The trade unions will no doubt be confronted with unprecedented diffi-culties. For the new generation of semi-adults, who are getting wages ten

---

[1] Ross and Hartman observe the same trend in Denmark, the Netherlands, the United King-dom, and West Germany. They call this the North European Pattern, First Variant. A. M. Ross and P. T. Hartman, *Changing Patterns of Industrial Conflict*, p. 74.

[2] W. Albeda, *De Rol van de Vakbeweging*, p. 27.

[3] 'These unofficial strikes ... reflect the strain which is inevitably experienced by the rank-and-file of the workers in adjusting to the changed functions of the trade unions in the modern society'. S. K. Saxena, *Nationalisation and Industrial Conflict, the Example of British Coal Mining* (The Hague, Nijhoff, 1951), pp. 96, 107.   [4] *Sozialistische Monatshefte* (1909), p. 82.

times higher than in peacetime and and are experiencing freedoms they will never know again, are being drained of any feeling of solidarity and ability to adapt themselves to the ordered economic struggle. A 'trade unionism of the immature' will be born.[1]

Our conclusion, therefore, is that in the European welfare state the difference from the past does not lie in the occurrence of wildcat strikes as such, but in their increased frequency as compared with union led conflicts.

This change in the structure of the social conflict can also be observed in other welfare states. In Britain, nonunion action accounts for 90 per cent of all strikes and 70 per cent of all working time lost through strikes.[2] PEP reported in 1948 that, compared to only one union strike since the end of the war, 'several disputes have occurred in which, had the same grounds for complaint existed in prewar days, the strikers would certainly have received official backing'.[3] Similar trends can be observed in the Scandinavian welfare states.[4]

As United States statistics do not distinguish between official and unofficial strikes,[5] one has to look for other indicators of lacking trade union discipline than wildcat action. One which recently has become available is the rate of contract rejections, i.e. the union members' refusals to ratify contracts negotiated by their leaders.[6]

As we saw on page 80, cases of collective bargaining where a negotiator is actively involved show a consistent increase of rejections; between 1964 and 1967 their percentage has almost doubled.[7]

Although in a less spectacular way than through wildcat strikes, this trend in contract rejections supports the conclusion that in the United States trade union discipline is waning. It is another indicator that the American 'Great Society' seems subject to the same social afflictions as the welfare states of Western Europe.

---

[1] M. Weber, 'Parlamentierung und Demokratisierung', *Gesammelte Politische Schriften* (Munich, Drei Masken Verlag, 1921), p. 222.

[2] *Britain, An Official Handbook*, p. 475.

[3] Political and Economic Planning, *British Trade Unionism* p. 171.

[4] H. Holter, 'Disputes and Tensions in Industry', p. 257.

[5] We, therefore, have to fall back on observations like this one: '. . . U.S. unions . . . are on the whole rather better than ours at coping with wildcat strikes and rather tougher in the discipline meted out to their own members who take part in them. American unions are much more willing than British unions to strike officially . . . But if there are far more official strikes there than here, there are fewer unofficial ones.' M. Shanks, *The Stagnant Society* (London, 1961), Penguin, p. 133.

[6] 'Refusals to Ratify Contracts', address by William E. Simkin, Director of the Federal Mediation and Conciliation Service, at the Graduate School of Business, University of Chicago, 17 November 1967, p. 3.

[7] *Ibid.* p. 7.

Taking another look at Figure 8, viz. at *the drop in trade union stoppages in the welfare era*, it becomes clear that trade unionism has lost a powerful cementing factor. This is confirmed by an account of one of the few post-war union walkouts in the Netherlands, describing how, in the emotional climate of the strike, a personal bond develops between union leader and members which lasts long after the conflict:

Acceptance [of the strike leader] will even develop into hero-worship if he does his job intelligently, and gives up hours of sleep and family life. The latter sacrifice in particular inspires a kind of tenderness among the strikers, and as a result the figure of the strike leader easily takes on messianic features. It was not for nothing that the strike leader was called 'Messiah'.[1]

It is obvious that if the strike is gradually disappearing from union life, the organization will lose a valuable binding force. Heyde's observation, that the identive power of the German unions declined with the falling strike-rate,[2] suggests this to be a general reaction. Related attitudes are known even among members of Catholic and Protestant trade unions.[3]

The second aspect of Figure 8, viz. *the increase in the welfare state of wildcat strikes*, makes this problem considerably more serious. For it means that union members who are involved in this sort of un-authorized action identify themselves with opinion leaders outside the union, and so come into sharp conflict with the leaders of their own organization.

At the meetings of the wildcat Amsterdam transit strike in 1955, for instance, nearly every speech was directed against the labor union to which most of the strikers belonged. This union's report on the dispute states that 'It was virtually impossible for the union leaders to establish contact even with their own members (!) because of the heated atmos-phere, the constraint and obstruction of those who wanted the strike to continue.'[4]

Similar reactions occurred during a wildcat strike of Rotterdam con-struction workers in June 1956. Again, there were strong anti-union feelings: 'One of the speakers proposed leaving the union en bloc, and

---

[1] J. J. de Wit, *Correctie op de Eeuwgrens, het anachronisme van de Ommelanden, sociaal-psycho-logisch beschouwd* (Assen, Van Gorkum, 1957), p. 66.

[2] Ludwig Heyde 'Arbeitskampf,' in *Handwörterbuch der Sozialwissenschaften*, v, p. 298.

[3] On the basis of an empirical survey, De Koning found that the members of the Protestant Metalworkers Union took a great interest in articles about strikes and reacted to them in a favorable emotional manner. See J. de Koning, *De lezers van Het Metaalbedrijf* (Utrecht, Sociological Institute of the Federation of Protestant Unions, 1957).

[4] *Rapport naar de oorzaken, de achtergronden en het verloop van de staking van het Amster-damse gemeentepersoneel, maart–april 1955* (Amsterdam, Committee of the Dutch Labor Party, 1955), p. 39.

others expressed harsh criticism of the union executive . . . Their words were booed or applauded according to whether they were for or against the union.' British data indicate that wildcat strikes in which trade unionists turn against their leaders are not uncommon in the welfare state.[1]

Since unauthorized strikes, especially under Communist influence, are often provoked when they have an optimal disruptive effect,[2] trade union discipline can become an acute economic problem. Consequently, observers often equate the problem of apathy in trade unions with that of unofficial strikes. If some time passes without any wildcat disputes, it is accordingly assumed that the fundamental causes of the problem have also disappeared. We shall see that this view is mistaken.

Our conclusion is that when trade unions become integrated into the welfare state, arbitration and joint consultation may aid in the prevention of open labor conflicts. The Dutch strike data, as given in Figure 8, together with Ross and Hartman's analysis, confirm this. But unless labor aims at a democratization of the industrial structure, this will not eliminate the more fundamental conflict in *values* of the managerial elite and the industrial workers.[3] Inasmuch as there are indications that unionism has given up this latter ideal,[4] the roots of the social conflict are likely to remain. The implication is that the structural basis of the labor strike, e.g. the incongruity of values, will survive in Western society,[5]

---

[1] The unofficial seamen's strike in Britain in August 1960, for instance, was directed primarily against the executive of the National Seamen's Union. Ian Mikardo expresses a corresponding view: 'Many unofficial strikes are not against the employers but against the union's national executive or its national trade council.' I. Mikardo, 'Trade Unions in a Full-employment Economy', p. 153. As a reaction against this, the union's leaders often bitterly attack unofficial strikes. Saxena quotes William Lawther, Chairman of the British Mine-workers Union, in 1948: 'They (the unofficial stoppages) are wrong; they are criminal; they cannot be tolerated or excused.' And, in 1949: 'It is a crime against our people that unofficial strikes should take place.' S. K. Saxena, *Nationalisation and Industrial Conflict*, pp. 108–9.

[2] A. Sturmthal, 'National Patterns of Union Behavior', *Journal of Political Economy*, LVI, No. 5 (December 1948), p. 517.

[3] 'Wherever there are industrial enterprises, there is a quasi-group of the incumbents of the roles of domination, the latent interests of which are in conflict with those of a corresponding quasi-group of incumbents of roles of subjection.' R. Dahrendorf *Class and Class Conflict in Industrial Society* (Stanford, Stanford University Press, 1963), p. 251.

[4] In Britain: 'For special institutional reasons, the trade unions . . . have renounced, formally, the objective of industrial democracy as incompatible with their traditional role. From the idea of democracy there has been a steady retreat to the far more modest objective of joint-consultation which neither in theory nor in fact constitutes a challenge to managerial power.' P. Shore, 'In the Room at the Top', in *Conviction*, ed. N. Mackenzie (London, Monthly Review Press, 1958), p. 40.

[5] Sheriff and Cantril make some interesting comments on value-congruity in Communist industry: 'The worker in the Soviet system has the possibility of finding an extension of the values held by his local factory unit to the whole factory or the collective operation and, in turn, to the larger goal of the whole social organization. Thus the values which are for him personal values and which give him status in his own eyes and the eyes of his fellow workers

the only difference being that the more labor's integration proceeds, the more the social conflict will manifest itself in its wildcat variant.[1] An increase of nonunion strikes, however, could well threaten the very basis of the union's integration in the welfare state.[2]

MEMBERSHIP APATHY: THE PROBLEM OF INVOLVEMENT

So far, we have discussed two aspects of a voluntary organization's internal strength: the stability of its membership and the discipline in its ranks. In trade unions, this amounts to the ability to create the loyalty which keeps turnover low, and an identification with the leaders which prevents unauthorized action.

More important for the organization's strength, however, is a third factor, viz. organizational participation. The reason is that a high level of participation implies an exchange of views between leaders and members, open channels of communication, and a body of active opinion leaders maintaining contact with the rank and file. As the trade unions carry greater economic and political responsibilities, with their structure becoming more bureaucratic and their problems growing more complicated, these roles gain in importance. Upholding the members' loyalty and their discipline, participants will check both turnover and wildcat action.

Organizational participation : quantitative analysis

Organizational sociologists have discovered that even a comparatively small group of participants, acting as opinion leaders, can fulfill invaluable functions in the communication between the organization's power elite and its members. They have cohesive impact which stems from the fact that, at any social level, men are most receptive to advisers from their own social ranks.

In an American election, for example, a stratum of participants, comprising between 22 and 27 per cent of the electorate, decisively influenced

are part and parcel of or reflections of values of larger social organizations of which he and his immediate group regard themselves a part.' Muzafer Sherif and Hadley Cantril, *The Psychology of Ego-Involvements* (New York, John Wiley and Sons, 1947), p. 381. If this observation is correct, the Soviet system has, in this respect at least, achieved a more harmonious situation.

[1] Clearly, this removes the conditions necessary for a statutory ban on strikes, as advocated in some welfare states. To be effective, such a measure would have to be based on a sense of justice common to *all* parties. This could only occur in a fully integrated industrial society in which employers and employees share the same standards and interests and work toward common goals. The number of unofficial strikes is ample evidence that this is as yet a dream.

[2] This occurred in Holland, in 1963, when the ratio of union to wildcat strikes had risen to 1:57. In the rapid and widespread raise of wages that resulted, the Dutch trade union's existence was almost threatened.

the choice of the other voters.[1] Panel research showed that these opinion leaders, through informal chats at work or with friends, had greater political impact than any mass medium.[2] Because their influence is limited to their immediate social milieu, every level of society has its own opinion leaders. The traits of an opinion leader are, according to Katz, that he carries some authority as a person, that he has many contacts, and that he is better informed than those around him.[3] Socially, however, he must be considered and be trusted as a member of the in-group. 'They are like everyone else,' writes Berelson, 'only slightly more so.'[4] Opinion leaders often owe their expert knowledge to the attention they pay to press, radio, and television and to their attendance at the meetings of their party, union, association, etc. Consequently, much of the information disseminated via mass media reaches the masses through the opinion leaders: 'Ideas often flow from radio and print to the opinion leaders and from them to the less active sections of the population.'[5]

In this 'two-step' communication, the local meeting is an essential link, as the opinion leaders not only pass on facts and ideas but also the 'ethos' or feeling tone in which the argument is cast. This is of particular importance among manual workers, who are often very responsive to this element.[6] Since most affective communication takes place through personal interaction at meetings, the opinion leaders form a virtually indispensable factor in intra-organizational relations.

The role of the opinion leaders becomes more crucial as (*a*) problems become more complicated, (*b*) policies change more rapidly, (*c*) decision-making becomes more centralized, and (*d*) mass media give contradictory information. As all these conditions are fulfilled in contemporary industrial relations, they are particularly valuable in the trade unions. Only a large stratum of participants who not only follow the organization's policy but also assist in shaping it, can solve their communicative problems. We shall now establish the average percentage of trade union members who participate; our criterion will be attendance at meetings:

[1] R. E. Lane, *Political Life: Why People Get Involved in Politics* (Glencoe, Ill., Free Press, 1959), p. 53.
[2] For a detailed description of this phenomenon, see E. Katz and P. F. Lazarsfeld, *Personal Influence, the Part Played by People in the Flow of Mass Communications* (Glencoe, Ill., Free Press, 1955).
[3] E. Katz, 'The Two-Step-Flow of Communication: an Up-to-Date Report on an Hypothesis', *Public Opinion Quarterly*, XXI, No. 1 (Spring 1957).
[4] B. R. Berelson, P. F. Lazarsfeld and W. N. McPhee, *Voting: a Study of Opinion Formation in a Presidential Campaign* (Chicago, University of Chicago Press, 1954), p. 113.
[5] P. F. Lazarsfeld, B. Berelson and H. Gaudet, *The People's Choice: How the Voter Makes up His Mind in a Presidential Campaign* (New York, Columbia University Press, 1955).
[6] M. Benney, A. P. Gray, and R. H. Pear, *How People Vote: a Study of Electoral Behaviour in Greenwich* (London, Grove Press, 1956), pp. 133-4.

TABLE 9. *The average percentage of members attending a trade union meeting, in four different countries*

UNITED KINGDOM

1. A general study on British trade unionism gives an average of[1]	4 to 7%
2. In 16 unions affiliated with the TUC[2]	15 to 25%
3. A study of British trade unionism during an economic boom[3]	
always under	10%
and often under	5%
4. In a local TGWU branch, 1941–9[4]	4%

WEST GERMANY

5. A documentary study of the DGB reports that attendance at meetings varies between[5]	2 and 10%
6. Another figure, from different sources, reported in the same study	5 and 15%

UNITED STATES

7. In 13 local branches of a building workers' union 1956[6]	5 to 10%
8. A study on human relations in United States' trade unionism[7]	2 to 8%
9. In six local union branches in Columbus, Ohio, 1955[8]	10%
10. In a survey of sociological studies of trade unionism in the United States[9]	10%

THE NETHERLANDS

11. At a local branch meeting of the Roman Catholic Metalworkers Union[10]	10%
12. Annual meeting of the Utrecht branches of the following trade unions, 1962[11]	
(a) Dutch Transport Workers Union	3%
(b) General Dutch Building Workers Union	1%
(c) General Dutch Metalworkers Union	2%
(d) Protestant Transport Workers Union	17%
(e) Protestant Union of Workers in the Wood and Building Industries	2%
(f) Protestant Union for the Engineering and Electrical Industries	2%

[1] B. Roberts, quoted by T. E. Stephenson, 'The Changing Role of Local Democracy: the Trade Union and Its Members', *The Sociological Review*, N.S. v, No. 1 (July 1957).
[2] Political and Economic Planning, *British Trade Unionism*, pp. 25–6.
[3] I. Mikardo, 'Trade Unions in a Full-employment Economy', p. 157.
[4] J. Goldstein, *The Government of British Trade Unions*, p. 197.
[5] G. Triesch, *Die Macht der Funktionäre*, pp. 46–7.
[6] G. Strauss, 'Control by Membership in Building Trade Unions', *American Journal of Sociology*, LXI, No. 6 (May 1956), p. 529.
[7] L. R. Sayles and G. Strauss, 'What the Worker Really Thinks of His Unions', *Harvard Business Review*, XXXI, No. 3 (May–June 1953), pp. 99–100.
[8] G. W. Miller and J. E. Young, 'Member-Participation in the Trade Union Local: A Study of Activity and Policymaking in Columbus, Ohio', *American Journal of Economics and Sociology*, XV, No. 1 (October 1955), p. 36.
[9] L. Broom and P. Selnick, *Sociology* (Evanston, Ill., Row, Peterson, 1955), pp. 440–1.
[10] A. J. M. van Osch, *Tijdstudie over de werkzaamheden van de Districtsbestuurders van de Nederlandse katholieke Metaalbewerkersbond St Eloy* (stencil) (Utrecht, 1960), p. 21.
[11] Results of a study carried out by R. Stolzenburg and R. van der Vlist, assisting the author.

One conclusion is that the proportions of participants in these United States' and European trade unions show a close correspondence. Another is that, if participants are defined as members who attend local meetings, their number may be too small to ensure sufficient organizational cohesion.

With the average attendance at a local meeting of 2 to 10 per cent, we may consider this to constitute the percentage opinion leaders in the union. If we accept the findings that one opinion leader normally influences six or seven other members,[1] this means that, in the present situation, a union branch with 100 members has between two and ten participants, influencing between fourteen and seventy passive members.

Allowing for a certain degree of rotation, the present attendance at union meetings is probably one-third to one-half of the number necessary to hold the organization firmly together. The conclusion is that the percentage of participants in European and United States unions is not high enough for a strong relationship between local leaders and rank-and-file members.

Since historical observations are lacking in quantitative data, it is hard to determine whether or not this implies that trade union participation has increased or decreased during the last half century.[2] What does seem likely, however, is that, in the qualitative sense, i.e. in the organizational radius within which the participant carries authority and influences decisions, participation has diminished.

Organizational participation : qualitative analysis

In Chapter 2, we found that labor unions have become less overly idealistic and more involved in the technicalities of bargaining and joint consultation. Reasons for this are the institutionalization of the social conflict, the decrease in social inequality, and the rise of social security systems. Although to be welcomed from an economic and social point of view, this change seems psychologically difficult for some participants to accept. 'The enemy has left the battlefield and suddenly everything has turned complicated and ambiguous', Crossland complains. 'Instead of about flagrant, glaring abuses we now have to get excited about the balance of payments, economic incentives and how to increase our production.'[3]

A negative aspect of this is that the members are seldom any longer sufficiently acquainted with trade union policy to take an active part in the movement; their actual knowledge is gradually lagging behind what is necessary for participation. The extent and structure of this lag are illustrated by the results of a survey of 400 workers in Utrecht, Holland, who

[1] Figures given by R. E. Lane, *Political Life*, p. 54, on the basis of an AIPO survey during the 1954 United States elections.
[2] There is one form of union activity, however, where participation has definitely decreased. Membership involvement in strikes has been generally declining for almost sixty years. A. M. Ross and P. T. Hartman, *Changing Patterns of Industrial Conflict*, p. 39.
[3] C. A. R. Crossland, 'De socialistische partijen en de toekomst', *Socialisme en Democratie* (11 November 1959).

were either members or ex-members of a socialist union. In a semi-structured interview they were asked the following questions:

1. Do you know what the term 'joint consultation' means?
2. Do you know why your union changed from a craft union into an industrial union?
3. Do you know what the latest wage demands of your union are? (These had been stated.)

Although the standards in grading the answers were lenient, the level of knowledge was equally poor for outsiders and trade unionists. The results for various economic categories are given below.

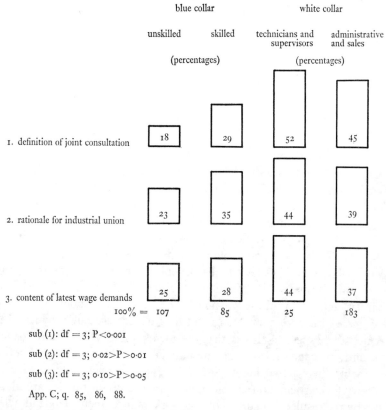

sub (1): df = 3; P<0·001

sub (2): df = 3; 0·02>P>0·01

sub (3): df = 3; 0·10>P>0·05

App. C; q. 85, 86, 88.

FIGURE 9. Knowledge of trade union policy in various socioeconomic categories.

The results of the survey permit the following conclusions:

(*a*) With the exception of the technicians and supervisors with regard to the first question, the majority in each category has insufficient knowledge to give a valid answer.

(*b*) The two white collar categories have consistently greater knowledge of trade union policies and problems than the blue collar workers.

(*c*) Among the blue collar workers, the skilled have greater knowledge of union affairs than the unskilled and semi-skilled workers.

(*d*) Among the white collar workers, the technical and supervisory staff have greater knowledge of union affairs than the administrative and sales staff.

An interesting outcome is that a group which is 'white collar' in status (supervisors, technicians, draftsmen, etc.) but whose work brings them in frequent interaction with manual workers, have greater knowledge about union matters than the historically older administrative and sales staff. Working on the borderline of the blue and white collar milieus, these employees are evidently in the best position to acquire knowledge about social issues. According to this criterion of social insight, the supervising and technical group of employees will contain the greatest number of potential union participants, and the unskilled manual workers the fewest.

The low level of knowledge leads to the conclusion that the problems of advanced industrial society become so complicated that the man in the street loses the ability to participate in its organizations. Marx refers to the loss of control over one's working conditions as 'Entfremdung' or alienation,[1] a concept which Weber has extended to politics.[2] There can be no doubt that organizational alienation, among those who are affected by it, is the condition which immediately precedes nonparticipation. This causal link becomes clear in the following responses, each of which, in its own way, mentions powerlessness or ignorance as the reason for nonparticipation.[3] They express organizational alienation in its most concrete form:

'As an ordinary member you have no influence on actions . . .'

'You've got no say anyhow, it's the man at the green table who decides things.'

'You may want this, that or the other, but as one of the rank-and-file you can't do a scrap. I feel so helpless, meetings and membership yield so little, everything is cut-and-dried before you go.'

'I'm not interested anymore. Most things are arranged before the members even know it. Years ago we all took part, had some action, organized meetings, and everybody could have his say. But today you only read in the paper what they've fixed, and next week you get the details in the union journal. I have always worked for the union, and taken part. But in the present situation I don't feel like it anymore.'

[1] K. Marx, *Economic and Philosophic Manuscripts of 1844*, Moscow, Foreign Languages Publishing House, n.d., pp. 72–3 and 77.

[2] M. Weber, 'Der Sozialismus', *Gesammelte Aufsätze zur Soziologie und Sozial-politik* (Tübingen, Mohr, 1924), pp. 492–518.

[3] This material is from an unpublished survey by the author.

Both, figures and responses indicate that the increasing complexity of the social system has reduced the radius of voluntary participation, and that this, in turn, has led to a smaller number of participants in unions and political parties.[1] The psychological background of this trend will be analyzed in Chapter 5.

CONCLUSION

On pages 87–9 above, we noted that during the last two decades trade union apathy has received more public attention than before. We found it to be the subject of concern in Europe and the United States among scholars and newspapermen as well as among labor leaders. Now, after our survey of its three symptoms, it is time to examine why the anxiety has grown.

If we again go over our data on membership turnover, wildcat strikes, and union meetings, it becomes clear that this concern cannot entirely be explained by rising figures. With regard to turnover, for example, we have no certainty that it is higher today than in the past; Thönessen's data, in fact, indicate that formerly it may have been as high. Similarly with regard to participation at meetings: although we hold our hypothesis, 'qualitative decline of participation leads to quantitative decline', to be true, we have no hard data which confirm it. Only with regard to unofficial strikes is there statistical evidence that at least in some welfare states they have increased. But this does not explain the worry about trade union apathy in countries where strikes are still in the hands of the unions. And none of these facts explain why, although apathy in *other* organizations may be considerably greater,[2] it gets much less public attention.

These circumstances make it likely that the cause of this growing anxiety lies not only inside, but also *outside* the unions, viz. in their changing role in society.[3] For although labor's size, financial resources, and economic experts have always given it an important voice in the nation's affairs, this was never accompanied by the formal integration in National Economic Councils, Presidential Committees and National Bargaining Boards which is occurring today. In this role, officially representing the working population, the unions' voice is gradually assuming the authority of a semipublic institution in society. Whether this institution is democratic, however, depends mainly upon the level of participation within its ranks. This integration makes union apathy a major

---

[1] For a quantitative analysis of this relationship, see M. van de Vall, 'Das Problem der Partizipation in freiwilligen Organisationen' in J. Matthes, *Soziologie und Gesellschaft in den Niederlanden* (Luchterhand Berlin Verlag, 1965), p. 255.

[2] M. van de Vall, 'Clients, Consommateurs ou Coopérateurs?' *Coopération, idées, faits, techniques* (April, May, and June 1962).

[3] J. H. Kaiser, *Die Representation organisierter Interessen* (Berlin, 1956), pp. 90 f.

threat to a democratic welfare state, and is a reason for growing public concern.[1]

There is also ground for concern *within* the unions.[2] For while the big corporations have been strengthening their economic position by large-scale expansions during the last twenty years, the trade unions have not grown correspondingly. This relative increase of management's power, together with the problems of loyalty, discipline and involvement in the unions, is according to Drucker, causing an 'anxiety neurosis' in our labor organizations.[3]

---

[1] B. M. Telderstichting, *De publiekrechtelijke bedrijfsorganisatie in Nederland* (The Hague, 1958), p. 11.

[2] 'Developments in the most recent past show that great watchfulness is necessary. There is a distinct tendency for the trade-union movement not to receive the attention and esteem it is entitled to expect by virtue of its position and responsibilities.' C. W. van Wingerden in the *Preface to the 22nd Report of the Dutch Socialist Trade Unions, Covering the Period from 1 January 1959 to 31st December 1961* (Amsterdam, 1962), p. 13.

[3] P. F. Drucker, *The New Society* (New York, Harper & Bros., 1950), p. 123.

PART II

Micro-sociological analysis

4. Toward the union : Joining

INTRODUCTION

At the macrosocial level, in the relationship of unions to society, labor underwent intensive changes. We saw in Chapter 1 how the nineteenth-century class structure developed into a status society in which socio-psychological issues gained in importance. Chapter 2 showed how the labor movement's reaction to this change was increasing integration: from a social opposition group it grew into a policy-shaping institution, an incorporated pressure group which prefers negotiation to the strike. In addition to its concern for the workers, there was a growing awareness of the interests of industry and of society as a whole. Briefs regards these 'established' unions as a fundamentally new phenomenon and as essentially different from trade unions of the past.[1] In Chapter 3, we analyzed their major problems.

At the microsocial level, in the relationship of unions to members, the change was no less extensive. We have already met *objective* changes, viz. in the members' actual link with the union, the services it performs, the problems it faces, and the means it uses to solve them. In this chapter, we shall see how these are accompanied by *subjective* changes, and how they affect the member's needs and desires, his image of the union, and his reasons for joining. In countries where trade union membership is a voluntary matter, based upon the organization's power to attract the working population, these subjective factors have an impact on the influx of new members, on the union's internal strength, and its membership turnover. Since the power of a labor organization, even when integrated with society, is ultimately grounded in the size of its membership and power to hold its members, these subjective changes have a direct bearing upon the position of the unions in the welfare state. In this situation, compulsory systems such as the closed and the union shops, have undoubtedly a stabilizing effect. But they have also the disadvantage of concealing the subjective basis of the organization, not only from the social scientists but from the trade union's leaders as well. Voluntary unionism enables us to better analyze the union's subjective functions with respect to the working population.

---

[1] G. Briefs, *Das Gewerkschaftsproblem gestern und heute* (Frankfurt am Main, Fritz Knapp Verlag, 1955), p. 23.

A PARADIGM OF MOTIVATION

When a worker applies for union membership, his action is usually the outcome of a decision-making process in which the major elements involved are:

(*a*) the image he has formed of the union;

(*b*) the needs he wishes to satisfy through the union;

(*c*) the social environment which directly exerts pressure to encourage or obstruct his application and indirectly influences the content of image and needs.

Image, needs and environment are closely linked; together, they compose the psychological field in which the applicant's motives develop. By the motives we mean the inner guiding processes which determine behavior toward an end or goal, in this case, membership in a trade union.[1] The image comprises the activities which the union performs for the benefit of individual, group and society as well as those factors which together make up 'the movement'. These are the social group (members, shop stewards, officials), the organization's structure (branch, union, federation), and the aims and ideals (for example, full employment and social justice).

The needs can be divided into 'egocentric', i.e. those which are directed primarily toward the individual's own interests, and 'sociocentric', i.e. those which include the interests of fellow-workers and/or the entire community. There are certain problems in the use of the sociological survey for establishing these needs. First, because some, such as the need for security, may be subconscious and only indirectly related to the trade union. This difficulty, however, can be overcome by deducing the members' needs from the motives he gives for his decision to join. A second complication is that a worker may join a union for more than one reason: manual workers gave an average of 3·8 motives and white collar workers an average of 3·9. The basic motive was found by going over the answers (see Appendix B) with the respondent and getting him to state which motive, in his own opinion, was the major factor in his decision.

Finally, in the social environment, distinctions may be made as to:

(*a*) family, whether own or parental (family environment),

(*b*) employer, supervisor, and fellow-workers (work environment),

(*c*) friends, neighbors, and acquaintances (leisure environment).

All of these elements play a major part in the decision-making process that precedes the application to join a union. The way in which they are related is shown in the paradigm below.

---

[1] P. F. Lazarsfeld and M. Rosenberg, *The Language of Social Research* (Glencoe, Ill., The Free Press, 1955), p. 394.

After the decision has been made and the employee has joined the union, the possibility arises that he will gradually identify himself with the organization and begin to participate, that he will attend meetings and even become a voluntary official. His original image of the union will thereby gain in depth and distinctness. On the other hand, he may find the reality disappointing; the organization may not supply his needs and, in the case of voluntary membership, he may leave. Each of these phases is dealt with in a separate chapter. Chapter 4 analyzes the parts which environment, image, and needs play in enrollment.[1] Chapter 5 examines apathy and participation within the unions; and Chapter 6 is devoted to the members' reasons for leaving.

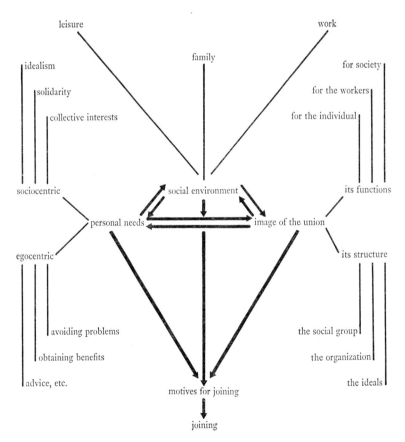

Paradigm of the factors playing a role in the decision to join a voluntary organization.

[1] Partly published as M. van de Vall, 'Trade Unions of the Welfare State as Seen by their Members', *Trade Union Information* No. 38 (OECD, Paris).

THE UNION'S IMAGE

How the image is formed

The media which transmit the trade union's image also play an important part in determining its content. The young worker whose first contact with the trade union is through his father's experiences will get a different picture than the one who first hears of it from his supervisor. We may assume that these media chiefly affect the 'feeling tone' of the cognitive outlook.[1] Another significant factor is the age at which the initial confrontation occurs. Research among new members reveals that most blue and white collar workers first heard of the trade union before reaching adulthood.

TABLE 10. *Age at which new members first heard of the union*

First Heard of Trade Union	Blue collar workers %	White collar workers %
Between 5 and 12 years of age	26	28
Between 13 and 17 years	48	37
At 18 or older	13	23
Did not remember	13	12
TOTAL	100 (136)	100 (68)

Since 44 per cent of these new members (the difference between blue collar and white collar workers is statistically not significant) formed an image of the union within five years of leaving primary school, it is evident that the first contact often occurs during adolescence. Since in most countries the schools pay little attention to the trade unions, the young worker first hears of the organization when entering employment. This conclusion is confirmed by other findings (see p. 140).

Of the various media which contribute toward shaping the union-image, personal contact is by far the most important: in the case of blue collar workers, this occurs mainly through parents; in the case of white collar workers, through colleagues as well.[2]

---

[1] '... the ethos, the predominant feeling tone, depends upon the cultural process through which the individual goes. Not only are the impulses molded, but the inner core and the flow of feeling into the cognitive outlook are likewise shaped.' G. Murphy, *Personality, a Bio-Social Approach to Origins and Structure* (New York, Harper & Brothers, 1947), p. 846.

[2] This does not prove that union members more frequently heard of the union through personal contacts than did nonmembers. For this, it would have been necessary to introduce a control group, which was impossible for both methodological and practical (i.e. financial) reasons in this case. Although this comment will not be repeated each time, it applies to every table in Ch. 4.

TABLE 11. *Media through which new members first learned of the union*

First Learned of the Union	Blue collar workers %	white collar workers %
Family environment:		
Parents, relatives, etc.	44	39
Work environment:		
Supervisor, fellow workers, etc.	23	37
Other media:		
School	10	9
Publicity	1	0
Miscellaneous:		
Newspapers, radio, etc.	6	13
Did not remember	16	2
TOTAL	100 (136)	100 (68)

Table 11 shows that the trade union does not make its initial impact upon a youngster via an intellectual source, through the press, books, radio, or television. The greater majority first learn about it through individuals: father tells son, older workers tell young ones. The fact that the role of fellow workers and supervisors is greater among white collar workers may be an indication that the latter's image of the union takes shape less gradually and is less conditioned by family tradition. To some extent, this may lead to weaker emotional ties with the organization.

Although the trade union's own media are barely mentioned in the first encounter, they cannot be dismissed as irrelevant in decision formation. A majority of 51 per cent of the blue collar workers and 66 per cent of the white collar workers ($0.05 > P > 0.02$) stated that they had read about the union before joining. This difference again suggests that manual workers join the union relatively more often out of family tradition, and technical or administrative employees more often out of rational motives.

Content of the image

Among status groups

When analyzing the image which new members have of their trade union, one must bear in mind that the aims and activities which they perceive do not completely coincide with those upon which they base their decision to join. Among the many factors which contribute to the image, there are usually one or two which are decisive in the motivation, while the others remain in the background. Still, a man's perception of the union must correspond to some extent with the needs he hopes to satisfy through membership. If this is not the case, the union will lose its attractiveness to potential members, the flow of new members will diminish, and membership will drop.[1]

The nature of the link between image and motives was examined in our survey of new members of the Dutch Federation of Trade Unions. They were asked questions about: (*a*) their image of the union's aims and activities, and (*b*) the benefits they expected in return for their dues. Figure 10 summarizes the answers to question *(a)* :[2]

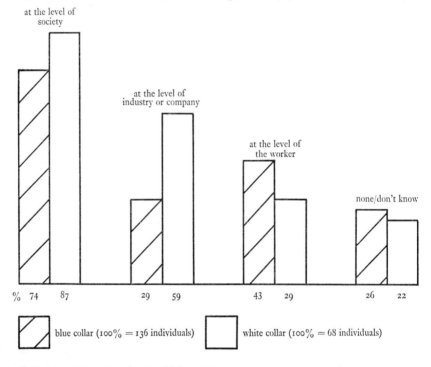

%   74   87   29   59   43   29   26   22

blue collar (100% = 136 individuals)   white collar (100% = 68 individuals)

Total of percentages > 100 owing to multiple answers

FIGURE 10. New members' conception of the functions of the union.

The results allow for the following conclusions:

1. In both the blue and white collar workers' image of the union's goals and activities, those which are related to the entire welfare state hold first place. To state this in more concrete terms, there is a belief that

[1] 'An ideology is not able to make a widespread way among the masses unless, in however distorted and deceptive a form, it expresses actual needs and interests and hopes of the masses and corresponds, at least in some measure with the actual state of social conditions and possible directions of their development.' J. Burnham, *The Managerial Revolution* (London, Penguin Books, 1954), p. 52.   [2] Based on questions 10 and 11, App. B.

concern for the economic cycle, the distribution of national income, prevention of unemployment, and supervision of wage and price levels demand most of the union's attention.

The member's image of the 'established' trade union is, therefore, dominated by activities which extend far beyond his own individual interests. Now, since the European unions are politically more active and more integrated with national policies than are their United States counterpart, this conclusion may well be restricted to the first. Lack of comparable United States data precludes a more definite statement.

2. The differences between the blue and the white collar workers' images of the union mainly concern activities or goals which are considered of lesser importance. The union's activities at the level of the company or industry (such as collective bargaining) are mentioned second by white collar and third by blue collar workers. The latter, on the other hand, attribute greater importance to services rendered by the union to the individual member. Figure 11 will show, however, that this image of activities and goals is not identical with the decisive factor for joining the union.

When examined in the same conceptual framework, we find all the aspects of the *image* also to be present in the *motives* for joining the union. The only notable shifts occur in the relative frequency in which the aspects are mentioned.

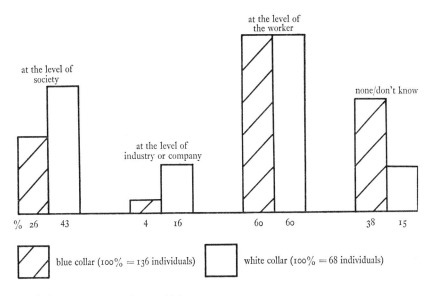

Total of percentages > 100 owing to multiple answers

FIGURE 11. Functions of the union as a motive to join.

Figure 11 shows which of the union's benefits were mentioned by blue and white collar workers as their motives, a few days after they applied to the union, i.e. the answers to question *(b)*:[1]

Again, two conclusions can be drawn:

1. In the perception of both the blue and white collar worker, the main benefits he receives in exchange for his union dues are those which the organization can give him as an individual. As European unions play no role in hiring,[2] these amount to assistance and advice in the case of a dispute between employee and management. From the point of view of their own membership, both categories of workers regard these individual benefits as more important than the union's functions in behalf of groups or society.

2. As with the image, the motives of blue and white collar workers differ only with regard to activities which they consider to be of lesser importance. A clear instance of this is that only 15 per cent of the white collar workers could see *no* advantages in membership, whereas more than a third of the blue collar workers, viz. 38 per cent replied to this effect. Other survey findings have demonstrated that this is linked to the common tendency for unskilled manual workers to join the union because of tradition and social pressures, without having any clear idea of its actual advantages.[3]

If we now compare the findings of Figures 10 and 11, we find that they exhibit the following trends:

1. Of the two groups, it is the white collar workers (87 per cent $>$ 73 per cent and 43 per cent $>$ 26 per cent) who have greater regard for the union's activities, aims, and benefits at the macrosocial level (i.e. of society). They may, accordingly, be expected to show greater interest in the national policies of the trade unions in the welfare state. This is not without some bearing upon the recruitment of potential participants in the organization.

2. Since the white collar workers are also more concerned with the aims, activities, and benefits of the union at company or industry level (59 per cent $>$ 29 per cent and 16 per cent $>$ 4 per cent), it may be concluded that this group has a greater interest in the *collective* functions of the trade union, i.e. those activities which benefit an occupational group, employees in general, or the entire nation. This finding is in conflict with

---

[1] Based on questions 28 and 29, App. B.

[2] In the United States, union hiring halls exist in construction, the printing trades, and the maritime industries. In Western Europe, hiring occurs almost exclusively through public employment agencies.

[3] For similar findings, see J. Haveman, *De ongeschoolde Arbeider* (Assen, van Gorcum, 1952), pp. 41 f.

the sociological theory that members of the new middle class, even within the union, display a highly individual attitude.[1] This divergence from the prevailing view can be explained in various ways. One explanation is that, because white collar workers are exposed to managerial pressure against membership in a trade union, they join only if they have deeply felt social and idealistic motivations. We have seen that white collar workers who belong to a union more often have working class backgrounds than do nonmembers in their group (see page 31). It is possible that this rise from, and familiarity with, a working class existence breeds a more progressive outlook. This explanation claims, in effect, that the union members among white collar workers tend to be an 'idealistic elite'. Another explanation is that administrative and technical employees have benefited less from the new affluence, relatively, than manual workers. Growing awareness of this economic lag may lead to a greater appreciation of the union's collective functions. Although the two explanations are not mutually exclusive and may supplement each other, the former seems more likely.

3. The union's collective aims and action at the level of the company or industry occupy second place in the white collar workers' image and third place with the blue collar workers (Figure 10), but as a motive for joining they hold only third and fourth place (Figure 11). Thus, both groups reveal a divergence between their image of the union and their motives for joining.

The low assessment of collective bargaining, one of the union's major activities, can again be attributed to different causes. An explanation is that many members feel that in the sector of bargaining the trade union of the welfare state has already achieved its primary objectives. In these days of social security, almost all industrial workers are covered by a collective contract, and this part of the union's work has now become less spectacular. An additional reason may be that employers are devoting greater attention to human relations, engaging personnel officers and social workers whose duties overlap the trade union's traditional tasks, and introducing appeal systems in the company. The employee may view the former process as a *fulfillment* and the latter as a *loss* of the union's tasks in industry.

4. In Figure 10, the blue collar workers are more concerned with the union's work on behalf of the individual (43 per cent > 29 per cent) than

---

[1] '*In the union* or out of it, for it, against it, or on the fence, the white collar employee usually remains psychologically the little individual scrambling to get to the top, instead of a dependent employee, experiencing unions and accepting union affiliation as collective means of collective ascent.' C. W. Mills, *White Collar: the American Middle Classes* (New York, Oxford University Press, 1951), p. 39 (my italics).

are the white collar members. As a motive for joining, individual benefits are mentioned equally often by both groups in Figure 12 (60 per cent = 60 per cent). However, comparing their *basic* motives (Table 13), we find the same trend as in Figure 11: 44 per cent of the blue collar workers against 22 per cent of the white collar workers joined the organization *primarily* because of its individual services. Both results support the hypothesis that the blue collar worker feels considerably less secure in the bureaucratic superstructure of the welfare state than his white collared colleague. Consequently, he feels a greater need for individual help.

5. That the manual workers more frequently lack an image of the aims, activities, and benefits of the union (26 per cent > 22 per cent and 38 per cent > 15 per cent) indicates that their perception of them is less clear-cut than is that of the white collar workers. This finding is in agreement with another: blue collar workers stated more frequently that they were members of the national federation while white collar workers more often named the specific union[1] (df = 2; χ^2 = 6·14; 0·05 < P < 0·02). Both results justify the conclusion that the blue collar worker's image of the union is vaguer than the image held by the administrative or technical employee.

6. Finally, the divergences between Figures 10 and 11 indicate that the influx of new members cannot be attributed primarily to the union's macrosocial actions. Although some influence of the union's role at the national level cannot be denied, the major causes of the gain or loss of members must be sought in the on the job situation of the individual worker and in the ways in which the union increases his security. The trade unions' macrosocial action has an important bearing upon membership only if a man can relate it to his working life.

Among different age groups

With the proportion of white collar workers in the labor force increasing, with manual work becoming more technical, and with the blue collar workers gradually conforming to the culture pattern of the new middle class, the distinctions between the two categories will diminish with time. The differences between the age groups are, at the same time, subject to a reverse process: the more the pace of social change increases, the more the dividing line between successive generations gains in prominence. One may well speculate as to whether the differences between a blue and a white collar worker, both of whom are sixty years of age, are not less pronounced than those between two blue collar workers of thirty and sixty years respectively.

[1] See question 9, App. B.

For this reason, the answers about the aims and activities of the union and the benefits of membership have also been analyzed according to age. The replies received from each age group are given in Table 12. The answers to the question about the aims and activities are on the left in each column, and those about the benefits of trade union membership are on the right.

TABLE 12. *The frame of reference in which workers view the actions and benefits of the trade unions, by age groups**

Aspects named	20 and under Aims and Activities	Benefits	21–30 years Aims and activities	Benefits	31–40 years Aims and activities	Benefits	41 and over Aims and activities	Benefits
Unknown and none	25	20	10	12	13	12	9	10
Individual level	20	52	27	57	25	48	14	43
Industry level	22	3	18	4	25	15	20	9
Society level	32	24	45	27	38	25	57	40
All answers 100% =	(59)	(51)	(143)	(129)	(61)	(53)	(104)	(78)

* The modal figures have been placed in frames; in view of the low content of cells, percentages were computed over answers instead of individuals.

We see that all age groups show the trends already noticed in Figures 10 and 11, e.g. that in response to questions about the union's aims and action, functions at the level of society are most frequently mentioned; however, when responding to questions about the benefits of union membership, the modal category in all four age groups shifts to 'individual benefits.'

When comparing the four traits of the 'union image' among the generations, a more latent trend becomes apparent. While 'no image' appears relatively most frequently among the youngest, individual union functions (grievances) are relatively more often mentioned by the second age group. Aims and benefits at the level of the occupational group or company (bargaining) are relatively more popular among the third age group, while the union's role in society (in behalf of the welfare state) is relatively more often mentioned by the oldest generation. Although there is no *linear* correlation between the variables 'age' and 'frame of reference,' this pattern in the modal figures, based upon two different sets of questions, is sufficiently consistent to be more than incidental.

For its explanation, one can reason in two different ways. From the *psychological* point of view, the trend can be accounted for by the fact that a person's interests are wider when he is older. It is the tendency later in life to view himself and the things and people around him in a broader social context. The psychiatrist Rümke describes how a man in his 'presenium', i.e. one passing the age of forty, more often relates himself to the community as a whole. At this stage, he will only find satisfaction in his activities for a voluntary association, a political party, or a trade union if related to the larger society.[1] The answer of a forty-six year old store clerk illustrates how this process may lie behind the observed trend:

When you're young, *you feel more on your own*; you're more dependent on yourself, *as an individual*. Then you don't bother much about a union, and you hardly know anything about it either, it doesn't concern you. *Later on you see things in a wider context*, and then you realize the importance of being organized. You realize that a man on his own doesn't mean very much.

This worker's mental growth is shared by thousands of his generation; from this it could be inferred that the trend under discussion, and particularly the comparative absence of a trade union image among the younger generation, is a normal psychological phenomenon. If the above trend reflects mere age change within a static culture, the trade unions in the welfare state have little cause for concern.

The situation is different, however, if this comparative lack of an image of the trade union among the younger workers has *historical* causes. This hypothesis is also supported by facts.

In Chapter 1, we observed a change in outlook in the younger generation in the welfare state; Schelsky called the process 'Individualisierung',[2] and Lockwood and Zweig referred to it respectively as 'privatisation'[3] and 'personalisation'.[4] Their basic tenet is that the proletariat of the nineteenth-century class society worked through *collective* action for a *new* society, whereas the young workers of the welfare state prefer to improve their position by *individual* effort in society *as it is*. As a result, the latter are less governed by sentiments of solidarity and collective unity, and accept the existing social services and organizations without attachments or ideals. This now could also be a reason for the lack of a trade union image among the younger members. The answer of a twenty-six year old clerk supports this historical explanation:

If I had been living then, in my father's time, *I too would have fought for better*

[1] H. C. Rümke, *De levenstijdperken van de man* (Amsterdam, 1950).
[2] H. Schelsky, *Die skeptische Generation* (Düsseldorf, 1958).
[3] D. Lockwood, 'The New Working Class', *Archives Européenes de Sociologie*, No. 2 (1960), p. 254.
[4] F. Zweig, 'The New Factory Worker', *The Twentieth Century* (May 1960).

social services, holidays and so on. But this isn't any longer necessary, and *now I honestly wouldn't know what to fight for.* And anyway, the government does an awful lot. Sickness benefits and unemployment insurance, *that's all arranged by the government.* You don't need a union for it any more.

This is almost a verbatim illustration of Schelsky's statement that the young worker of today tends to display a 'consumer attitude' toward the trade union, accepting its benefits without much gratitude or enthusiasm.[1] This is reinforced by the union's integration into national policy and by the centralization of bargaining, which remove its major roles further from the worker's private life. Moreover, many of the concrete benefits of union membership are now offered, in whole or in part, by state and industrial welfare programs. Such basic changes in our culture may also account for the fact that the union image is blurred for a generation which is familiar only with the welfare state.

Which of these two explanations is correct, the psychological or the historical one, cannot be established with any certainty; most probably both factors are at work, each reinforcing the other.[2] It is to be expected, therefore, that the blurring of the trade-union image among the younger age groups will continue. Training programs or propaganda will only partially reverse the process, as information which is not accompanied by personal, concrete experience has little cognitive impact.[3] This makes the above trend one of the most urgent problems of the trade unions in the welfare state. The only adequate remedy will be to bring the union's policies and functions back within the worker's concrete experience.

THE MOTIVES FOR JOINING

A general survey

Even more fundamental than the worker's image of the union are, in the case of voluntary membership, the needs underlying his decision to join. Indeed, the content of the image can often only be explained in terms of his needs.[4] As already stated, however, these needs must be inferred from the motives which the members give for joining. A comparison of these motives among white and blue collar workers reveals a rather high degree

[1] H. Schelsky, *Die skeptische Generation*, p. 272.
[2] For a similar problem of analysis, see P. F. Lazarsfeld, 'Methodological Problems in Empirical Social Research', *Transactions of the Fourth World Congress of Sociology*, II, p. 243. Also Samuel A. Stouffer, 'Communism, Conformity and Civil Liberties', in *Sociological Research*, ed. Mathilda White Riley (New York, Harcourt, Brace and World, 1963), I, p. 267.
[3] L. Festinger, 'Informal Social Communication', in L. D. Cartwright and A. Zander, *Group Dynamics* (Evanston, Ill., Row Peterson, 1960), p. 286.
[4] 'Needs, rewards and punishments can even determine a simple visual perception', D. Krech and R. S. Crutchfield, *Theory and Problems of Social Psychology* (New York, McGraw–Hill 1948), p. 88.

of similarity; the motivation patterns of the two groups differ only in details.[1]

TABLE 13. *The motives and the basic motive leading to union membership among blue and white collar workers*

	Blue collar workers Motives	Basic motive	White collar workers Motives	Basic motive
A. Egocentric motives				
1. To avoid personal problems in the work environment: friction, dismissal, etc.	76	40	65	23
2. To obtain individual benefits, such as promotion	2	1	10	3
3. To obtain benefits outside the work environment	13	2	10	3
4. For personal information and advice	12	1	7	0
5. For psychological reasons, e.g. prestige	0	0	1	1
TOTAL (%)		44		30
B. Sociocentric motives				
1. Also for the workers in my firm, my team, occupation, etc.	29	5	35	12
2. In the interest of society, all employees the workers, society, etc.	21	4	20	3
3. Being organized makes us powerful, unity is strength, etc.	25	0	24	6
4. For solidarity's sake, so as not to be a parasite, etc.	39	11	40	9
5. Out of social duty, because one *ought* to be a member, because it's the accepted thing, etc.	7	3	3	1
6. Out of idealism, for a better society, a happier world, etc.	21	1	20	1
TOTAL (%)		24		32
C. Social control				
1. Influence of parents	48	12	46	7
2. Influence of fellow workers	42	11	37	15
3. Influence of wife	16	2	12	1
4. Influence of superior/boss	11	4	18	7
5. Influence of friends	4	2	7	1
6. As a result of house call	7	1	12	7
TOTAL (%)		32		38
		100% = 136 individuals		100% = 68 individuals

The data suggest differences and similarities between the blue and white collar workers. Among the white collar members the sociocentric

[1] For the data upon which this information is based, see questions 12–17, App. B.

basic motive dominates over the egocentric basic motive (32 per cent > 30 per cent), while this is reversed among the blue collar members (24 per cent < 44 per cent). Or, while it takes the first place among the blue collar workers, the egocentric basic motive takes the last place among the white collar workers.

At the same time, 'conflict insurance' is in both groups by far the highest single motive, with 76 per cent among the blue collar and 65 per cent among the white collar members. Depending on the data chosen for comparison, two conclusions are possible: one is that both groups are highly dissimilar in their motivation, the other is that they are predominantly similar. Data from West Germany reveal the same situation. There, also, both groups of workers are mainly attracted by the 'conflict insurance' of the union, with again the blue collar workers showing a higher propensity toward this motive.[1] The blue collar workers' relatively greater interest in the union's benefits for the individual member appears a rather general trait.

The predominance of sociocentric basic motives among the white collar workers can be attributed to two single basic arguments: (B 1) union membership brings advantages for one's entire occupational group (12 per cent > 5 per cent) and (B 3) to obtain certain benefits it is necessary to have sufficient power (6 per cent > 0 per cent). An unexpected outcome is that the solidarity argument (B 4) is almost as common among white collar workers as among manual workers. This again refutes Mills' thesis that the white collar trade union member is more egocentric than the man who works with his hands. The data indicate on the contrary that in his attitude to the union he is *less* egocentric, and often more similar to the traditional image of the trade union member than the blue collar worker of today.

About one-third of the members joined primarily at the insistence of others, particularly because of personal influence in the family or at work. If the influences of superior and fellow workers are grouped together as 'social control in the work situation', it appears that white collar workers (22 per cent) are more susceptible to this factor than manual workers (15 per cent). There is, therefore, some ground for the hypothesis that the company is rather more of a 'closed shop' for the former or that white collar workers are more liable to be under pressure when joining a union. Taken together, the frequencies of sociocentric motives and social control seem to suggest that white collar workers who join the union are influenced more often either by idealism or by social coercion. The implication for the trade union is that its white collar members are often of

[1] *Arbeiterjugend, Gestern und Heute*, ed. H. Schelsky (Heidelberg, 1958), p. 348.

opposite type: members whose motivation is relatively low and members with a higher than average involvement.

As for differences between the generations, contrary to what we usually consider the spirit of youth, it is not the younger age group which is most strongly motivated by idealistic-collective aspirations, but the oldest.

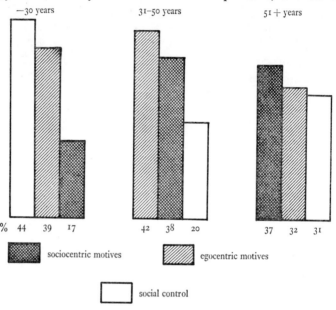

df $= 4$; $\chi^2 = 9.8$; $0.05 > P > 0.02$

FIGURE 12. Relation of age to motive for belonging to the union.

This, however, should not lead to the conclusion that the younger age groups of the welfare state have no ideals: the most that can be inferred is that they show little responsiveness to labor's contemporary goals. Summarizing, younger workers tend to join the union relatively more on account of personal influence, the middle-aged weigh individual interests most heavily, and older workers are relatively more often moved by collective and idealistic reasons.

To find out whether there is a correlation between these motives and attachment to the union, the members of each of the groups were asked if they expected in the future to discontinue their membership. The answers give an indication of the strength of the members' ties with the organization. While no difference was found between the workers whose basic motive was 'egocentric' or 'social control', with 23 per cent of both groups thinking it likely that they would leave at some time, the corresponding figures for those with 'sociocentric' motives was only 12 per cent (df $= 2$; $\chi^2 = 9.54$; $0.01 > P > 0.001$). This indicates that socio-centric motives lead to the strongest bond with the union. This conclusion is challenged by the fact that Figure 12 showed a link between socio-centric motives and increasing age, so that the above findings may also be influenced by the age factor. However, when the breakdown is repeated with the age factor kept constant, the correlation remains:

TABLE 14. *Connection between motives and attachment to the union.*
Age kept constant

	Up to 30 years			Over 30 years		
	Sociocentric	Egocentric	Personal Influence	Sociocentric	Egocentric	Personal influence
Expect to leave	16%	27%	24%	11%	20%	19%
100% =	(19)	(44)	(50)	(35)	(35)	(21)

In both age groups, the workers with sociocentric motives have the strongest attachment, since they least frequently expect to leave the organization. Although the underlying reasons will be examined at a later state, we may already conclude that the 'Entideologisierung' described in Chapter 1, i.e. the loss of idealistic vigor among the younger workers, tends to weaken their ties with the union.

The egocentric motives

We found in Chapter 2 that the welfare state leads to an expansion of the union's collective functions, while the organization's services to the individual member decline. Table 12 demonstrated, however, that for many members the union's greatest attraction *still* lies at the individual level. This leads to the question of what role the various objects of trade union policy, ranging from the individual worker to society, play in the motivation to join. Could it be that the further the benefits of trade union policy are removed from the individual worker the smaller their part in his decision to join? This hypothesis is confirmed by an analysis of six reference groups which appear in the new members' motives (Figure 13).

Among both blue and white collar workers, references to one's own individual interests are the most frequent, followed by considerations involving one's family (wife, parents). The importance of the work group (colleagues) is also rather widely mentioned. References to the industrial community are relegated to fourth place, while categories such as 'the working class' or 'all employees' hold fifth place.

In contrast to the worker's image of the union as dominated by macrosocial functions (see Figure 10), society is mentioned least often in his reasons for joining. Although no historical statistics are available, it seems not unlikely that the relative frequency of such concepts as 'working class' and 'society' was higher at one time, but that they have suffered from the unions' de-politization and the creation of the welfare state.[1]

percentage

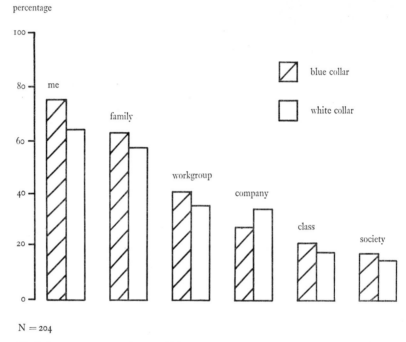

N = 204

Total of percentages > 100 owing to multiple answers

FIGURE 13. Reasons given for joining the union.

Table 13 confirms the fact that nearly all blue collar workers and the great majority of white collar workers have personal interests in mind when they join a trade union. Indeed, nearly half (44 per cent) of the members from the one group and nearly a third (30 per cent) from the other join *primarily* for this reason. Of the five egocentric submotives, one

---

[1] There are indications that this is a general tendency. An example is the following observation from the United States: 'In the midst of marked economic progress, *general* dissatisfaction is at a minimum. Under such conditions (rising incomes, price-level stability, full employment) workers' protest is likely to take mainly the form of plant grievances, which are individual or small group complaints about particular local actions by management.' Richard A. Lester, *As Unions Mature* (Princeton, N.J., Princeton University Press, 1958), p. 43. At p. 34, Lester reports that the number of grievances in the automobile and rubber industries has risen in recent years, even in absolute terms. *It may justly be concluded that as a result of modern affluence employees experience fewer collective and a greater number of individual problems.*

completely overshadows all the others, viz. the desire to avoid, by means of union membership, the consequences of individual conflict in one's work environment. Because even (or perhaps especially) in the welfare state, union membership seems to rest largely upon this need, we shall now explore it in more detail.

Unions as 'conflict insurance'

Analysis of the content of motive (A1) reveals that the union's most highly valued service to the worker is its 'conflict insurance', i.e. the provision of legal and material assistance in the case of individual grievances. Examples of this are conflicts about unfair treatment, unjustified dismissal or demotion, underpayment and incorrect application of social legislation. A deeper psychological background to this motive, as the following comments reveal, is the worker's fear of a threat to his security:

'You can't achieve anything on your own.'

'Because alone you can't begin much . . .'

'There would be nobody to fall back on.'

'Because we are weak compared with the bosses.'

'You'll never manage alone.'

'Then you're not on your own any longer.'

'So that you're not without protection.'

'Otherwise you're right on your own.'

'Otherwise they can do as they like with you.'

The deepest feeling behind these comments is the anxious fear of standing alone and defenseless against economic powers stronger than oneself. Despite the widespread use of human-relations skills by management, many employees are aware that there is no question of true democracy in modern industry[1] where 'principles of inequality and subordination still dominate over those of freedom and equality'.[2] This awareness is reflected by the fact that 75 per cent of the blue collar workers interviewed and 65 per cent of the white collar joined the union partly in order to avoid individual troubles.

It may be concluded, therefore, that vague but intense feelings of anxiety about individual difficulties at work constitute the psychological basis in which voluntary membership in a trade union is rooted. This means that for many workers the trade union assumes the function of an

---

[1] 'For me, "human relations skill" has a cold-blooded connotation of proficiency, technical expertness, calculated effect.' Malcolm P. McNair 'Thinking Ahead: What Price Human Relations?' *Harvard Business Review*, xxv, No. 2 (March–April 1957), 15–39.

[2] F. J. H. M. van der Ven, 'Het arbeidsconflict', *Sociale Wetenschappen*, ii, No. 3 (April 1959).

insurance company within the sphere of employment. Some mention this explicitly:

> 'I joined as a kind of *insurance*. In case there's any trouble.'

> 'In my last job the foreman was much tougher on you if you weren't in the union. There it was *safer* to be a member.'

> 'It's stupid not to be in the union. There are people who don't have any *health* insurance or *fire* insurance. Someone just had his house burnt down, and he was not insured.'

That the last respondent mentions his state health insurance, private fire insurance, and the trade union in the same breath indicates how much, in his view, they fulfill complementary functions. Together, they serve, according to Weisser, 'to insure against future dangers which threaten one's existence'.[1] Another conclusion is that, for these members, trade union membership will often satisfy unspecified emotional needs rather than specific material desires. This, again, occasionally becomes explicit:

> 'Well, you get a kind of *feeling* that you're not alone. Otherwise you don't really know where you're headed. It gives you a certain *sense* of security in your work.'

The conclusion that for many workers union membership meets an emotional need for personal security is also supported by less explicit responses:

> 'It backs you up when you're in trouble.'

> 'Membership gives you protection.'

> 'If something goes wrong, they'll help you.'

> 'They help you if you're in the right.'

> 'Now you can assert your rights.'

> 'You get help and backing if you need them.'

> 'The union is behind you.'

> 'You can always go to them for help.'

> 'You've got an institution you can turn to.'

Such concepts as help, protection and backing indicate that the satisfaction workers expect in return for their dues—generally about 2 per cent of their income—is a general feeling of security.[2] The vagueness of

---

[1] G. Weisser, 'Soziale Sicherheit,' *Handwörterbuch der Sozialwissenschaften*, p. 396.

[2] In the United States, this is probably accompanied by another need which plays a less prominent part in European trade unionism: the need to obtain another job when dismissed. The union's role as an employment bureau can be a very significant one. In California, Garbarino reports: 'The importance of the union as a source of job information was substantial.' As a proof of this, he points out that 60 per cent of all members had obtained a new job through the union, and that for non-colored members the figure was as high as 73 per cent. See T. W. Garbarino, 'The Unemployed Worker during a Period of Full Employment', in *A Sourcebook on Unemployment Insurance in California*, App. D(1).

this feeling ties in with the fact that many have no clear notion of the dangers against which they want to be protected: 25 per cent of the members were unable to elaborate their hazy answers.

Sociologists in the United States and Germany report similar trends, the latter particularly among younger workers.[1] Schelsky, for instance, concludes that the generation of the affluent society views the usefulness of the union mainly in terms of 'a significant benefit for *private* interests'.[2] The similarity to observations in Holland indicates that this tendency is general in modern labor,[3] and that the basic differences in union membership in Europe and the United States are less than generally assumed.

Of the other motives in Section A of Table 13, the one closest to the one above is the expectation of information and advice, since the problems on which advice is desired are largely dismissal, personal disputes, and loss of wages. As further evidence of the relationship, this consideration is also mentioned more frequently by blue collar (12 per cent) than by white collar workers (7 per cent). Yet, its virtual non-occurrence as a basic motive indicates that it is mostly regarded as an incidental advantage.

The need for security

The need for 'conflict insurance' is the result of a combination of indirect conditions and direct causal factors, as is often the case in sociology. Important conditions are the growth and equalization of national income, the public social security program, and increasing industrial welfare. For, surprisingly, the quest for security seems less a reaction to the economic

---

[1] (*a*) In the *United States*, Purcell reports that workers in Chicago are in the union because it prevents them from 'being pushed around', enables them to 'go over the boss' head', provides 'someone to talk to', and gives 'protection for our people'. T. V. Purcell, *The Worker Speaks his Mind on Company and Union* (Cambridge, Mass., Harvard University Press, 1953), p. 150.
(*b*) In *West Germany*, Lohmar reports: 'When discussing the tasks and work of the trade unions with Hamburg apprentices we frequently heard the claim that they provide security for one's old age in the form of a pension or other assistance,' Lohmar in H. Schelsky, *Arbeiterjugend*, p. 240.

[2] H. Schelsky, *Die skeptische Generation*, p. 468. Elsewhere (p. 272), he quotes the social researcher S. Braun: 'This type has no moral relationship with the trade unions: the unions are a power, and as such they must prove themselves through concrete benefits: a comprehensive unity of interests with the working community must be their identity card.'

[3] This tendency is also general in another dimension, manifesting itself not only among employees in their formal membership in the union, but among housewives in their informal relationships with their neighbors. In his investigation of neighbor contacts, Klages met the need for 'a willingness to help, which in the great majority of cases does not imply help with concrete and immediate problems but *the security that there is a potential reserve of aid to which one can turn in the case of undefined future needs.*' H. Klages, *Der Nachbarschaftsgedanke und die nachbarliche Wirklichkeit in der Grosstadt* (report) (Cologne, 1958), p. 156 (my italics).

depression of the 1930s than to modern affluence and social legislation. With rising income and stable employment leading to the installment purchase of family property (house, car, refrigerator, television set), the horror of poverty assumes greater proportions. Also, as one's life expectancy increases, the need to provide for one's old age augments. And as the rate of industrial accidents and illness drops, one takes them less for granted and wishes to be insured against them.

Another condition is the transition from nineteenth-century social structure, with its fairly static division into two classes, to the finely graduated 'status society', with its hectic social mobility. Sociologists in various countries have pointed out that this change in social structure may have increased the need for status security.

1. Following the French sociologist Friedmann,[1] Titmuss in Britain has studied the psychological effects of social security and believes that as social differentiation within a society increases, the people become more aware of social inequality; and the more involved they feel with the existing social strata and their position within the stratification, the more anxious they become about incompetence, failure, or social decline.[2]

2. Similarly, there is the observation based on empirical research, that 'the degree of dissatisfaction with their lot is often less among the people in severely depressed social strata in a relatively rigid social system than among those strata who are apparently better off in a more mobile social system'.[3]

3. Both observations are linked to the law of social psychology which states that setbacks not shared by others in one's social environment ('relative deprivations') have a deeper frustrating effect than those which are also suffered by the other members of one's group.

In the affluent society, as observed in Chapter 1, social ascent is dominant and, thus, gradually assumes the character of a general norm; a slip down the social ladder, consequently, may easily bring with it the odium of social inferiority. This certainly holds good for dismissal and unemployment, as Garbarino found was the case with unemployed workers during a period of full employment. Someone who is out of a job while everyone else is working is soon regarded as inferior by his peers.[4] It is the kind of phenomenon which Parsons has in mind when he

[1] G. Friedmann, 'The Social Consequences of Technical Progress', *International Social Science Bulletin*, IV, No. 2 (1952), p. 254.
[2] R. M. Titmuss, *Essays on the Welfare State* (London, Allen & Unwin, 1958), p. 54.
[3] R. K. Merton and A. S. Kitt, 'Contributions to the Theory of Reference Group Behavior', in *Continuities in Social Research: Studies in the Scope and Method of the American Soldier*, ed. R. K. Merton and P. F. Lazarsfeld (Glencoe, Ill., The Free Press, 1950), p. 90.
[4] T. W. Garbarino, 'The Unemployed Worker during a Period of Full Employment', App. D (1.)

observes a 'social angst' in modern family life, manifesting itself in strong defensive reactions against any decline in status.'[1]

In addition to indirect conditions, there are also causal factors, viz. developments in the technical and labor sectors which actually increase the frequency of individual setbacks and, as a result, threaten individual security. The reality of such developments and the fact that the company is not always able to help are confirmed by industrial management. J. G. Bavinck, for instance, a director of N. V. Philips of Eindhoven, about the social consequences of automation:

Although it can be stated that the changeover has taken place without any serious hitch, and that the policy followed was therefore successful, we are conscious that many employees are finding things difficult; this is because at this hectic and busy time they cannot use their talents sufficiently, because they fear *that in the course of the many changes to which they have to adapt themselves they may lose their jobs or their status,* and because they are afraid they will fall behind in technical knowledge or will not be equal physically to their jobs. Difficult as it is, personnel policy must also respond to needs such as these. *We are very well aware that in this we are only partially successful.*[2]

Although it is not clear whether this refers to blue or to white collar workers, the mechanization of office work[3] justifies the supposition that anxiety about personal employment problems is not uncommon among administrative employees. It is not inconceivable that other factors, such as the introduction of rational working and control techniques for office work, add to their individual problems.

Bavinck's statement that employers are only partially able to prevent individual problems offers a striking correlation with the conclusion drawn from Table 12 that both blue and white collar workers join the union primarily to avoid such troubles. This influx, however, is checked by industry's efforts to deal with the problems through *internal* company services (personnel department, company social work, internal arbitrating bodies). The mere awareness that these exist will keep many white collar workers from joining a so-called *external* organization like the trade union.

The above experiences indicate that problems caused by automation will rarely be solved *within* the company, even when under enlightened

---

[1] T. Parsons, 'The Social Structure of the Family', in *The Family, Its Function and Destiny*, ed. R. N. Anshen (New York, Harper & Brothers, 1959), p. 235.

[2] *De Philips Koerier*, 4 October 1961 (my italics).

[3] It has been pointed out by J. Engelfriet that, if European firms were more willing to pool their experiences with the mechanization of office work, this development could proceed much more rapidly than is generally expected. (See *Algemeen Handelsblad*, 'Bank en Verzekerings-wezen' edition, 19 January 1960.)

management.[1] The requirements of retraining and relocating a large number of workers go far beyond the scope of management, and can only be met by public funds and planned industrialization. In these 'external' areas the union, with its political influence, is certainly as useful for uprooted workers as management.

The 'social control' motives

The observation that no human being lives in a social vacuum is especially pertinent to the potential member's relationship to the union: family tradition, chats with fellow workers, the example of his friends, and the advice of superiors all play their part. Sometimes these social influences are so powerful that the employee joins only to escape their pressure. In such cases, of course, membership can hardly be called 'voluntary'. The fact that many workers conform to social control in the matter of union membership should not cause a great deal of concern. The social sciences have long since demonstrated that all group life in which we participate affects our thought and behavior.

With regard to the structure of this process of control, it has been shown that primary groups such as parents, play groups, and work teams, at first only succeed in changing the individual's *behavior*; later, they effect changes in his *perception*; and only at the final stage will he conform in his *values and norms*. 'We come to the view', Murphy writes, 'that any specifiable adult group uses its way of gentle or forcible coercion to impress upon the young what they should do, perceive and value.'[2] The reason why they conform is that to be accepted in one's social environment is one of the most powerful and constant human needs.[3]

The implication is that many workers join the union in order to occupy a psychologically safe position among the members of their group, i.e. in order not to be isolated or despised as a 'parasite'. Evidence of this is that 82 per cent of the blue collar and 81 per cent of the white collar workers mentioned persons in their immediate environment who had influenced their decision to join. Since 32 per cent and 38 per cent, respectively, gave such influence as their basic motive, it may be concluded that at least one-third joined mainly on account of the convictions

---

[1] For a similar example in the United States see A. H. Raskin, 'The Obsolescent Unions', in *Industrial and Labor Relations*, ed. A. Fraser Isbester (Boston, Mass., D.C. Heath and Company, 1967), p. 35.

[2] G. Murphy, 'The Internalization of Social Control', in *Freedom and Control in Modern Society*, ed. M. Berger, T. Abel, and C. H. Page (New York, Van Nostrand, 1954), pp. 3–17.

[3] " . . . for many of us the possibility of even a single instance of rejection by another presents a terrible threat and one to be carefully guarded against." Warren Bennis *et al.* (eds.), *Interpersonal Dynamics, Essays and Readings on Human Interaction*, rev. ed. (Homewood, Ill., The Dorsey Press, 1968), p. 212.

of others. In the light of what has gone before, it is clear that for these workers joining is merely an adjustment of outward behavior, which influences neither their image of the union nor their assessment of its value.

Among the unskilled and the skilled

Although the part played by social control among blue and white collar workers is almost equal, there are marked differences *within* the blue collar group, i.e. between unskilled and skilled workers. Here, however, we come up against an unresolved theoretical controversy in modern sociology.

(I) It has been pointed out that, with regard to the influence of primary groups on union membership, there is a difference between skilled and unskilled manual workers. Among the unskilled, this theory states, relatives and fellow workers exert a greater influence on a man's decision than among the skilled. According to this hypothesis, one of the reasons Communist trade unions have a greater impact upon unskilled workers is that agitation within small groups forms a substantial element in their propaganda.[1]

(II) Other sociologists find themselves at variance with these conclusions. According to them, the receptiveness toward primary group influences observed among unskilled workers may also exist among other sections of the population. 'If one concerns oneself exclusively with unskilled workers', writes an observer, 'one may easily come to look upon certain characteristics observed as typical of unskilled labor, whereas in reality they exist in any small group.' He comes to the conclusions that statistical data only partially support hypothesis (I). In cases in which unskilled workers really do take a different attitude toward such formal organizations as the trade union, these sociologists claim that a greater receptiveness to primary influences (explanation I) does not apply.[2]

Taking the influence of the primary group as an independent variable, the factor 'skilled or unskilled' as an intervening variable, and union membership as a dependent variable, hypothesis (I) can be expressed diagrammatically as follows:

Hypothesis I.

[1] J. Haveman, *De Ongeschoolde Arbeider*, pp. 41 f.
[2] J. A. A. van Doorn, *De Proletarische Achterhoede* (Meppel, Boom, 1954), pp. 36 f.

If we now check this hypothesis against our own results and compare the two blue collar groups with the white collar group we find the basic motive of 'social control' distributed as follows:

TABLE 15. *Influence of primary social control as the basic motive for joining the union: white collar, unskilled and skilled workers*

Basic motive	Unskilled manual workers %	Skilled manual workers %	White collar workers %
Primary-group influences	50 (100% = 38)	24 (100% = 96)	38 (100% = 68)

(df = 2; χ^2 = 13.76; P < 0.001)

Unskilled workers among these new trade union members mentioned the influence of primary groups, such as family and fellow workers, twice as often as did skilled workers; in this respect, they differ even more markedly from the skilled than from the white collar group.

If theory (I) (which, in this respect, has been proved correct) is followed further, we find that, in addition to skill, it mentions age as a variable sensitive to primary-group influences. This is illustrated with an example showing that the younger unskilled workers are often subjected to severe pressure to join the union. With age as a second intervening variable, this hypothesis (II) can be expressed as follows:

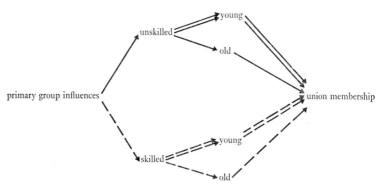

Hypothesis II.

In concrete terms, a worker who is both young and unskilled will be under the impact of two variables and show an extremely high receptivity to primary group influences, while the older skilled worker will be the least receptive to such form of social control. When checked against the interview data, we find that hypothesis (11) is also corroborated:

TABLE 16. *Influence of primary social control as a motive for joining the union in manual workers, by age-groups*

Basic motive	Unskilled manual workers		Skilled manual workers	
	30 and under %	31 and over %	30 and under %	31 and over %
Primary-group influences	58 (100% = 24)	36 (100% = 14)	34 (100% = 50)	17 (100% = 48)

(df = 2; χ^2/comb. = 6·31; 0·05 > P > 0·02)

Whether the worker joins the union mainly in response to social pressure is determined not only by his being unskilled or skilled (58 per cent > 34 per cent and 36 per cent > 17 per cent) but also by his being younger or older than thirty (58 per cent > 36 per cent and 34 per cent > 17 per cent). The impact of this for the trade union is that young unskilled workers are rather uncommitted and that their membership will be often limited to outward appearances. To strengthen their ties with the organization, ways must be found to instill a more positive image of the union. Opportunities for occupational training of young unskilled, as offered by the German trade unions, might produce this effect.[1]

The three major forms of social control will now be considered in detail.

Influence of parents

In his analysis of the political influences to which the individual is subjected during his lifetime. Hyman concludes that, of all the agencies of political socialization, the parental home is the most powerful.[2] The same applies to the trade union, with parents being the most frequently mentioned of all personal influences on membership. This correlates directly with the fact that, among the new members, the fathers of 66 per cent of the blue collar workers and 59 per cent of the white collar workers *also* belonged to a union.

Apart from the indirect ways in which parents influence the behavior, perception, and norms of their children, parents of two-thirds of the new

---

[1] See '*Op weg naar volwassenheid*', quoted by J. A. A. van Doorn, *De Proletarische Achterhoede*, p. 30.

[2] Herbert H. Hyman, *Political Socialization: A Study in the Psychology of Political Behavior* (Glencoe, Ill., Free Press, 1959), p. 69.

members played a more direct role in the decision for membership. As might be expected, this parental pressure shows a negative correlation with the member's age.

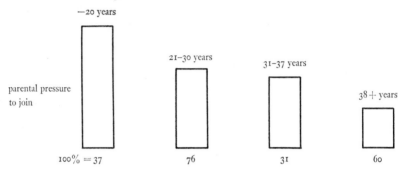

W/σ = 5·21; P < 0·001

FIGURE 14. Relation between age and parental pressure to join.

That the majority of the youngest age-group conforms to parental wishes in the matter of trade union membership parallels the development of their political loyalties, and this is attributed by Lane to the insecurity inherent in adolescence.[1] With regard to the theory that the young person is influenced by his parents in three phases (viz. first, *behaving* like his parents, then, *perceiving* the environment as they do, and, finally attaching the same *value* to things), some responses indicate that in the case of union membership parental influence often does not go beyond the first phase.

'My mother gave my name in. *I didn't know she had done it.*'

'My father has been a member for years, and he thought I ought to join as well. So I did. *But it's sheer waste of money.*'

'Well, you know, I joined *because my father really forced me to.* He thinks it is everyone's duty.'

'My mother put my name down for the union. *No, I didn't talk to anyone; my mother fixed everything.*'

These are illustrations of what we call 'incomplete socialization': although the parental influence has affected their son's behavior, it had no impact upon his perception or evaluation. Obviously, these young workers will only be marginal members; and if the union wants to retain

[1] '... generally for normal, non-marginal adolescents, with ego's not yet hardened and defenses still not quite developed, a reality-testing apparatus still inexperienced, a career to make, a husband still to catch and a "self" to discover, conformity and low involvement offers the greatest rewards.' R. E. Lane, *Political Life: why People get involved in Politics* (Glencoe, Ill., Free Press, 1957), p. 217.

them, it will have to convince them of the benefits of membership. This task, however, is frequently neglected by the union or left to incidental experiences as illustrated:

'My father has always been in the union, so I found it natural to join as well. First I was too young to realize exactly why I had joined. *Later on, when there were some difficulties over wages*, I saw that it is worth being a member, because they support you.'

Individual problems with dismissal, wages, fringe benefits, holidays, etc., are not daily occurrences, however, and many European workers leave their unions before they are confronted with them. Our survey of former union members, in Chapter 6, shows that this is more than hypothesis: of those who left the union within a year of joining 70 per cent had never become convinced of its practical value.[1]

Influence of colleagues

The largest part of the worker's day is spent in his work group, i.e. in the primary group of fellow workers at factory or office. This group determines to a great extent what he considers a reasonable day's work, the enjoyment he finds in his work, his attitude toward his supervisor, and his opinion of the trade union. On this last point, he may be *indirectly* influenced, positively or negatively, by the ways in which union members differ from nonmembers as colleagues, as superiors, and so on. Of the new trade union members interviewed, 40 per cent were of the opinion that there was a distinct psychological difference between members and nonmembers. The great majority thought the trade union members quieter, more balanced, easier to get on with, calmer, more skilled, better at their jobs, older, or in higher positions. This subjective impression finds support in reality, as Chapter 5 will show.[2]

But there are also more *direct* influences: 42 per cent of the blue collar and 37 per cent of the white collar workers joined the union under some form of influence from their fellow workers. In fact, this was the basic motive for 11 per cent of the blue collar and 15 per cent of the white collar members. This indicates that colleagues have less influence upon trade union membership than do parents. Parental influence, moreover, is of the nature of gradual socialization, whereas the influence by fellow workers tends to be of a more coercive nature. This can be inferred from such responses as:

'People were always putting a lot of pressure on me. I joined the union purely *to stay on good terms with my colleagues.*'

[1] See p. 183.
[2] See p. 163, which shows that active trade union members are more socially integrated and less frustrated than apathetic ones.

'At the insistence of a workmate. In fact under *severe pressure*. Not being married I don't see so many advantages in it.'

'At work they really *insist on* it, although it's not actually compulsory.'

'My workmates *insisted* I should do it; about half a dozen of them.'

'At the machine plant there were twenty-seven on the production line and *they were all* in the union. So I joined too.'

'When I *started work* there they asked at once: Are you one of us? Aren't you going to join the union?'

'Every day they come to talk to me. One of them, a real hard one, *pestered the life out of me.*'

These answers show how the work team often exerts informal coercion upon a newcomer to make him join the union. When he conforms, he does so less because of the benefits he expects from membership than because he wants to be positively evaluated by his fellow workers. Particularly in the initial stage of membership, members with this instrumental motivation will feel little attachment to the organization.

This has been confirmed by a survey of members of a European metalworkers union: 23 per cent of those who joined primarily at the insistence of others left again because of 'lack of interest', as against 9 per cent among the other members.[1] Such members, when they change jobs and escape the control of their colleagues, will frequently terminate their membership. This is probably one reason why many European workers who are transferred to another union after a change of occupation or employer, fail to take up membership in the new organization.[2]

Coercing fellow workers to join a union is an old and widespread European practice. The Webbs noticed it as long ago as 1894,[3] and today no less than 70 per cent of British trade union members consider it a legitimate form of control.[4] There are some indications, however, that the content of this influence is gradually changing from predominantly positive to predominantly negative.

Of the trade unionists in Utrecht, only 5 per cent felt that they were on more pleasant terms with members than with nonmembers. When compared with the friendly atmosphere among trade unionists seventy years

---

[1] 'According to the comparison of members and ex-members, those who stated that they joined the union under pressure from fellow workers proved a negative selection with regards to membership.' S. Poppe, *Conceptrapport over het bij onze enquête naar het ledenverloop verzamelde materiaal* (The Hague, ANMB), p. 23.

[2] This figure is taken from a series of articles which the former general secretary of the NVV, G. K. Jansen, published in the journal of the local federations, *Over en Weer*, in 1955.

[3] S. and B. Webb, *The History of Trade Unionism* (London, 1894), p. 432.

[4] W. E. J. McCarthy, *The Closed Shop in Britain* (Berkeley, University of California Press, 1964), p. 3.

ago—'Friendships are made, numerous "sing songs" and smoking concerts arranged; and the joke and the friendly glass, the good cheer and the conviviality, all presented great attractions to the young workman'[1]— one may well wonder whether nowadays the pressure within the work group to join the union has not obtained a more negative content. This hypothesis also finds support in the following remark of a forty year old tool cutter: 'You used to be able to tell your friends you were in the union. It was more or less an honor. Nowadays nonmembers are made out to be parasites and subjected to a lot of pressure to join.'

The trend indicated by these data may have an important bearing on the members' ties with the union: a worker who joins primarily to avoid a negative evaluation by his work group will not easily develop a favorable image of the organization. Negative social control will provide less personal satisfaction among members of an organization than control with a positive content.

Closely related to control by fellow workers is influence by the worker's superior: this factor is mentioned by 11 per cent of the blue collar and 18 per cent of the white collar workers who joined the union, and was the basic motive for 4 per cent and 7 per cent respectively. Among new women members, this factor is more than two times as common (27 per cent) as among men (11 per cent) ($df = 1$; $\chi^2 = 5.51$; $0.02 > P > 0.05$). As with the influence of parents, the influence of a superior shows an inverse correlation with age ($W/\sigma = 2.51$; $P < 0.05$). However, at the higher levels of white collar work, the superior more often functions as an obstacle than as a stimulus to union membership.

Influence of wife

A fourth person who played a part in the new member's decision is his wife: she was mentioned by 16 per cent of the new blue collar and 12 per cent of the new white collar workers, but her influence was rated as a basic motive by only 2 per cent of the former and 1 per cent of the latter.

Data from the surveys among new and ex-members indicate that among blue collar workers the housewife has both a more negative *and* a more positive influence on union membership than she has among white collar workers. The difference is statistically significant with regard to leaving the union, not with regard to joining. However, among both blue and white collar workers, the wife's influence on membership is much more often negative than positive, which shows that she is an important factor in membership rotation.

[1] S. and B. Webb, *The History of Trade Unionism*, p. 433.

The sociocentric motives

Of the three major groups of motives, social control, the egocentric reasons and the sociocentric reasons, the last correspond most closely to the trade-unionist goal of improving the workers' lot by means of collective action. Although different at first sight, all sociocentric motives have the common trait of transcending the worker's individual needs, partly because the interests involved are shared with others, and partly because they are founded on moral duty or ethical values. Members with such sociocentric motives are of great importance to the labor movement, because it is from among their ranks that both the voluntary and the paid officials will be recruited. An indication of the quality of their membership is that even on joining they feel already a close attachment to the union. When asked about their future membership, for instance, workers with sociocentric motives indicate more frequently that they expect to remain in the union:

TABLE 17. *Expectation of remaining in the union*

	Blue collar workers		White collar workers	
	Sociocentric motives %	Other motives %	Sociocentric motives %	Other motives %
Expect to remain in the union	80	76	100	82
	(100% = 20)	(100% = 116)	(100% = 12)	(100% = 56)

Not tested owing to empty cell.

These figures correspond with United States findings that members with idealistic motives are most dedicated to the trade union. Tannenbaum, for example, states that 'support for broad union goals corresponds perfectly with the level of membership participation',[1] and Dodge comes to the conclusion that 'members who exhibited a more pro-union orientation tended to display greater political activity'.[2] In their study of political consciousness in a union, Seidman, London, and Karsh come to similar results.[3] Taken together, these European and United States observations indicate this to be a general trend.

[1] A. S. Tannenbaum and R. L. Kahn, *Participation in Union Locals* (New York, Row, Peterson, 1958), p. 122.

[2] R. W. Dodge, 'Some Aspects of the Political Behavior of Labor Union-Members in the Detroit Metropolitan Area' (mimeograph), p. 2.

[3] 'Whereas all the leaders and the active members interviewed agreed that the union should be active politically, only half of the inactives shared such views, and then mostly with reservations as to the type of activity that should be undertaken or the issues that should be acted on.' J. Seidman, J. London, and B. Karsh, 'Political Consciousness in a Local Union', *Public Opinion Quarterly*, XV, No. 4 (1951), p. 692.

Among some groups of members

The fact that sociocentric sentiments are the basic motive for 24 per cent of the blue collar and 32 per cent of the white collar workers suggests that they are more common among the latter. If the blue collar group is subdivided according to skill, this link between idealist motives and social status becomes still clearer:

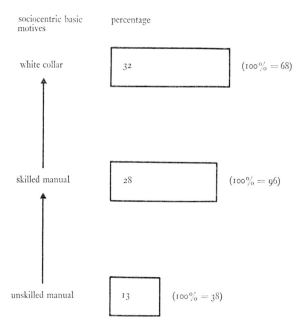

sociocentric basic motives   percentage

white collar   32   (100% = 68)

skilled manual   28   (100% = 96)

unskilled manual   13   (100% = 38)

$W/\sigma = 2\cdot19$; $P = 0\cdot02$

FIGURE 15. Relation between social status and sociocentric motives for joining the union.

Since observations by United States researchers, including Sanford[1] and Wyant and Herzog,[2] point in the same direction, this correlation seems to exist for both European and United States labor. Additional data indicate that it even exists *outside* the unions, viz. in political life. Lane in his review of sociopolitical research found that the higher a person's status, the more concerned he was with political values and ideals.[3] It is likely, therefore, that the above correlation represents a general sociological trend.

[1] F. H. Sanford, 'Public Orientation to Roosevelt', *Public Opinion Quarterly*, xv, No. 2 (1951), 189–216, quoted by R. E. Lane, *Political Life*, p. 123.
[2] R. Wyant and H. Herzog, 'Voting via the Senate Mailbag—Part II', *Public Opinion Quarterly*, v, No. 4 (1941), pp. 616–24, quoted by R. E. Lane, *Political Life*, p. 126.
[3] R. E. Lane, *Political Life*, pp. 126–7.

Other variables, apart from social status, also have a bearing on socio-centric motives. Sex is one of them: while 28 per cent of the new male members named motives in this category, the corresponding figure for females was only 13 per cent (df = 1; χ^2 = 12·64, 0·01 > P > 0·001). Age is another factor: the younger members of both the white and the blue collar groups are clearly less inclined to sociocentric motives:

TABLE 18. *Idealism related to age*

| | Blue collar workers | | White collar workers | |
	30 and under %	31 and over %	30 and under %	31 and over %
Sociocentric motives	5 (100% = 75)	26 (100% = 61)	8 (100% = 39)	31 (100% = 29)

(df = 2; χ^2/comb. = 38·35; P < 0·001)

In the welfare state, it is not the young who come to the union with high ideals. On the contrary, sociocentric motives are extremely rare among members of the younger generation: among the older blue collar workers they are over five times as common, and among the older white collar workers nearly four times as common. This may well be how the trend toward individualization manifests itself in the established trade union.[1]

Although neither women nor young workers are, at present, important in the unions, these findings are relevant for the role of idealism within the labor movement. In the next ten years, the proportion of female workers will undoubtedly rise and, at the same time, the older generation will gradually give way to the young. Thus, these results have an empirical bearing on the declining role of trade union ideals in the welfare state. We shall now examine some sociocentric motives in detail.

Collective interests

Motives which refer to more than the member's individual interest can be divided into two categories: (1) those involving other employees in one's firm or occupational group, and (2) those involving wider social groups, such as all workers, or the entire nation. Table 13 shows that the first category is mentioned by 35 per cent of the white collar and 29 per cent of the blue collar workers, and is the basic motive for 12 per cent and 5 per cent of the two respective groups.

[1] See pp. 36 f.

This confirms our observation (see Figures 11 and 12) that the supposedly 'individualistic' white collar workers in the union are often more concerned with collective interests than are the blue collar workers. It corresponds also with the positive attitude among white collar workers toward collective bargaining (see p. 31).

All these findings indicate that office workers and technicians may not be unwilling to pursue collective interests and that their strong personal ambitions may well be accompanied by an appreciation of organized action. The resistance among white collar workers to the industrial union is probably based more on status and career considerations than on a rejection of its goals.

This assumption is supported by the fact that several white collar groups, indeed, are affiliated with industrial trade unions, e.g. book-trade employees, civil servants, engineering and scientific employees, merchant-navy officers, professional musicians, dental technicians, police, salesmen, and restaurant staff. The problems they bring to the unions are, in many cases, issues of collective interest.

A sample of their demands includes: higher wages, a collective contract, longer holidays, minimum holidays, salary instead of tips, protection against unqualified persons in their occupational group, shorter working hours, introduction of a new rank, security of employment, and abolition of the apprentice system.

Less frequent are the motives of category (2), which relate to such wider social groups as 'the workers', 'the labor force', 'society', etc. These are mentioned by 21 per cent of blue collar and 20 per cent of white collar workers. Their major theme is the prevention of unemployment; other issues are: a higher standard of living, old-age pension, earlier retirement, lower prices, defense of the workers' economic position, doing more for all workers, and scaling wages to performance. Notwithstanding the vagueness and diversity of these motives, they share one striking trait: the absence of explicit references to the social conflict. This is in line with Dahrendorf's theory that the class conflict has lost its encompassing nature and has become isolated within the social system of the plant.

Solidarity

In addition to common interests, voluntary trade unionism is also rooted in the existence of common emotions. One of its strongest bases, for example, has always been the solidarity of working men. Although the welfare state constitutes a new social environment, this is still the case: 40 per cent of the new union members mentioned some aspect of 'unity'

6

as a reason for joining and for 10 per cent this was the basic motive. But before conclusions can be drawn, it must be stressed that this motive cannot automatically be equated with the sentiment which, in the past, has impelled thousands of workers to great sacrifices. For, in many cases, the present motive is nothing more than an inner projection of negative social control: the argument 'You *mustn't* be a parasite' being transformed into 'I don't *want* to be a parasite'. Workers joining the organization for this reason only want to avoid being identified with the group's opponents. The following response illustrates how external pressure and one's own conscience are blended in this 'negative solidarity':

'You really *couldn't do anything else* but join. When everybody does it, and your boss insists on it into the bargain. And *of course you're a dreadful parasite* if you aren't in the union and then get the benefit of a wage increase or something.'

But alongside this partly negative motivation, there are also responses which show a more positive sense of identification with one's fellow workers:

'. . . to join the others. Together we are strong.'

'In reality it is more to support people who in their jobs are more in need of it than I am.'

'There are some people without work. That concerns me too, they are people close to us.'

'It is really a duty towards the man who pays his union dues.'

In the last response the feeling of positive identification has moved into an internalization of the group's values, i.e. a sense of duty and inner calling. From the organization's point of view, this is probably one of the most valuable motives among its membership. The gradual transition from social coercion to value internalization (or moral duty) can be depicted in these four stages:

Increasing strength of motivation

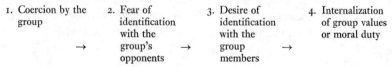

1. Coercion by the group	2. Fear of identification with the group's opponents	3. Desire of identification with the group members	4. Internalization of group values or moral duty
→	→	→	

This motive of a sense of moral duty seems to be more frequent among blue collar (7 per cent) than among white collar workers (3 per cent). Valuable as it may be, it is rather rare: for only 3 per cent and 1 per cent respectively was it the basic motive. There is little doubt that the members' ties with the union would be greatly strengthened if the incidence of this intrinsic motivation could be increased.

Idealism

In the idealistic motives of union members, three different themes can be detected; the most fundamental are the *moral principles*, i.e. the underlying social ethics from which the ideals derive their nourishment. Behind vague terms such as 'equal opportunity', 'improvement', and 'concern', one discerns a humanist ethos and sometimes, as in 'social justice', only a single ethical value. Such fundamental principles lie, partly conscious, behind many of these motives.

Secondly, there is the *social concern*, which is more immediately directed toward one's fellow human beings and which can even develop into a crusading spirit. This aspect of trade union idealism is less abstract or contemplative and involves an active striving. Sometimes, this need for action has an existence independent of any aim toward which it is directed: 'You can strive for a goal, can't you', one member answered 'without being quite sure what it is!' The opportunity to release his concern into action provides enough satisfaction to keep him from pondering about its aims.[1]

Thirdly, there are the *idealist goals*, the union ideals in the true sense. When people live in an economy of full employment and social security, these social ideals become easily blurred. Among union members, this takes the form of a differentiation resulting in the trends of orthodox idealism, conservative idealism, and modern idealism.

(1) *Orthodox idealism.* The ideals of these members stem from the Marxist period in the labor movement, described on page 46. Orthodox idealists belong mostly to the prewar generation and have difficulty in understanding modern labor. The influx of white collar members into the labor movement, labor's participation in national policy, and the rejection of Marxist traditions and symbols led to their alienation from the movement. Born before World War I, they still live very much in the social climate of the class war, as the following response shows:

'With the world situation as it is, the power will ultimately come to the workers. They need to be united if they are going to reap the fruits.'

In this view, the working class is still in conflict with the bourgeoisie and peaceful cooperation is out of the question. This image of society as a conflict-situation is often accompanied by an eschatological vision. This is evident from the reaction of a sixty-year-old steelworker to one of the pictures shown during the interview:[2]

---

[1] Analyzing the biology of motive patterns, Murphy found that 'awareness of the end is not the prime or essential condition for motivation; so far as consciousness is concerned, it is the *conative, impulsive* aspect that is essential'. G. Murphy, *Personality*, p. 126. This observation in biopsychology seems to coincide with ours in voluntary participation.

[2] See App. B, picture I.

'It makes you think of the song "The Glorious Day is coming When the People Break their Bonds". The trade union movement in the light of the dawn! The worker in the picture sees the symbol of the new socialist society. It could very well be me!'

Symbols, songs, and metaphors like 'breaking bonds', 'the dawn', and 'the new socialist society' occupy a major place in this orthodox idealism and are responsible for its continuing intensity. Closer examination shows it to linger chiefly among the older unskilled workers.

(2) *Conservative idealism.* That one can be both conservative and idealist is shown by those members whose ideal is mainly to preserve what the trade unions have achieved. This form of idealism dovetails with the official contention that economic conservatism is in fact the major policy of trade unions in the welfare state.[1] The way conservative members feel about this is evident from such reactions as:

'I am a member on principle, we don't want the prewar condition again.'

'I feel it my duty to help in the fight to keep what we have achieved.'

'Of course we can't be satisfied with things as they are, there is still a lot to be done. But nor should we forget what has already been achieved.'

'Our parents got it for us, our job is to keep things as they are, and if possible to improve them.'

The way they formulate these aims leads to the impression that such members are more concerned with preserving what has been achieved than with improving existing conditions. Since they are concerned neither with the tangible content of their ideals, nor with their chance of realization, the emphasis is, naturally, on the past.

(3) *Modern idealism.* Although the conservative idealists are more modern than the orthodox, the only idealists who are 'modern' in the proper sense of the word are those who see *new* trade union ideals even in the welfare state. Besides such economic goals as economic security, and a higher standard of living, their idealism also includes hopes for socio-cultural achievements. Take, for instance:

'I am sorry that the unions mainly serve material interests, such as salary questions. Idealism should occupy a more prominent place. What matters is the uplifting of human beings, but at present the union is just a place for bargaining.'

'We must struggle for freedom of thought and speech, and particularly for more democracy and freedom in industry.'

---

[1] 'The unions are primarily, but still not exclusively, an economic defense organization', Adolf Sturmthal, *Workers' Councils* (Cambridge, Mass., Harvard University Press, 1964), p. 7. Also C. de Galan, *De Invloed van de Vakbeweging op de loonshoogte en de werkgelegenheid* (Leiden, 1957), p. 172.

'. . . there is also the question of why the blue collar employee should have to work longer hours than the office worker. The latter may be more necessary, but my father has to leave for work while I'm still asleep. There's something unfair about that!'

Such statements should guard us against concluding that the absence of trade union ideals is a result of the workers' materialistic attitudes. For even the welfare state seems to offer them ideals which the union could pursue. The cultural emancipation of the working population, a change of the authority structure in industry, and the abolition of out-dated social distinctions can be regarded as moral principles essential to present-day trade unionism. If the unions of the welfare state could bring these principles together in a coherent view of society, close enough to the workers' experience to give it meaning in their eyes, this would stimulate their willingness to participate in the organization.

5. In the union: Participation[1]

Historically, there are three stages in the sociological approach to voluntary, democratic organizations: the theoretical, the impressionistic, and the empirical approach.

The first or idealistic stage goes back to the eighteenth century, when thinkers like Rousseau and Montesquieu were theorizing about the citizen's participation in the democratic state. Their position was radical as well as idealistic: to them, a government that claims to express the will of all the people should allow every citizen to take part in political decision-making. Diderot and d'Alembert accordingly defined democracy as 'the system of government in which *every* citizen submits to an assembly of which *everyone* is a member'. The possibility of political apathy did not fit in this theoretical model.[2]

The second stage followed in Germany, one hundred and fifty years later, when Michels, familiar with democratic reality in the socialist parties of Europe, made the observation that relatively few citizens are sincerely interested in the common good. From impressions based on participant observation, he concluded that only a *dwindling* minority of a party's members take part in making decisions. Political apathy plays a major role in this impressionistic model, and is seen as the reason that democracy in large organizations will ultimately end in the oligarchic power of the leaders over the apathetic mass.[3] This 'oligarchic law of large organizations' had supporters until the middle of the twentieth century. One of the best known was Burnham, who, in *The Managerial Revolution*, foresaw that the democratic parliament—unable to resist the oligarchic forces of the welfare state—would disappear after World War II.[4] Today we know that Michels' impressions lacked representativeness and that, as a result, his predictions were too gloomy. For the 'dwindling' group of participants still forms the hard core of contemporary democracy.

The third, or empirical, stage was developed in the United States after

---

[1] Partly published as Mark van de Vall, 'Voluntary Participation in Democratic Organizations', *Studies in Sociology*, ed. Milton C. Albrecht, *Buffalo Studies*, III, No. 2 (December 1967), 43–68.
[2] A. Naess, *Democracy, Ideology and Objectivity* (Oslo, 1956), p. 100.
[3] R. Michels, *Zur Soziologie des Parteiwesens in der modernen Demokratie, Untersuchungen über die oligarchischen Tendenzen des Gruppenlebens* (Leipzig, 1911), pp. 49–50.
[4] J. Burnham, *The Managerial Revolution* (London, Penguin Books, 1954).

World War II. Social scientists applied their research techniques to political participation and demonstrated that democracy, like the arts, religion, and science, is sociologically an elite phenomenon, owing its existence less to the indifferent many than to the interested few. Democracy, it was found, as a system of organized decision-forming in which leaders are to some degree responsive to nonleaders, operates even with a comparatively low level of participation.[1] The empirical model is the only one accounting for *both* apathy and participation in the democratic process. Empirical sociologists, such as Katz and Lazarsfeld,[2] Berelson[3], and Lipset, Trow, and Coleman,[4] demonstrated that Michels' two poles of 'democracy' (with total participation) and 'oligarchy' (with absolute power of the leaders) constitute only a normative polarity. Their findings showed it to be at variance with reality, since most democratic organizations belong to an intermediate form. In this empirical 'polyarchy', neither the members nor the leaders alone are decisive, but leaders and active members, by means of the democratic rules, keep each other in a balance of power.[5]

An example of a polyarchic organization is given by Abma, who describes how a proposal, by the executives of a European teachers association, to affiliate with the Federation of Trade Unions brought only 18 per cent of the members to the meetings; this minority, however, voted to reject the proposal.[6] An organization which is confronted with apathy among 82 per cent of its members on such an important issue diverges radically from the concept of 'Démocratie' in eighteenth-century France. On the other hand, the activity of the 18 per cent who *do* participate is so successful in controlling the leaders that this organization cannot be called an oligarchy in Michels' sense.

The polyarchic organization differs from the oligarchic in that, in addition to the powerful leaders and the passive membership, there is a third group, the active participants. By their two-way communication within the organization (*controlling* from members to leaders and *informing* from leaders to members), they act as its democratic core. The larger and the more active this group, the closer the organization approaches the ideal

[1] R. A. Dahl, 'Hierarchy, Democracy and Bargaining in Politics and Economics', *Research Frontiers in Politics and Government* (Washington, D.C., Brooking Institution, 1955), p. 59.
[2] E. Katz and P. F. Lazarsfeld, *Personal Influence* (Glencoe, Ill., Free Press, 1955).
[3] B. R. Berelson, P. F. Lazarsfeld and W. N. McPhee, *Voting* (Chicago, University of Chicago Press, 1954).
[4] S. M. Lipset, M. A. Trow and J. S. Coleman, *Union Democracy: the Internal Politics of the International Typographical Union* (Glencoe, Ill., Free Press, 1956).
[5] R. A. Dahl and C. E. Lindblom, *Politics, Economics and Welfare: Planning and Politico-economic Systems resolved into basic social Processes* (New York, Harper & Brothers, 1953), Chs. 10 and 11.
[6] E. Abma, 'De NOV en de Socioloog, verslag van een onderzoek van de Landbouwhogeschool', *Het Schoolblad*, xv, No. 17 (May 1960), *passim*.

of the democratic theorists. The smaller its number and strength, the more the organization moves toward the oligarchic pole.

Inasmuch as our pluralistic welfare states[1] are controlled largely by polyarchic organizations, the existence of a broad and active stratum of participants is essential to a democratic structure. This refers not only to participation in political parties but also to participation in other organizations, including trade unions.

Using the results of several studies, the group of organizational participants will be analyzed in greater detail. First, we shall explore the size of the participating membership in the trade unions; second, its social structure; third, some traits in the participants' personalities; and, finally, the various motives leading to voluntary participation.

THE SIZE OF THE PARTICIPATING GROUP

Since they are concerned mainly with organizational *apathy*, most surveys record only the extent of nonparticipation, i.e. the number of members who never attend union meetings. The percentage of participants can be inferred from the figures for nonparticipation, and this reveals considerable similarity in the size of the participating group in the various countries, as shown in Table 19.

The general situation is that just over half of all trade union members in the various countries are *completely apathetic*, while the rest are occasional participants, members who regularly participate, or voluntary officials.

Taking regular attendance at meetings as a criterion for participation, the size of the participating group is probably between 10 per cent and

---

[1] H. J. Laski, 'The Pluralistic State', in *The Foundation of Sovereignty and Other Essays* (New York, Harcourt, Brace and Company, 1921).

FOOTNOTES TO TABLE 19

[1] S. M. Lipset and J. Gordon, 'Mobility and Trade Union Membership' in *Class, Status and Power: A Reader in Social Stratification*, ed. R. Bendix and S. M. Lipset (Glencoe, Ill., Free Press, 1953), pp. 491–500.
[2] C. Bear-Rose, 'Morale in a Trade Union', *American Journal of Sociology* (1950), pp. 167–74.
[3] L. R. Dean, 'Social Integration, Attitudes and Union Activity', *Industrial and Labor Relations Review*, VII (1954), 48–58.
[4] Political and Economic Planning, *British Trade Unionism*, (London, 1948), p. 31.
[5] S. K. Saxena, *Nationalization and Industrial Conflict* (The Hague, 1955), Tables VII and VIII, pp. 167–8.
[6] J. Goldstein, *The Government of British Trade Unions* (London, 1952), p. 202.
[7] A. Mausolff, *Gewerkschaft und Betriebsrat im Urteil der Arbeitnehmer* (Darmstadt, 1952), p. 100.
[8] Research by the author, App. A (6).
[9] Research by the author, App. A (3)
[10] H. Wagenfeld, *De toestand van de vakbeweging in de Tielerwaard* (report of the Gelders Komgronden Commissie), p. 7.
[11] Survey carried out on behalf of the Dutch Steelworkers Union by S. Poppe, one of its employees.

TABLE 19. *Size of participating and nonparticipating groups in the trade unions in four different countries*

UNITED STATES

1. In Oakland, California, an area with one of the highest trade union densities in the United States:[1]

	Blue collar workers	White collar workers
Never attended a union meeting	50%	54%

2. In a large industrial union in the United States, in the Midwest, based on the reports of 27 shop stewards on their local branches:[2]

Members uninterested in union affairs	50%

3. In three firms having a total of 635 union members:[3]

Rarely or never attended a union meeting	54%

UNITED KINGDOM

4. In 16 unions affiliated with the TUC, based on information up to 1943:[4]

Rarely or never attended a union meeting	50%
Occasionally attended	30%
Regularly attended	20%

5. In two branches of the NUM, totals of those who never participated:[5]

In branch A	53%
In branch B	62%

6. In a branch of the Transport and General Workers Union:[6]

Never attended a union meeting	65%

GERMANY

7. In a representative sample of 219 union members at Darmstadt, 1949–50:[7]

Never attended a union meeting	38%
Occasionally attended	44%
Regularly attended	17%

THE NETHERLANDS

8. Of 22,363 Rotterdam members of the NVV, in 1955:[8]

Attended no union meetings in previous session	59%
Attended one meeting	15%
Attended two or more meetings	26%

9. In two representative sample of members of the Steel Workers Union and the Clerical Workers Union, Utrecht local, in 1956:[9]

	Blue collar workers	White collar workers
Attended no meetings in previous session	51%	66%
Did attend, but did not take part in discussion	30%	13%
Joined in discussion, or active in other ways	19%	21%

(If these findings are adjusted to the proportion in which blue and white collar workers are represented in the NVV, i.e. 6:1, the percentage of nonparticipants is found to be 53%).

10. In a survey of CNV and NVV members in 15 villages around Tiel:[10]

	Noncommuters	Commuters
Never attended a union meeting	46%	70%
Occasionally or regularly attended	54%	30%

11. In a national random sample of 626 members of the Steel Workers Union (ANMB) in 1954:[11]

	Ordinary members' meetings	Meeting about collective wage agreement
Never attended	58%	55%
Occasionally attended	29%	31%
Regularly attended	13%	13%

See page 154 for footnotes.

20 per cent of the total membership, while 30 to 40 per cent attend only at important meetings when, for example, the collective agreement is being discussed. Owing to rotation, the attendance per meeting is somewhat below the quoted figure, and thus, the findings broadly correspond with Table 9 of Chapter 3. Further, the data indicate a greater apathy among members who commute (70 per cent) than among the noncommuters (46 per cent). The reasons for this are that the journey is tiring and that the commuter gets home late; a more important factor is the lack of relevance to the commuting member of the discussions at the local branch meetings.

A third conclusion is suggested by comparing the figures for Tiel, Utrecht and Rotterdam, indicating an inverse correlation between urbanization and participation. This tallies with Dutch surveys in welfare organizations[1] and with social research findings in France[2] and in England.[3] It is therefore justifiable to speak of a more general trend and of a prospect of increasing apathy in the trade unions with increasing urbanization.[4]

THE STRUCTURE OF THE PARTICIPATING GROUP

In sociology, the relationship between social structure and cultural pattern is well recognized. It is to be expected, therefore, that changes in the structure of the labor force, e.g. the increase in the percentage of white collar workers, will be reflected in various cultural traits. One such trait is democratic participation: a widely known characteristic of white collar workers is that they are more organization-minded than blue collar workers. Observations in France,[5] the United States,[6] and Holland[7]

---

[1] E. Abma, 'Participation in Community Services', *Sociologia Ruralis*, I (1960), pp. 43–50.

[2] 'L'apathie des coopérateurs est beaucoup plus fréquente et plus grave dans les grandes coopératives que dans les petites'. G. Laserre, 'Le fonctionnement de la démocratie coopérative', *Revue des études coopératives*, XXIX, No. 108 (April–June 1957), p. 79.

[3] G. N. Ostergaard and A. H. Halsey, 'Democracy in British Retail Cooperatives', *Archives Internationales de Sociologie de la Coopération*, I (1957), pp. 65–72.

[4] In this context it should be pointed out that although Stinchcombe suggests urbanization to be positively correlated with organizational *competence*, the above data suggest it to be negatively correlated with organizational *participation*. The intervening variable leading to this negative result is probably willingness to participate. Arthur L. Stinchcombe, 'Social Structure and Organizations', in *Handbook of Organizations*, ed. James G. March (Chicago, Rand McNally, 1965), p. 152.

[5] O. R. Gallagher, 'Voluntary Associations in France', *Social Forces*, XXXVI, No. 2 (December 1957), 160.

[6] 'The middle classes belong to more organizations, are better informed, have greater facility with the verbal means of influence, and participate in elections more than do the working classes.' R. E. Lane, *Political Life* (Glencoe, Ill., Free Press, 1959), p. 227. See also J. C. Scott, 'Membership and Participation in Voluntary Associations', *American Sociological Review*, XXII, No. 3 (1957), 315–26; and M. Axelrod, 'Urban Structure and Social Participation', *American Sociological Review*, XXI, No. 1 (February 1956), 15–16.

[7] CBS, 'Verenigingsleven', *Vrijetijdsbesteding in Nederland, Winter 1955–56*, p. 5 (Zeist, De Haan, 1957), p. 18.

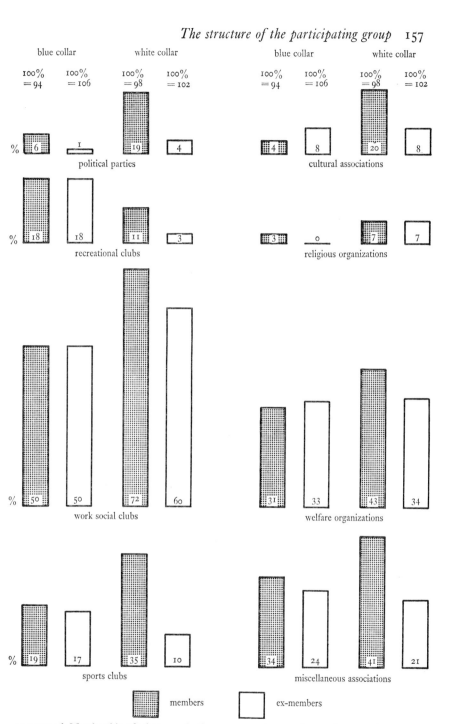

FIGURE 16. Membership of other organizations among union members and ex-members.

confirm this observation. At first sight, the trade unions seem to be an exception to this rule. Chapter 1 showed that the proportion of white collar members in organized labor was well below that of manual workers. *Within* the unions, however, the rule manifests itself with undiminished force: white collar union members are more association-minded than their unorganized colleagues.

Figure 16 provides a comparison of the extent to which both blue and white collar members and ex-members of trade unions belong to various kinds of associations. Not only do white collar employees predominate in seven out of eight types of association, but it is the trade union members among them who are most organization-minded, having the highest percentage of membership in six types of association or organization. Closer analysis shows this not to be limited to formal membership: they also tend to *participate* more actively than others in each of the six types of association. The conclusion is that those members of the white collar group who join a trade union form a select group from the point of view of organization-mindedness.

As for trade union participation, Table 20 allows for a fourfold classification of participants, viz. blue and white collar workers in public services and in private industry. These four categories show considerable differences with respect to the lowest criterion of participation, attendance at meetings.

TABLE 20. *Attendance at union meetings*

	Blue collar members		White collar members	
	Government service	Industry	Government service	Industry
	%	%	%	%
Attended one or more union meetings in past session	88	42	50	31
100 per cent	3,566	12,455	2,287	2,067

df = 3; P <0·001. See App. A (6): Rotterdam Survey.

This cross-classification shows that high attendance at trade union meetings does not apply to *all* white collar members: civil servants attend considerably more often than do salaried employees in industry whose participation, in fact, proves to be the lowest of all four groups.

In the history of labor, with its thousands of cases of workers' protest, it seems rather surprising that union members in public service should show the highest level of participation. Nor is this restricted to the Low

Countries; similar observations in Scandinavia suggest it to be a more general trend.[1]

On second thoughts, this may be understandable. We have seen that, compared to the widespread rise of incomes and fringe benefits in the private sector, conditions in the public sector have generally been lagging behind. With the strike weapon denied to them, public employees have few means of protest against this trend except increased union participation. It is one more illustration of how the welfare state constitutes a new social environment for the labor organization.

Although with regard to attending meetings we found no general predominance of white collar workers, there is a difference at higher levels of participation, e.g. filling voluntary posts. By virtue of their greater intellectual abilities, reflected in their knowledge of union affairs,[2] the white collar workers even tend to oust the manual workers from voluntary office. This is shown in Figure 17 (page 160), which covers a representative sample of unpaid union posts in the Rotterdam union branches.

At the lower, intermediate, and higher levels of voluntary office the white collar members (cf. the 23 per cent line) are over-represented, and this is more marked at each succeeding level; conversely, the blue collar members (cf. the 72 per cent line) are increasingly under-represented. Studies of the French and Dutch labor parties have also revealed this trend in other sectors of the labor movement.

These two processes, the increase of white collar and the decline of blue collar members in voluntary posts, need not be *directly* connected, since both could result from a third, antecedent variable. The results of three different studies suggest, however, that there is a direct causal link. M. Duverger, in his research of local branches of the French Socialist Party, states that, for psychological reasons, domination of one group— whether blue or white collar—always causes nonparticipation in the other.[3] The greater activity of white collar workers in a Dutch political

---

[1] 'At the same time as relations between employers and workers have been stabilized in an atmosphere of mutual confidence, increased activity and disquiet is found to prevail among one large and expanding group of wage earners, previously not very organization-minded, namely salaried employees *and particularly social servants.*' 'A feeling has spread among public servants and other non-manual workers that they are being squeezed between the powerful organizations of skilled and unskilled workers, on one hand, and private employers and their organizations, on the other.' *Freedom and Welfare, Social Patterns in the Northern Countries of Europe*, ed. G. R. Nelson (Copenhagen, 1953), p. 140.

[2] See Fig. 9, p. 106.

[3] 'Dans une section à prédominance bourgeoise, les ouvriers se sentent isolés au milieu de gens qui partagent leurs opinions politiques, mais non leur mentalité, leurs préoccupations quotidiennes, leurs réactions instinctives; de même, les "bourgeois" dans des sections à prédominance ouvrière. La diversité sociale des adhérents paraît donc être un obstacle au développement du militantisme. On serait tenté de dire: plus le milieu est homogène, plus l'indice de militantisme est élevé.' M. Duverger, *Les Partis Politiques* (Paris, 1951), p. 136.

organization (Labor Party) is, similarly, a direct cause of nonparticipation among its manual workers.[1] Finally, we found that while *passive* blue collar members were least in favor of white collar members in their union, among the white collar workers the *active* ones least favored blue collar workers in their organization. This leaves ground for the conclusion that if the passive blue collar workers would become more active in the organization, major resistance would come from the active white collar workers; and, reversely, that increased participation on the part of the latter would meet with little enthusiasm among the former.[2]

Together, the facts point toward one conclusion, viz. that the trend towards under-representation of blue collar members in voluntary trade union office is, in part, directly caused by overrepresentation of members of the new middle class. Once started, this type of self-perpetuating process is hard to halt.

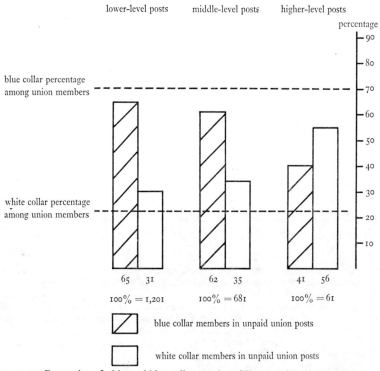

FIGURE 17. Proportion of white and blue collar members filling unpaid union posts.

[1] M. van de Vall, 'Sociografie van een doorbraakafdeling' (Report for the Dutch Labor Party) (Amsterdam, 1953), p. 33. cf. App. A (7).
[2] For further conclusions, see M. van de Vall, 'Non participatie in Vakbeweging', *Sociologisch Jaarboek*, XIII (Amsterdam, Het Koggeschip, 1959), p. 132

THE PERSONALITY OF THE PARTICIPANT
The psychological approach to trade union participation includes two diametrically opposite theories about the personality of the active union member. The oldest is the Marxist view, major elements of which are found in the *Communist Manifesto*.[1] There, Marx and Engels put forward what can best be described as the 'frustration-aggression hypothesis of trade union participation'.[2] The theory is this: after the exploited (= frustrated) workers have entered into conflict (= aggression) with the employer and in their blind rage, have smashed the machines with which they work (= displacement), 'the collisions between individual workers and individual bourgeois take more and more the character of collision between two classes. Thereupon the workers begin to form combinations (trade unions) against the bourgeoisie.' According to this hypothesis, therefore, the trade union participant is frustrated in his material conditions, in his needs for security, and in his status aspirations.

Opposed to this is the view of the revisionist theoreticians. As far back as 1899, Bernstein observed that the members who took an active part in union life were not the most deeply frustrated, i.e. the unskilled workers, but rather the slightly better-off skilled craftsmen.[3] Elaborating this, the sociologist de Man argued that not resentment and frustration but the more positive motives of belongingness and morality form the psychological background to union participation. 'Even as regards attitudes there is a wide rift between Marxist theory and trade union practice', writes de Man.[4] 'Apart from a warrior in the class struggle the participant is also, even primarily, a human being, familyman, citizen, neighbor, colleague, even—as theorists often forget—a worker: a man in a factory who is also concerned with other things than the class struggle, and with other relationships than the one between exploiter and exploited.'

It is clear that the revisionist hypothesis views a positive social attitude as the psychological background to trade union participation. By comparing active and passive blue collar members in a local branch of a Dutch labor organization, we shall try to find out which of the two hypotheses is correct.[5]

In the frame of reference that any individual uses to evaluate his social

[1] K. Marx, *Communist Manifesto*, p. 31.
[2] J. Dollard, *Frustration and Agression* (London, Routledge and Kegan Paul, 1944).
[3] E. Bernstein, *Die Voraussetzungen des Sozialismus und die Aufgaben der Sozialdemokratie* (Stuttgart, 1899), translated as *Evolutionary Socialism* (New York, Schocken, 1961).
[4] H. de Man, *The Psychology of Socialism* (London, Allen and Unwin, 1928), p. 328.
[5] Discussed in greater detail in M. van de Vall, 'Das Problem der Partizipation in Freiwilligen Organisationen', in *Soziologie und Gesellschaft in den Niederlanden*, ed. Joachim Matthes (Berlin, Luchterhand Verlag, 1965), pp. 251–67.

position, a major element is his status as compared with that of his parents, especially his father's. Someone who has risen higher socially than his father will be more satisfied with his status than the man who, though perhaps socially outranking the first, has dropped below his father's social position.

Investigating the occurrence of this indicator of frustration among active and passive members of the labor organization, we find the following figures.

TABLE 21. *Social mobility and participation*

Status compared with father's occupation, in own view	Participants %	Nonparticipants %
Lower	7	40
Same or higher	93	60
	(100% = 38)	(100% = 38)

(df = 1; χ^2 = 11·08; P < 0·001)

Although a minority in both groups consider themselves to be of lower social status than their father, this minority is significantly smaller among the participants. It may reasonably be assumed that within this category, therefore, there will be less social resentment based upon this factor.

A related element is whether the worker feels he has progressed sufficiently in his career, i.e. in his own work environment. The man who in our 'status society', does not have a successful career will easily be regarded as a failure. Such a man may be inclined to put the blame on factors external to himself, i.e. on factors in his social milieu. The view that participation in the trade union is no form of displaced aggression against one's environment is supported by the fact that more participants (85 per cent) express satisfaction with the progress in their careers than do nonparticipants (71 per cent). A related phenomenon is the attitude towards other aspects of the work situation. Asked whether they like or do not like their present work and why, the participating members (91 per cent), again, responded more favorably than the nonparticipants (79 per cent). The workers' evaluation of their incomes follows the same pattern: although the majority of both active and passive members are satisfied with their wages, 61 per cent of the former reply favorably as compared with 52 per cent of the latter. It is interesting that these participants earn an average of four dollars a month *less* than their passive fellow members! This confirms the conclusion that the participants take a more favorable attitude than the nonparticipants toward their work situation.

The above findings, however, relate only to the worker's immediate family and work environments. Now the question arises whether or not the same correlations appear in a wider social framework.

Whether or not participants and passive members differ about present-day industrial relations was checked on the basis of the following questions: (1) 'What do you think of the relationship between workers and employers in society?' (The respondent could refer to the situation in his own firm.) (2) 'Has this relationship changed since the war?' (3) 'Do you think that in the future there should be a different relationship?' and 'if so, could you say why?'

The results are tabulated below.

TABLE 22. *Opinion of labor–management relations and participation*

Opinion of labor-management relations	Participants %	Nonparticipants %
Largely favorable	73	45
Largely unfavorable	27	55
	(100% = 40)	(100% = 38)

(df $= 1$; $\chi^2 = 6\cdot08$; P $< 0\cdot01$)

Together with the other figures, this table confirms the revisionist hypothesis that participants in trade unions have a more favorable attitude than nonparticipants toward society, toward the work community, and toward their own social position. For a multivariate analysis of the validity of this correlation we refer to Appendix D, page 224. Since Gadourek confirms that participants show greater upward social mobility, see better prospects for the future, and are more satisfied with their career,[1] and Spinrad reached identical conclusions in his comparison of thirty-five trade union studies in the United States,[2] it is, in all probability, a general trend.[3] Instead of being frustrated and alienated, the

[1] I. Gadourek, *A Dutch Community* (Leiden, 1956), p. 313.

[2] W. Spinrad, 'Correlations of Trade Union Participation', *American Sociological Review*, xxv, No. 1 (February 1960), 237. Also of interest here is Lane's conclusion: 'People who are satisfied with their communities and feel integrated in the community life are more active in politics than those who do not: Integration, not alienation, forms the basis of most political motivation in the modal non-crisis American politics'. R. E. Lane, *Political Life*, p. 166. For a more recent review of research on union participants, with similar conclusions, see Arnold S. Tannenbaum, 'Unions', in *Handbook of Organizations*, ed. James G. March, pp. 745–50.

[3] The problem of cause and effect has not been considered here, i.e. the question whether positive attitudes lead to participation or whether active participation leads to positive attitudes. Most likely is that the two variables are interdependent.

modern trade union participant is more satisfied and integrated into society.

After this outline of some of the basic personality traits of the active trade unionist, we shall turn to the specific motives that lead to participation in democratic organizations. Our analysis is based on surveys of a labor organization and a political organization in the Dutch welfare state.[1]

THE MOTIVES FOR PARTICIPATION

Studies of voluntary participation show an antithesis between a predominantly psychological hypothesis which views democratic activity primarily as resulting from a particular pattern of intrapsychic processes, viz., a democratic personality, and a sociological hypothesis which regards it as resulting from the interaction of common human needs and their satisfaction by the organization. Representative of the psychological approach is Bonger[2] whose hypothesis, 'democracy is above all a matter of character', weighs the personality of the participant most heavily. This predominantly European[3] hypothesis implicitly distinguishes between democratic and authoritarian personalities; its assumption is that an organization will be more democratic when it counts a larger number of democratic personalities among its members.

Representative of the sociological approach is Lane who, in his review of modern sociopolitical research, concludes that participation depends on the satisfaction by the organization of six common human needs. These needs are: the pursuit of economic gain, the need to belong, the need to understand, the relief of intrapsychic tensions, the pursuit of power, and the need for self-esteem.[4] In this hypothesis the responsibility for participation has shifted to the organization, since the better it satisfies these human needs the more participants it will have. Since the desire for economic gain relates primarily to paid work and intrapsychic tensions are of too subconscious nature to be reached by sociological research, we shall restrict our analysis to the remaining four needs. We shall also demonstrate however, that there is one more need relevant to voluntary participation in democratic organizations.

---

[1] The unions are the Dutch Steelworkers Union (ANMB) and the Dutch Union of Administrative Employees (Mercurius). The political organization is the Dutch Labor Party.

[2] W. A. Bonger, *Problemen der Demokratie, een sociologische en psychologische studie* (Amsterdam, 1936), p. 26.

[3] This refers to T. W. Adorno and to M. Horkheimer, co-author and editor of *The Authoritarian Personality* (New York, Harper & Brothers, 1950). Both have since returned to Europe.

[4] R. E. Lane, *Political Life*, Chs. 8 and 9.

The need to belong

When man is referred to as a 'social being', the implication is that the sympathy of his fellows, i.e. interpersonal affection, is necessary for his mental health. In Horney's view,[1] the desire for social acceptance—in reaction to life in modern, competitive society—has almost become modern man's obsession. Whether this is true or not, it is quite certain that the normal adult, in his adjustment to his social milieu—parents, wife, children, friends and fellow workers—experiences satisfactions which are beneficial to his mental well-being. It is our hypothesis that his contacts in meetings and on committees with members of his clubs and associations help satisfy this 'need to belong'.[2]

This is substantiated by the answers of those trade union members who never attended union meetings but did participate in other associations (see survey, App. A (6)). Interviewed about their reasons for this, about one-third (32 per cent) mentioned motives of social contact. Examples are:

'The . . . is more a recreational club, you feel more at home there, it's smaller and you get to know the people better. In the union I always feel a bit out of place because I don't know anyone.'

'There are so many people I know in the arts social club. It's much nicer if you know the people a bit. That's why the club meetings are much pleasanter than the union ones.'

Sometimes the specific wording suggests that social satisfaction functions as a stimulus toward deeper interest in the organization. In the following answers, for example, the members, first state (1) that they do not have any friends in their branch and, then conclude (2) that they are not interested in the union:

'I prefer the . . . because (1) *I know far more people there*, and feel much more at home, It (2) *also interests me more.*'

'In the hiking club we are always together. At the meetings (1) *you know your fellow-members better.* And anyway (2) I have *no interest* in union affairs.'

'I prefer going to the meetings of the Youth Club, because (1) *I know all the people there well* and get on fine with most of them. The union (2) *doesn't interest me much.*'

[1] K. Horney, *The Neurotic Personality of our Time* (New York, W. W. Norton & Co., 1937), p. 35.
[2] M. M. Shaw, 'A Comparison of Individuals and Small Groups in the Rational Solution of Complex Problems', in *Readings in Social Psychology*, ed. Maccobby, Newcomb and Hartley (New York, Holt, 1958), and Dorwin Cartwright, 'Influence, Leadership, Control', in *Handbook of Organizations*, ed. J. G. March (Chicago, Rand McNally, 1965), p. 33. See also, in the context of labor organizations, A. S. Tannenbaum and R. L. Kahn, *Participation in Union Locals* (New York, Row, Peterson, 1958), p. 9.

A similar correlation was found among the members of a political party who, while living in a small community participated in local branch life, but after moving to larger city lapsed into apathy:

'Previously, in B., (1) I attended all meetings and (2) I was more interested in the party. That was *because* I knew far more people there.'

The sequence of (1) having social contacts and (2) being interested in the organization may point to a causal relation. This is supported by Lipset's survey of the United States typographical union: there it was found that new members either get involved in the social life of the union or remain socially isolated and that the former *as a result* of their social involvement become interested in union affairs.[1]

In these political and labor organizations, satisfaction of the need for social acceptance precedes participation. The implication is that, so far as the members' motives are concerned, such latent functions of the organization as the satisfaction of individual needs often outweigh its manifest function, e.g. the realization of the common goal.[2] An important consideration for the trade unions is that the strength of this 'need to belong' is different in various segments of the population.

Social status and the need to belong

It has been found, in Western Europe and the United States, that blue and white collar workers often differ with respect to the feeling tone of their social contacts, including their contacts with fellow participants. Blue collar workers, for instance, orient themselves often primarily to the individual personalities around them and only secondarily to their job or rank. Even in his relationship with a bureaucratic organization, according to Miller and Riessman,[3] the blue collar worker views himself first and foremost as related to persons and not to abstract roles, positions, or organizational status. Zweig calls this the trait of 'personalization' among modern factory workers.[4]

This is in contrast to the basic attitude of white collar workers who, according to Merton, are often governed by a 'norm of impersonality' in their daily work.[5] Parsons has observed that, in the white collar work situation, where technical competence often is decisive, the personal elements of group life often fade into the background.[6] The conclusion

---

[1] S. M. Lipset, M. A. Trow and J. S. Coleman, *Union Democracy*, pp. 92–3.
[2] Robert K. Merton, *Social Theory and Social Structure* revised and enlarged edition (Glencoe Ill., Free Press, 1957), p. 63.
[3] S. M. Miller and F. Riessman, 'The Working Class Subculture: A New View', in A. B. Shostak and W. Gombers, *Blue-Collar World* (Englewood Cliffs, N.J., Prentice-Hall, 1964), pp. 24–36.   [4] F. Zweig, 'The New Factory Worker', *The Twentieth Century* (May 1960), p. 397.
[5] R. K. Merton, *Social Theory*, p. 157.
[6] T. Parsons, *Essays in Sociological Theory* (Glencoe, Ill., Free Press, 1949), p. 193.

is that blue collar workers in a large, voluntary organization will be inclined to stress the personal aspect of interaction and white collar workers the more functional aspects.

When both blue and white collar workers belong to the same organization, for example a political party of trade union, this difference will have a direct influence on the satisfaction of their need for social acceptance. A concrete example is offered by a political organization which recently received an influx of white collar members.[1] As a result, human relations grew more formal: the use of first names, once widespread among the members, became restricted to one's own status group, and members came to know less about each other as persons. Many blue collar members felt this as a severe deprivation:

'Formerly, the party was not so big, but the comradeship was different; that has all gone now. There used to be a lot of socializing with the others, now one just says Hello and that's all. There isn't the social spirit there used to be.'— Coachbuilder.

'The middle class doesn't understand the worker. The difference between then and now is too great, I can't stand it.'—Lathe operator.

'. . . and I haven't much contact any longer. None of the committee ever comes along to say what's wrong. The committee members used to come along and talk to you, but not anymore. You pay your dues and that's that. Formerly at the meetings people used to know each other: "Hi, John, Bill, Tom!" Now it's all office workers and civil servants.'—Milling-machine operator.

The white collar worker's tendency toward a more functional social climate, on the other hand, is illustrated by a university-trained civil servant's response to a blue collar member's complaint at a branch meeting that the party had neglected him during his illness. The blue collar member, a hopper worker, complained:

'When you are that ill you sometimes want to talk to somebody. I was ill for eight months, and even admitted to hospital, but they forgot all about me. I was deeply hurt.'

After the meeting, when members were discussing the charge, the civil servant, who often had shown himself to have a well-developed social conscience, remarked:

'I didn't think the complaint was right. What does he expect? Surely that isn't the job of a political party. For pastoral care he needs a clergyman. That isn't what you join the party for, that's a job for the church.'

This illustrates how, in European blue collar life, the local labor party branch used to function as a 'Gemeinschaft', a community whose social and emotional ties provide enough psychological gratification to make

[1] See App. A (7).

membership an end in itself; whereas, for the more functionally-minded white collar member, it has more the character of a 'Gesellschaft', an organization serving aims external to its immediate group life. Such differences in attitude, deeply rooted in the basic personalities of both categories of members, easily lead to tensions within the participant group.

The need to understand

Social psychologists have shown that individuals often feel a need to reduce the chaotic social world around them to a more comprehensible cognitive structure. 'Man is an organizing animal', observe Krech and Crutchfield,[1] implying that man's search for intellectually meaningful patterns is not limited to the Rorschach ink blot, but extends to his social situation.[2] Politics is one means to satisfy this need, as is illustrated by the way Marxist theory served and, for many, still serves[3] to reduce their social world to a systematic, comprehensive model. Activity in one's labor organization is another; our hypothesis that participation in trade unions meets the need for social insight is supported by such responses as:

'I go mainly to the union meetings to learn, so that I know about what is being discussed . . . Usually I go when financial matters are being dealt with.'

'I prefer the union meeting, you pick more up there. You learn something, and then you can join in discussions at the factory and express your views.'

'I go to seven meetings out of ten, to know about conditions in the plants, wages, and things like that.'

Conversely, members who do *not* find their need for insight satisfied easily lapse into organizational apathy. Our analysis of political participation indicates that this reaction is not uncommon in political organizations. The following remarks illustrate this:

'Politics? It doesn't interest me any more, I don't understand what it's about any longer. Frankly it leaves me cold now.'

'You can hardly concern yourself with the party any more, you cannot understand what it's all about.'

Thirty-six per cent of the union members covered by our survey of

[1] D. Krech and S. Crutchfield, *Theory and Problems of Social Psychology* (New York, McGraw–Hill, 1948), p. 86.
[2] Murphy calls this the quest for form: 'The ordering of events in time and space gives satisfaction', Gardner Murphy, *Personality* (New York, Harper & Brothers, 1947), p. 359.
[3] *For Germany:* 'The specific educational background of the worker in industry is undeniably of predominantly Marxist origin. The range of information which he has acquired is determined largely by the Marxist conception of society.' H. Popitz, H. P. Bahrdt, A. E. Jüres, and H. Kesting, *Das Gesellschaftsbild des Arbeiters* (Tübingen, 1957), p. 86.

For Holland: 'The fact, observed in other parts of Holland, that the old anti-clerical Marxism is still most effective among manual workers and that at their level the . . . spiritual renewal of socialism is least apparent, is also clearly evident in Twente, particularly in Enschede.' P. Smits, *Kerk en Stad* (The Hague, 1952), p. 278.

participants (App. A (3)) stated similar motives, so that this trend manifests itself rather strongly in the trade union movement. As a result, such members cease to participate in this influential organization and, at best, transfer their activities to less important but simpler associations. To illustrate this, some members who did not participate in their union but were active in other organized groups, gave the following reasons:

'The problems you have to deal with in the ball club can be understood by an ordinary man. But not union matters, because I don't know enough about them.'

'The staff social club, the sheepdog association and the volleyball club are much more within my horizon. The union is so big and complicated.'

In this transition to participation in simpler associations, four phases can be distinguished. The first is that the member finds it harder to understand the technicalities of the organizational action; this implies that the meeting fails in its educative task, since the member's insight into the problems of union and plant is not increased. Such lack of knowledge leads, in the second phase, to the discussions at the meetings passing more and more over his head. He becomes unable to take an active part in policy-making; he feels superfluous and stays away from meetings. In the third phase, he is apathetic toward the organization and, if he is among the most active workers, he will turn toward associations within his own horizon. The fourth phase, found mainly among blue collar workers, occurs when the one-time participant experiences a sense of social impotence, feeling that participation in the organization is denied to him *because* he is a manual worker. This resignation is evident in such comments as:

'These things have become much too complicated for the ordinary worker. They no longer mean anything to him.'

'Activity in the union? That's more for office workers, because they know more about administration.'

Once members have this feeling, it becomes virtually impossible to involve them in the organization, despite modern methods of education and training. People with a sense of social impotence ('Ohnmacht'), according to Fromm, have lost all interest in the very knowledge that would bring about their emancipation.[1] Apart from the fact that it undermines the psychological foundation of democratic participation, those who are governed by 'Ohnmacht' tend to form an irrational element in

---

[1] E. Fromm, 'Zum Gefühl der Ohnmacht', *Zeitschrift für Sozialforschung*, VI (1937), 114. For empirical confirmation of this observation, see Herbert H. Hyman, 'The Value System of different Classes, a Social Psychological Contribution to the Analysis of Stratification', in *Class, Status and Power*, ed. Reinhardt Bendix and Seymour Lipset (Glencoe, Ill., Free Press, 1953), pp. 426–42.

democracy, less susceptible as they are to rational arguments and more susceptible to emotional suasion.[1]

Another effect of differences in social insight is that they tend to create misunderstanding between blue and white collar members of the participant group.

Social status and social perception

In Chapter 3 we found that white collar workers know more about the labor movement than do either skilled or the unskilled blue collar worker; their knowledge of trade union problems was consistently greater.

Further, there are indications that the *content* of their social perceptions also differs. The nature of this difference may be clarified by the concept of 'partial thinking'. This means that one perceives one's social environment as consisting of compartments, each with its own content, its own norms, and its own pattern of behavior.[2] This kind of social perception, in which the areas of religion, economics, politics, culture, and science are distinguished both cognitively and behaviorally, is relatively new. According to Mannheim, it originated in the second half of the nineteenth century, and he allows for the probability that it has not yet permeated all strata of society. This finds support in two empirical studies, which showed differences in social perceptions between white and blue collar workers. In a political organization (the Dutch labor party), it is shown by the contrasting ways in which the two types of participants view a celebration (Labor Day). While blue collar workers regard this as an *integral* part of their total political attitude, many white collar workers take the compartmental view:

'What I object to in Labor Day is that it is more a cultural than a political occasion. And cultural occasions should be kept apart from politics. The cultural aspects of Labor Day mean nothing to me.'—Teacher.

'Labor Day? It has a social function, it is a token of community, with a play element added. Although I am a member of the party, I don't feel myself a member of this community, so I don't go.'—Lawyer.

These members of the new middle class distinguish between the political, social, cultural, and play elements in organizational life and take a separate attitude toward each of them. By contrast, in the blue collar participant's perception these kinds of abstract segments are almost entirely absent. From his schooldays less familiar with abstractions like

---

[1] R. Bendix, 'Social Stratification and Political Power', *American Political Science Review*, XLVI, No. 2 (June 1952), p. 369.

[2] K. Mannheim, *Man and Society in an Age of Reconstruction* (London, Routledge and Kegan Paul, 1946), p. 164.

'social functions', 'the play aspect', and 'community', he perceives his social environment in a more preanalytical way, and his response to the organization is often predominantly emotional. Since politics, the trade union, Labor Day, etc., are for him indivisible aspects of one integrated whole, he views compartmentalized reasoning as unrealistic. A typical response is:

'They (the intellectuals) chop life up in many pieces; they separate politics from one's outlook on life and from culture. It's just theory for me; it isn't passionate or real enough.'—Factory foreman.

For these skilled workers it is evident that the elimination of social and cultural elements from their participation implies a loss of satisfaction. It is for this psychological reason, and not for political reasons, that they dissociate themselves from the white collar participants. As a result, they often long for the past:

'The member of the (pre-war) Workers' Party got far more out of his membership and found much more satisfaction than the member of the (postwar) Labor Party.'—Park attendant.

'I prefer the old Workers' Party. In my mind, I fully accept the Labor Party, but in my heart I still prefer the old party. The intellectual approach makes problems too complicated.'—Fitter.

If the active white collar members, in their analytical approach, distinguish and reject segments of the organization which less well-educated participants intuitively regard as indivisible, the situation is ripe for misunderstanding. And when, at the time, this difference in perception coincides with dissimilarities in income, social status, and command of language, the conditions for conflict are present. Although such discord between blue and white collar participants is not uncommon, it is rarely caused by political issues. The fact that participation is voluntary and the fact that the members wish to realize a common goal makes a political dichotomy unlikely. The data show that most such misunderstandings are of a sociopsychological nature.[1] Since Duverger,[2] in his survey of the French socialist party, comes to similar conclusions, this seems a general trend.

The need for self-esteem

For many participants, the prime motive is the desire neither for social contact nor for social insight, but rather a semiconscious need for a positive self-image, i.e. for self-esteem.

The desire for self-respect is, according to Allport,[3] an almost insatiable

[1] M. van de Vall, 'Sociografie', (See also App. A (7.) [2] M. Duverger, *Les Partis Politiques*, p. 136.
[3] G. W. Allport, 'The Psychology of Participation', in *Readings in Group Work*, ed. D. Sullivan (New York, The Association Press, 1952), p. 239.

need in modern man, explaining much of his behavior, including organizational participation. *Indirect* ways to this goal are the acquisition of power and status; one derives self-esteem from one's power over others and one's status among them. Both are powerful and they are related: Mulder[1] found the opportunity to wield power a primary determinant of satisfaction, and in Murphy's view,[2] the need for power is so closely integrated with the need for status that the two are often considered to be identical. The more fundamental need for self-esteem is their common basis.[3]

There is also a *direct* way of increasing one's self-esteem, as a result of a confrontation not with others but with oneself. This is the case when a man sets a high standard for himself and esteems himself to the extent that he meets his ego-ideal. Since this motive does not presuppose any relationship with others, it is less 'social' than the indirect motives. When a personal norm of this kind is based upon an ethical value, a political ideal, or a religious calling, we speak of a sense of self-fulfillment.[4]

The attraction of participation in a major democratic organization—such as a trade union—is that it increases the member's self-esteem in various ways, viz. through power, status, moral duty and a sense of purpose. We shall now analyze them.

Power and status

Like ego-needs in general, the desire for power can be satisfied either directly or indirectly. Sills gives an example of the *indirect* way when he describes how participants in a large organization found satisfaction in the fact that it was a powerful national association with hundreds of thousands of members.[5] Motivation in terms indicating massive force, such as 'tidal wave', 'battle', and 'crusade', illustrate how the individual's self-esteem was derived from the strength of the organization. Similar feelings of reflected power are found among active trade unionists; 7·5 per cent of them gave such answers as:

'... I prefer to serve on a committee in the union, because it's a lot more important. Much more originates from the union, it has more significance.'

'... the union meetings are more important: they concern social and individual welfare, and everything connected with the engineering industry.'

'... sooner to the union meetings, because what I say there has much wider consequences.'

[1] M. Mulder, *Group Structure, Motivation and Group Performance* (The Hague, Mouton, 1963), p. 52.
[2] G. Murphy, *Personality: a Biosocial Approach to Origins and Structure* (New York, Harper & Brothers, 1947), p. 244.   [3] R. E. Lane, *Political Life*, p. 235.
[4] D. Sills, *The Volunteers: Means and Ends in a National Organization* (Glencoe, Ill., Free Press, 1957), p. 235.   [5] *Ibid.* p. 240.

An active member of a labor organization has a feeling of sharing in its social and economic power and of contributing directly to the interplay of social forces; this indirectly increases his self-respect. The process was familiar to its founders[1] and still plays a role in the union's relationship to its members; anyone conversant with the terminology and symbols of modern labor knows the prominence of this power element.

Participation can, at the same time, satisfy the desire for power in more *direct* ways, e.g. in the communication between leaders and members. There is, for example, the voluntary official's power over members:

'I would prefer to hold office in the trade union; it would be nice to play the boss there.'

On the other hand, the case of the teachers' union (p. 153) demonstrates that there is also a power factor in the opposite direction, i.e. of the participant over the leader. A hint of this can be detected in:

'I shall be going to the next meeting, because they have to submit the new collective contract and the wage proposals to us.'

If the attendants of the meeting lose the possibility of exerting this type of influence, partly because decision making (collective bargaining) has moved to a higher level and partly because the leaders are not inclined to give in to members, it will cease to satisfy the need for self-esteem. Our analysis has already shown that the trade union in the welfare state, with its centralized bureacracy, is showing this tendency.

Related to the search for power is the quest for status which the participant may be able to satisfy within no less than three reference groups: among the rank and file (through knowledge acquired at meetings), among the other participants (by joining in the discussions) and among the leaders (by carrying out delegated tasks). Although participants often hesitate to mention explicitly the drive for status and prestige, it often becomes manifest when frustrated. When, for example, the members are deprived of the opportunity to make themselves heard at organizations meetings, their reactions are:

'At a union meeting you never know what to expect, if you will be able to join in the discussion or just have to listen.'

'If I go to meetings of the fishing club and say something, I can see that it has some effect. But in the union no one takes any notice of the individual.'[2]

---

[1] '... with the development of industry the proletariat not only increases in number, it becomes concentrated in great masses, its strength grows, and it feels that strength more.' K. Marx, *Communist Manifesto*, p. 30. See also the quotation from H. Roland Holst in Ch. 1, p. 35.

[2] This reply lends support to Murphy's contention (see p. 172), that the needs for power and status are closely linked, as in this motivation the desires for influence and for recognition are intermingled.

'A union meeting is more of a series of announcements, and it is really difficult to enter into argument with one of the officers because you don't know nearly so much. No, I don't often go.'

To be able to actively join in the discussions, to argue with the executive committee, to win an argument in front of the other members, in short, to be singled out from the crowd and acknowledged as an individual is a source of ego-strength to the participant. If he is deprived of this satisfaction, a strong motive for participation is lost.

Responsibility

The needs for power and for status become completely integrated if the participant is given official responsibility in the organization. By filling a voluntary office, he is formally endowed with power and status and takes part in the responsibility for its policy. In many individuals it will bring forth an entirely new motive, based upon the desire to be worthy of this trust. This occurs when a sense of *moral duty* joins power and status as an additional motive for participation. Of the union members interviewed, 25 per cent mentioned motives of this nature:

'Most of all I like going to meetings of my own associations because I feel more involved in them, and have to be present because of the office I hold.'

'I prefer going to the carrier pigeon association, if I don't go the whole thing will fall apart!'

'As a member of the basketball club's membership committee I have to attend a meeting every three weeks. And being a member implies that you are interested.'

These responses illustrate that a voluntary obligation, functioning as a moral duty, can become a strong motivational basis for participation. The group has expressed its expectations about the member; he makes these his own and tries to live up to them in order not to lose his self-respect. It leads to the paradox of an obligation being the basis of voluntary action. This new ego-ideal, based upon one's responsibility, plays a role chiefly at the higher levels of participation. March and Simon[3] have observed that participation increases as members identify themselves more closely with their organization, and the converse is also true. A response like 'Most of all I like going to meetings of my *own* societies . . . because I *have to* be there' suggests that the more scope for participation (power, status, purpose) the organization offers its members, the stronger their identification. A practical conclusion is that decentralization, or the transfer of power, status, and responsibility to lower participatory levels, increases social cohesion in an organization and leads to greater internal strength.

[3] J. G. March and H. A. Simon, *Organizations* (New York, Wiley, 1959), p. 72.

Sense of purpose

In the above cases, the participant increases his self-esteem via the social group, which endows him with power and prestige. The same augmentation occurs more *directly* when participation is for the sake of an ethical value or a political goal that has been introjected as an ego-ideal. To belong to a social movement the aims of which reach far beyond individual existence is, according to Sheriff and Cantril,[1] a source of deep satisfaction. It confers a wider meaning upon the member's life and strengthens his self-respect;[2] it may even develop into a life-purpose, a justification of existence. This type of motive is often influential among participants in labor organizations, with their strong idealistic tradition. It is seen in such comments as:

'I always go to the union meetings. One gets a view of the future and ideals.'

'It is nice to work together in the union towards a definite goal.'

'I go to meetings because the union tries to do something for workers in general, and because of idealism.'

In this form, the motive was mentioned by 20 per cent of the new trade union members, but for only 1 per cent did it play a central role in the decision to join. These figures hold for voluntary members of an idealistical European union. It is probably mentioned less frequently in the more 'job conscious' unions in the United States.[3]

Although the aims and ideals of the organization are explicitly mentioned in the responses above, this is not always the case. More often, they are implicit in the motives and discernable only in such expressions as 'fighting for social improvement', 'doing something for the workers', or 'helping your fellow men'. According to Nuttin,[4] this human urge to realize a higher potential in oneself, 'this need to give meaning to our life',[5] is central in the dynamic structure of personality, but is neglected in social and psychological research. This is confirmed by the fact that in studies of participation, social psychologists have devoted little attention to the factor of idealism.[6]

---

[1] M. Sherif and H. Cantril, *The Psychology of Ego-Involvements* (London, Wiley, 1947), Ch. 2.

[2] Starr observed that above the more simple human motives there exists a self-realizing motive, which is based upon the identification with humanity. This 'Promethean complex' might well be related here. Cf. E. H. Starr, 'Promethean Constellations', *Psychological Clinic*, XXII (1933), pp. 1–20.

[3] A. F. Siegel, 'The Extended Meaning and Diminished Relevance of "Job Conscious" Unionism', *Proceedings of the 18th Annual Meeting of the Industrial Relations Research Association*, ed. Gerald Somers (Madison, 1966), pp. 162–82.

[4] J. Nuttin, 'De dynamische structuur der persoonlijkheid en de psychoanalyse', *Ned. Tijdschrift v.d. Psychologie en haar Grensgebieden*, N.S., Pt. IV (1949), pp. 176–7.

[5] J. Nuttin, *Psycho-analyse en de spiritualistische opvatting van de mens* (Utrecht, 1949), p. 192.

[6] G. Murphy, *Personality*, p. 430.

Various responses suggest that ego-satisfaction is most intense when an organization offers its members an *idealistic sense of purpose* together with an opportunity for *responsible participation*. It was pointed out in Chapter 3 that, in postwar society, because of the 'Entideologisierung' and centralization of party and trade union policies, this combination is gradually disappearing. The result is that some participants withdraw from these organizations and turn to less complex groups which still allow for idealism and action:

'The . . . is an idealistic association, and not all that big, so you can really do something to help. The union is too big for me, you see. I am not talking about meetings, mind, but in the union you are just a small cog in a big wheel.'

'I prefer going to the Nature Conservation League, because I love nature and can take an active part.'

'I go to the meetings of the Temperance Union, because I can take an active part by recruiting members, doing rehabilitation work and so on. In the trade union there is really nothing for me to do any more.'

'I prefer going to the Salvation Army. Its goals appeal to me and I can do something for it. I do a lot of work for the movement, selling literature and so on'.

The 'idealistic association', the Nature Conservation League, the Temperance Union, and the Salvation Army are all groups with idealistic goals, which allow their participants to find a deeper sense of purpose. Each of these participants (who had become an apathetic member of his trade union) stresses that, by sacrificing time and effort, he is able actively to work for his ideals.

This switch to associations which, though less important, still offer opportunities for idealistic participation sometimes assumes socially useless forms. This is illustrated by one member's explanation of why he is apathetic in the labor organization, but active in the pigeon club. His comment on the first is:

'The union is dead, too many things are done for you and handed to you on a plate.'

In such an organization, he obviously sees little opportunity for satisfactory participation, for idealist content, and for active striving. His next comment, shows how, in reaction, he has looked to another association:

'The pigeon fanciers club, that's something really special. It's your hobby, and gives you something to do. You can build up a homing pigeon.'

Not only is the 'dead' union contrasted with the active participation in the other association, but there is also a hint of other things: in the 'building up' of this bird soon to fly back to him from afar, a deeper sense of purpose is implied. Transfer of ideals from an important organization that imposes passive membership, to a less valuable association that allows for active participation, is idealistic retrogression. It is a reaction to one's loss of central life goals, an individual response to trends of cultural anomie.

As many observers have pointed out, the conditions for idealistic retrogression are almost inherent in the modern welfare state. E. H. Carr,[1] for example, maintains that participation in contemporary democratic organizations is being drained of much of its content and responsibility. Referring to observations in Britain during the World War II, he concludes that, today, only wars and catastrophes give the individual the 'sense of meaning and purpose' which is the basis of democratic action.[2] The following reflections on the rescuers in the Dutch flood disaster of 1953 show this trend to be fairly general:

They, the rescuers, had been nonentities in the offices and plants of an obscure society, where the meaning of work and action remained unclear. They became stern irreplaceable heroes, whose every deed had a direct purpose and to whom every second was indispensable. This is the greatness which only calamities, wars, and floods seem able to inspire: the release of justifying one's own existence through an act, anonymous but unique; the release of existing for oneself and others without appearances or conventions.[3]

An indispensable condition for democratic participation is that it provides satisfactions which are lacking in the pursuit of one's individual interest. One of the most important of these satisfactions is a deep sense of meaning and purpose. In the past, the labor organization has been able to provide this. If, however, in the midst of the social changes which lead to the affluent society and the welfare state, this should temporarily disappear, the members' idealism will retrogress. The intellectuals will return to academe,[4] the workers will seek compensation in their clubs and sports, and the youngsters will confine themselves to their careers. Empirical studies confirm that the younger age groups in the Western welfare states do, indeed, show a tendency toward 'privatization'[5] or withdrawal from the established institutions. A pathological form of

---

[1] E. H. Carr, *Conditions of Peace* (London, 1942), p. 115.
[2] Carr bases this partly on the comments of the *Times* of London of 7 October 1940: 'Save when immediate tragedy comes their way, an enormous number of ordinary peaceable citizens are personally, at this time of horror and trial, extraordinarily happy. There is work to be done, now in this island, by them.'
[3] *De Ramp* (Amsterdam, 1953).
[4] H. Harris, 'Why Labor Lost the Intellectuals', *Harper's Magazine* (June, 1964), pp. 79–86; M. Neufeld, 'The Historical Relationship of Liberals and Intellectuals to Organized Labor in the United States', *Annals of the American Academy of Political and Social Science*, 350 (November 1963), pp. 115–28; S. B. Gottlieb, 'The Union Intellectual in the Labor Movement' (Panel Remarks, *IRRA Convention*, Boston, Massachusetts, December 1963), pp. 6–7.
[5] D. Lockwood, The New Working Class, in *Archives Européennes de Sociologie*, No. 2 (1960), p. 154.

retrogressive idealism is probably the idealization of withdrawal through drugs, in the 'hippie' culture.

It is now evident that the psychological hypothesis of 'democratic behavior as primarily a matter of personality traits' is both too one-sided and too static. The hypothesis is supported by the fact that a certain personality type, with such psychodynamic attributes as a strong ego-need and a positive attitude toward his social environment, is apparently predisposed toward democratic participation. However, such needs as the need to belong, the need to understand, and the need for self-esteem (whether via power, status, responsibility, or a sense of purpose) are common human traits and are not restricted to one personality type. Moreover, the data indicate that the mere possibility of satisfying them through a democratic organization suffices to arouse these needs in any individual. If, however, the organization does not satisfy them, even a democratic elite will lapse into political apathy. This finding tends to support the sociological hypothesis of voluntary participation, placing the major responsibility for democratic action with the organization.

BETWEEN DEMOCRACY AND OLIGARCHY

Whether or not the labor organizations in the welfare state will retain their democratic character has now been reduced to the question of whether or not they will offer their members the satisfactions which stimulate active participation. Formerly, this was probably the case. In the second half of the nineteenth century, European and United States workers generally had the opportunity, in their unions, to satisfy needs for acceptance, understanding and self-esteem. Although organizational apathy did exist, thousands could give greater meaning to their life by active participation in the union.

We saw, however, how 'principia media', deeply entrenched in changes toward the affluent society and the welfare state, weaken these satisfactions. The growing complexity of the societal process reduces the cognitive rewards of participation; the centralization and bureaucratization of our democratic organizations narrow the volunteer's access to status and power; and the 'Entideologisierung' drains the trade unions of their idealistic goals. The result is a process of circular causation:

(1) Because of growing complexity, bureaucracy, and centralization, common human needs are less satisfied through participation.

(2) Losing control over union affairs, more and more members lapse into organizational apathy.

(3) This increasing apathy results in a further centralization and accumulation of power by the organization's leadership.

(4) Because of this, participation is drained still more of its psychological satisfactions, ensuing in a loss of motivational resource.

(5) Increased apathy and retrogression of idealism among the rank and file are the result.

Whether the labor organizations of the welfare state will move toward the democratic or the oligarchic pole depends, in part, on the ability and will of their leaders to break this vicious causal circle. It depends *only* in part on them, however. For without changes in the social environment, counteracting its growing complexity, bureaucratization and centralization, the chances that even an active organizational leadership will be able to achieve this 'democratic democracy' are doubtful.

7

6. Out of the union: ex-members[1]

The members' relationship to the organization differs with the various labor movements. In Western Europe, it is largely voluntary, although—as we saw in Chapter 4—not always free from coercion; the members can, in principle, join or resign at will. Membership in United States unions is often compulsory, either through closed shops (employers can only hire through the union) or—increasingly—through union shops (employers can hire freely, on condition that the worker joins the union). There is little indication that voluntary membership renders trade unions less powerful,[2] and it undeniably makes them more democratic.

Compulsory membership often has the disadvantage of keeping the workers' feelings about the union or its policy hidden, even from observers within the organization. Labor leaders in Western Europe have learned to view fluctuations in membership as a highly sensitive barometer of the organization's standing with the rank and file. When this expression of disapproval is denied, feelings of discontent may explode at a least suitable moment, for example in large-scale defections during a strike.

Other aspects of the member-union relationship on both continents being quite similar, the motives which lead European unionists to leave the organization may well shed light on problems which remain beneath the surface in the United States. Such motives reflect more general processes in advanced industrial society. We have already seen how large-scale trends in the income structure and in the workers' subculture had the effect of moving individual needs into the foreground of the motivations for joining. We also found that the 'de-politicization' of modern life led to apathy within the organization. Similarly, the motives of ex-members show symptoms of the union's functional erosion and integration in the welfare state.

The ex-members' motives for resigning from union membership fall into three main groups. There are the *structural* motives, referring to the organization's situation in the structure of the welfare state, the *functional*

---

[1] This research project is described in App. A (4).

[2] A system of voluntary membership will often result in a relatively low proportion of union members per firm, over a large number of firms. Compulsory membership often has the effect of arousing greater managerial resistance, which results in a higher proportion of non-union-ized industries in newly industrialized areas. The first situation leads to broader trade union representation in the nation and, probably, to greater accumulation of union power.

motives, referring to the ways the union fulfills its functions in the members' lives, and the *policy* motives, directed against the organization's goals, policies or leaders. Each group consists of the following specific motives:

 (1) Structural motives:

  A. 'membership in the union is useless' (low gains).

  B. 'membership in the union is too expensive' (high dues).

 (2) Functional motives:

  C. 'the union gives insufficient assistance in individual problems at work.'

  D. 'I did not like the way the union treated me.'

  E. 'the union has too little concern for the individual member.'

 (3) Policy motives:

  F. 'I have objections to the union's leadership.'

  G. 'I have objections to the union's policy or principles.'

Three sets of motives and motive D will be subjected to quantitative analysis (Charts 1–4), using the following operational concepts:

 (1) *Frequency:* The frequency is indicated by the percentage of ex-members mentioning a motive as reason for resigning from union membership. Motive A was mentioned most often and Motive G least often. The charts present the motives in the order of their relative frequency.

 (2) *Centrality:* The centrality reveals the ex-members' degree of involvement in the organization before they resigned. It consists of two partially related indicators, presented in the second and third columns of the charts: (*a*) average length of membership and (*b*) level of participation in the organization. The level of participation is based upon the index which weighs each higher level of activity increasingly, e.g. attendance at meetings with Factor 1, voluntary tasks with Factor 2, performing an unpaid function in the union with the Factor 3. A motive with high centrality is more often mentioned by ex-members who were long-standing and active unionists and is viewed as having relatively high disintegrating effect among the rank and file.

 (3) *Alienation:* The alienation indicates the degree to which ex-members mentioning the motive are disaffected. The indicator used is the percentage of negative answers to the question whether, if asked, they would join the union again. A motive with a high alienating effect is viewed as instrumental in keeping unorganized workers from joining.

The charts being based upon ordinal scales,[1] only *relative* values are

[1] Scores in an ordinal scale have the strength of ranks. They may be replaced by different symbols (for example, letters instead of percentages or indexes) so long as their order remains unchanged. See S. Siegel, *Nonparametric Statistics for the Behavioral Sciences* (New York, McGraw-Hill, 1956), pp. 23–5.

presented in the four columns, i.e. the position of each motive compared with those of the other six. Chart 1, for example, indicates that Motive A: 'union membership is useless' is mentioned more often (first column), appears more at the periphery of the rank and file (second and third columns), and has a higher alienating effect (fourth column) than any other motive.

After the quantitative analysis of each set of motives and Motive D, there follows a qualitative exploration of their various nuances and sub-jective meanings. This approach is mainly illustrative and will, at best, lead to hypotheses for further research. The reliability of its conclusions is certainly lower than those drawn from the charts.

THE STRUCTURAL MOTIVES

The relationship between advanced industrial society, the trade union, and the workers' perception of them, is nowhere more manifest than in the struct-ural motives, viz. Motive A ('union membership is useless') and Motive B ('the union's dues are too high'). Both are rooted in doubts about the value of labor organizations for the individual worker in the welfare state.

Motives A and B: quantitative analysis

The importance of Motive A ('union membership is useless'—the low-gains motive) in membership erosion may be seen in the fact that it plays a role in the motivation of 40 per cent of the ex-members interviewed. Their conclusion is based upon two lines of reasoning. In the first, the ex-member refers to his changing individual position in the labor market; in the second, to changes in the union's role in present day society. These two approaches, explored in detail on pages 185–91, show the following frequencies:

TABLE 23. *The various types of 'low-gains' motive among ex-members*

1. *The worker's changed situation:*		
'it is useless in my job, position, rank'	15%	
'it is useless in the company I work in, in my occupation'	25%	
'it is useless because I am able to solve my problems myself'	24%	
		64%
2. *The union's changed situation:*		
'it is useless because government has taken over the union's role'	16%	
'it is useless because with the welfare state everything the union stands for has been realized'	20%	
		36%
TOTAL	100%	(90 answers)

That the ego-directed references dominate suggests that the worker usually experiences union membership as an individual affair, relevant mainly for his own individual position. Since we found a similar attitude among new members (Chapter 4), this seems to be a consistent re-action throughout union membership.

Motive A is mentioned more often ($0.02 > P > 0.01$) by white collar workers (49 per cent) than by blue collar workers (31 per cent) and this again coincides with a trend among new members. Chapter 4 showed that the white collar workers among the new members were less convinced of the value of union membership for their individual work situation. The above results suggest that in the case of the ex-members, these doubts were not removed by the facts of union membership. In the present endeavors of United States and European unions to recruit among the new middle class,[1] inadequate satisfaction of individual needs will be the biggest obstacle for white collar unionization.

Motive A is not only the most frequently mentioned but the ex-members mentioning it have also been in the organization the shortest time. While 63 per cent joined the union less than four years before, this figure was only 37 per cent among the ex-members for whom this motive did not apply. More detailed analysis shows an inverse correlation between length of membership and resignation because of this low gains argument.

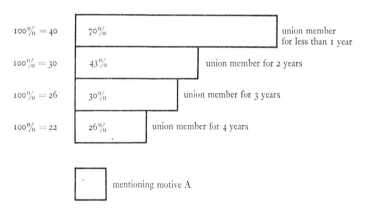

$W/\sigma = 12.5$; $P < 0.001$

FIGURE 18. Length of membership and 'low gains' motivation among ex-members.

That 70 per cent of those who resigned within one year did so because they considered membership 'useless' indicates that doubts existed before

[1] In the United States, for example, see 'Union Aide Predicts White Collar Gains', *New York Times*, 8 June 1967, p. 18C.

they joined. The ultimate fact of their joining, these negative feelings notwithstanding, presents us with a theoretically interesting situation. Individuals who are led to express outwardly an attitude (e.g. joining) which is discrepant with their actual private attitude (e.g. doubt) enter, according to Festinger,[1] into a state of 'cognitive dissonance'. To reduce this unpleasant condition, they will search for clues confirming the wisdom of the outward behavior or decision. If these are not provided, e.g. if the doubt is not disproved by the reality of membership, it is interpreted as a negative clue. The result will be that the dissonance increases. The way out is to make the outward behavior conform to the reinforced inner negative attitude: in other words, the member resigns, with little chance that he will ever join the organization again. This is confirmed by the high alienating effect of Motive A (column 4, Chart 1): while 82 per cent of the ex-members with Motive A expected never to join the union again, only 48 per cent of the other ex-members expected never to join again (P < 0.001).

The conclusion is that organizations should provide their new members with consonance, that is, they should remove their doubts and convince them of the wisdom of their decision to join *after* the decision has been made. This is especially important where membership is not entirely a voluntary decision but is partly based on such means of compulsion as closed and union shops.

Mentioned by 33 per cent of the ex-members, Motive B ('union membership is too expensive'—high dues) is as frequent among the young as among the old and among blue collar as among white collar

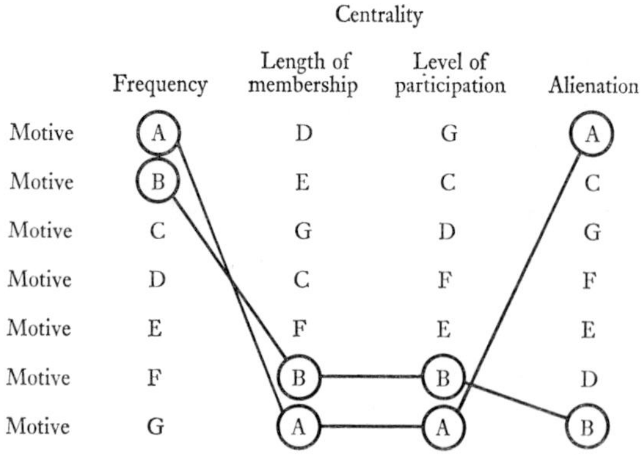

CHART 1. Ranking of Motives A ('membership of the union is useless') and B ('membership of the union is too expensive') compared with the other motives for resigning.

[1] L. A. Festinger, *A Theory of Cognitive Dissonance* (Evanston, Ill., Row, Peterson, 1957), *passim.*

workers. As the high-cost argument refers basically to *relative* costs, e.g. in relation to expected gains, it has much in common with Motive A. This is confirmed by the fact that ex-members with Motive B have a higher average income and the same standard of living (as indicated by possession of durable goods) and number of children as those without it. This affinity between Motives A (low gains) and B (high costs) is also reflected in their parallel positions in Chart 1.

Their high frequency and low centrality suggest that both motives are widespread and especially common among members with little attachment to the organization. The only discrepancy appears in the fact that Motive A shows the highest alienating effect and Motive B the lowest, indicating that doubts about the advantages of union membership are more harmful to the organization than objections to its financial demands. To strengthen these workers' ties with the union, an increase of benefits would be more effective than a reduction of dues. Asked what reduction of dues would induce them to rejoin the organization, 63 per cent of those with the high-costs motive answered that *no* reduction would induce them to return. This confirms the view that complaints about the high costs are basically complaints about the low individual benefits of union membership.

Motives A and B: qualitative analysis

Motive A: 1. The worker's changed situation

(*a*) '*It is useless in my job, position, rank.*' In deciding to join a union, most new members do so partly with reference to possible problems in their individual work situation. The ex-members, in their decision to resign, show a similar type of reaction. They weigh the chances of becoming involved in an individual conflict at work and also the chances of receiving support from the union. In this evaluation, two conditions will induce them to finally resign. One is that there is a real chance of an on-the-job conflict in the work situation, but that the interests at stake are low. This situation is often found among female workers:

'It [union membership] is not very important for a woman. A man, he needs it, if he gets laid off. A man works all his life. A girl works till she gets married.'

'I don't need a union. For the few years that I'll be working, it's no use. I'll be married pretty soon.'

'Women have no use for a union. We join for a couple of years, but then we marry. What can a union do for me?'

Although these workers reckon with the occurrence of individual problems at work, they do not consider the consequences sufficiently threatening to warrant protection by union membership. With the increasing proportion of women in the labor force, the question arises whether labor unions should not introduce a special membership for female workers.[1]

In the second situation, the interests are sufficiently serious, but the chances of individual on-the-job conflicts are considered low. This motive is found among workers who raised their occupational status to such an extent that they discard the possibility of being dismissed. Some examples are:

'I had no need for the union anymore. I got accepted by the Company's pension fund. So my wife thought we could as well quit.'—Industrial pharmacologist.

'I only joined to have my job protected. But I shouldn't have cared. When you're married, you look for security. But in my position you don't need it anymore.—Accountant.

'The very day they made me assistant manager I quit the union. At my rank I can't use it anymore. I'm now part of management.'—Assistant manager.

The awareness of needing protection by a union decreases with increasing status security. This may result from rising a grade, joining a pension fund, improving one's relationship with one's employer, getting promoted—especially from a blue collar to a white collar rank—or becoming part of management. That most of these reactions are from white collar workers indicates that—rightly or wrongly—this group is less fearful of being without protection against industrial despotism.

Hardly less crucial than obtaining higher occupational status is the fact of *aspiring* to higher status. The mechanism of 'anticipatory socialization', i.e. identification with a social group, membership of which one does not possess but to which one aspires, keeps many white collar workers away from an organization which defends the blue collar workers and challenges industrial power.[2] A young (and subordinate) clerical employee says:

'One joins a union for self-protection. Being a manager would imply not being in a union. That's why I left the union.'

Although of low status, this young white collar worker is identifying himself in advance with his superiors and their presumed negative

---

[1] According to Everett Kassalow, 'New Union Frontier: White Collar Workers', *Harvard Business Review*, XL, No. 1 (January–February, 1962), p. 51: 'Special appeals and structures for the relatively greater number of women in this area will be necessary.'

[2] R. K. Merton and A. S. Kitt, 'Contributions to the Theory of Reference Group Behavior', p. 84.

attitude towards the union.[1] And this not without reason. While managements usually accept the unionization of their manual work force, they tend to view the union membership of white collar workers as a sign of lack of integration in the company.[2] The facts, however, point in the opposite direction. In a study of 400 young white collar workers in a large European corporation we compared the union members with the nonmembers in their group with the following results:

(*i*) White collar union members showed a more positive attitude toward the collective contract than nonmembers ($P < 0.001$).

(*ii*) White collar union members had been with the company longer than nonmembers of the same age ($P < 0.001$).

(*iii*) White collar union members showed greater satisfaction in their work than nonmembers ($0.3 > P > 0.2$).

(*iv*) White collar union members showed a greater inclination to advise friends to come to work in the company than did nonmembers ($0.3 > P > 0.2$).[3]

These results suggest that the union members among the white collar workers are more integrated in the company than their colleagues outside the organization. And it means that management's negative image of white collar union members is quite unrealistic. However so long as it induces management to keep white collar workers from joining a union, it will be real in its consequences.

(*b*) '*It is useless in my company, occupation.*' The situation in the company or occupation can also cause the member to resign. In these cases, two different lines of reasoning can again be detected. The first is that, in the worker's eyes, the union does have a worthwhile task in the company, but lacks the power for its successful execution. In the second situation, the union has sufficient power but lacks, in the worker's eyes, a worthwhile task in the company to which it can be applied. Illustrations of the task-but-no-power situation are:

'In my company the union is of little use. They can't do a thing for you. Unless they would have at least thirty members. What am I paying for then?'

'The majority in our plant is not in a union. So the union has no voice.'

'They can't do much for me. Because they have only a few members in the plant.'

'We have many women in our mill—they'll never join. So, even if the union would give it a try, the boss wouldn't budge.'

[1] S. M. Lipset, M. A. Trow, and J. S. Coleman, *Union Democracy*, p. 174, footnote 12, find a similar inverse correlation between social aspiration and *participation* in the union.
[2] See also p. 32, footnote 1.
[3] M. van de Vall and J. Roelands, *De jonge Philipsbeambte*, p. 30.

That modern unions are integrating themselves in the welfare state does not imply that they are also integrating with modern industry. The union is, in many plants, still struggling for a recognized role—often without much success. Critics of the omnipotence of modern labor organizations usually confine themselves to their macrosocial position and neglect their position in the plant. But in many companies, the union is so weak that it leads its members to resign.

Diametrically opposite to these complaints are the complaints about the powerful organization that apparently lacks the functions to which to apply its power. These power-but-no-task arguments are encountered among younger workers, whose experiences are restricted to the welfare state:

'It's all very smooth in our company. Everything is so well organized that you don't need a union anymore. We have no problems in the plant.'—Welder.

'I've no use for the union in my company. I'd like to see first what they can do for my money.'—Bookkeeper.

'Ours is a small plant. If you're on good terms with the boss, you've no need for the union. I hate spending my money for nothing.'—Polisher.

Peaceful labor relations are so normal in the lives of these young workers that they fail to apprehend the role the union plays in this peace. And this is often supported by management's inclination to settle grievances internally, i.e. without the interference of the union. Ideas of industrial humanism and systems of appeal within the company often successfully replace the settlement of grievances by the union.[1] A side-effect of this policy is that, in cases in which union representatives do get called in, the problem has practically become insoluble.[2] Obviously, this does not serve to strengthen the image of the union in the workers' eyes.

Motive A: 2. The union's changed situation

We saw that the transfer of functions to other agencies is often viewed as a loss for the union. The reaction to this loss is usually stronger the further the member is removed from the core of participants. At the periphery of the rank and file, it may even lead to the decision to resign. Such ex-members tend to contrast the past—

'Before the war the union did a lot of good.'

'In the past you knew what the union did for you.'

'Before the war . . . the union was powerful.'

[1] W. G. Scott, *The Management of Conflict* (Homewood, Ill., Richard Irwin, Inc., and Dorsey Press, 1965), pp. 78–80.

[2] Dutch union officials view this as a factor in downgrading the union in the workers' eyes. See J. H. Buiter, C. Poppe, and H. Wallenburg, 'Lager Vakbondskader als Communicatieschakel', *Socialisme en Demokratie* (January 1962).

with the present union—

    'Today, unions are superfluous.'

    'A labor union has no say anymore.'

    'The union doesn't do much for you anymore.'

—and draw negative conclusions. All of these workers have in common that they refer to a process, the conditions, scope, and content of which are seldom clear to them. At best, they see only one aspect; four such aspects are detected in the motives. They refer to the transfer, obscuring, loss, and realization of union functions.

(*a*) *Transfer of functions.* Of all functional changes in trade unions, none has made a deeper impression upon members and ex-members than the transference of unemployment insurance to the public administration. The ex-members' perception of it is vague and they are unclear about the agency that has taken over the function, suggesting: social security, the unemployment office, the municipality, other agencies, welfare, the politicians, the unemployment law, social assistance, and the Labor Department.

But however uncertain their perception, their evaluation is simple, showing only two variations. Some view it as a real loss and blame the union for having allowed itself to be shelved:

'Before the war the union had more power, and was more active. Today it is too easygoing. It is just heading to a dead end.'

Others are less pessimistic or even applaud this trend, conceiving it as the realization of cherished ideals:

'Today everything has been arranged. The unions don't have to strike anymore. They are just superfluous today. It's almost ideal now. What's there left to improve?'

But apart from whether these members deplore or applaud the trend, their reaction is the same. They feel that the union's usefulness in their life has been diminished to such an extent that they decide to leave the organization.

(*b*) *Obscuring of functions.* In Chapter 1 we saw how centralized bargaining increases rank-and-file apathy in union affairs. At the fringe of the rank and file it has still another effect, viz. that bargaining loses its reality in the workers' perception. The less the union contract is a matter of their immediate concern, the less relevant to them is information about wage policy, bargaining, and income distribution:

'The present situation is O.K. and they shouldn't always talk about work conditions and things . . .'

The centralization of union functions can even affect perception to the extent that some ex-members lose the ability to recognize union functions when they see them. This happens, for example, when the collective contract is viewed as a substitute for the union:

'I have quit because I see the contract replacing the union.'

'Our company has its own collective contract. If that stays as it is today, who needs the union?'

These are extreme examples of what we designate as functional obscuration in large organizations. Although the contract is usually recognized and appreciated as a result of union work, the above remarks illustrate that the centralization of functions can have the effect of totally obscuring the role of the union in the life of the individual worker.

(*c*) *Loss of functions.* While unemployment insurance is often voluntarily transferred from the unions because they are unable to meet its rising cost, functions *within* the company are sometimes lost less voluntarily. Although the introduction of 'human relations' into industry is based partly on industrial humanism, there is little doubt that, at the same time, it is also partly motivated by plain anti-unionism. At present, the unions are still losing ground in the company to internal appeal systems, managerial grievance committees, and review boards.[1] This explains the following reactions:

'Today, if you're good in your work, you don't need the union. If I consider my wages too low *I can always talk to my boss.*'

'I've no need for the union anymore. I'm now able to help myself. *I now see the boss myself to discuss what I need.*'

'I joined the union because I thought I might need them some time, against management. But it was never necessary. Oh, sometimes there was some trouble. *But I could always manage that myself.*'

'No, *I fight for myself.* I don't need the union for that. *I can pretty well manage alone.*'

'And even if there would be trouble I expect to handle that myself. *There are other ways of appeal nowadays.*'

These comments show a high degree of individualism and, at the same time, a lack of emotional involvement with the ideals of the organization. Such macrosocial trends as increasing employment opportunities together with such microsocial factors as effective 'human relations' in the plant

---

[1] '. . . most of the firms that adopted one aspect or another of employee welfare programs did oppose unions (except company unions) and considered membership as evidence of disloyalty. And the proponents of welfare programs certainly stressed their union discouraging effects.' M. W. Reder, *Labor in a Growing Economy* (New York, John Wiley and Sons, 1957), p. 62. See also W. G. Scott, *The Management of Conflict*, p. 94.

have the effect of bolstering the confidence of the workers.[1] Against this background, the security provisions offered by the union lose in attractiveness, while the company's personnel office is increasingly viewed as a substitute.[2]

(*d*) *Realization of functions.* A number of workers react to the fact that with the welfare state, long-standing goals in the area of social security have been realized. Ex-members of the union either do not perceive what ideals are left or deny that the remaining union goals justify their membership:

'When I joined, everything the worker needed *was already obtained.*'

'The union has been great in the past. But now, *having arrived where we are,* unions don't make much sense.'

Today, everything is cared for. Unions don't have to fight anymore. *They are more or less unnecessary.* It's almost perfect. There's nothing left for them to improve.'

These reactions are symptomatic of the ideological situation of the west-European unions and, to a lesser extent, of the more 'job-conscious' United States labor unions. They are the psychological side of the *Entideologisierung* of Western labor, mentioned in Chapter 1. We saw, in Chapter 5, that among participants this decline of idealistic perspective may lead to organizational apathy or retrogressive idealism. Among members at the periphery of the rank and file, it is one of the reasons for resigning.

Motive B: The high cost of membership

The high-cost motive presents the rational aspect of trade union membership in its purest form. The obscuring of union functions again plays a crucial role in this motivation, as the ex-members ask repeatedly, 'What do they do for the money?' For example:

'The dues are high, and they don't do very much with them.'

One characteristic of this motive is its increasing urgency when the continuity of payments is interrupted, for example, by a sudden increase

---

[1] This is true both in western Europe and in the United States. According to a United States observer: 'As the cold climate of fear in the plant gives way to the warm sunlight of company paternalism, an employee can be easily persuaded that his new-found dignity reflects management's belated recognition of those talents he always possessed. The resurgence of such self-confidence encourages loyalty to the company and more critical scrutiny of the union's collectivist ideology.' P. E. Sultan, *The Disenchanted Unionist* (New York, Harper & Row, 1963), p. 16.

[2] British observers note: 'Employer paternalism has in some firms even made the unions' role of opposition seem unnecessary. In ICI it is the firm's personnel staff rather than the unions who usually seem the more sensitive to the men's complaints.' G. Cyriax and R. Oakeshott, *The Bargainers, a survey of modern British Trade Unionism* (New York, Praeger, 1961), p. 124.

or a backlog of unpaid dues. The reason is that it confronts the member anew with the degree of his sacrifice:

'I've always paid one-eighteen, and then the dues got raised to one-sixty. That's exactly a hundred cents too much. I see no revenues for one-sixty.'

Although raised only forty-two cents, this member now suddenly realizes that this is one hundred cents more than he is willing to pay. Similar reactions are found when arrears have to be paid. No less than 24 per cent of the manual workers (mainly the unskilled and semiskilled) mentioned a backlog in dues as a reason for resignation.

Some conclusions

The social conflict has been subject to three trends in the welfare state. One is the relative decline in social friction, resulting from such fundamental changes as a stabilization of the economy, a more equal income distribution, greater opportunities for ascending socially, and increased social security.

Second, societal integration has had the effect of transferring and obscuring the functions of the unions. At the same time, 'industrial welfare' and 'human relations' are competing for the union's role within the plant. In newly industrializing areas of the United States, for example, profit sharing combined with nonunionization is a rapidly spreading type of industrial relations.

The third trend is basically derivative. It is the worker's growing inclination to perceive industrial society in terms other than those of a social conflict. As they are less aware of being exploited or oppressed, the new working generations lack their parents' drive to conceive of the industrial system as a conflict between exploiters and exploited, or oppressors and oppressed.

Together, these three trends are the basic reason for the high frequency of structural motives among ex-members of the unions, denying the organization's valuable role in the welfare state.

This leads to the question whether the apparent disappearance of the social conflict really causes the union to lose its functions within the industrial firm. This does not seem very likely. Even an efficient system of 'human relations' is not able to eliminate authoritarianism, eradicate injustice, or solve all interactional conflicts in shop or office. The question is only whether or not the unions are able to adjust themselves to deal with such problems.

In Western Europe, workers' councils, members' committees, and labor directors are enhancing the union's role in the areas of promotion policies, technical innovation, and profit sharing. They are also thwarting the companies' claims to treat such issues exclusively as matters of 'human relations', that is, by management.

Such functional adjustment meets only one serious problem, viz. that a large number of these issues are of an individual character, while unions over the last hundred years have been specializing in collective bargaining, not in their members' individual problems. The next section will show that settling individual grievances is one of the weak areas of modern trade unionism and another important cause of membership erosion.

THE FUNCTIONAL MOTIVES

In the next three motives mentioned, the worker reckons with real problems in his work and, in his view, the union could very well solve them. His objections are against the way the organization fulfills, or rather does not fulfill, this task.

While the structural motives were generally vague and cast in general terms, the functional ones are based on specific experiences and often elaborated in great detail. In the quantitative analysis, we shall first show the relative positions of Motives C and E in Chart 2, and then those of Motive D in Chart 3.

Motives C and E: quantitative analysis

The relative importance of motive C: 'The union gives insufficient assistance in individual problems at work' is indicated by the fact that it is mentioned by 28 per cent of the ex-members. Half of these refer to wage-problems, the others to problems of illness, incapacity, dismissal, promotion, hours of work, or discord with superiors.

Compared with the structural motives, Motive C is more specific, usually related to on-the-job problems and often based upon the worker's own observations. The ex-members mentioning Motive C are older and have often shown some interest or even participation in the organization. With their greater attachment to the union only a serious experience could move them to resign.

This is, to a lesser extent, also the case with Motive E: 'I did not like the way the union treated me.' Mentioned by 21 per cent of the ex-members, it is again more frequently mentioned by the middle-aged: 61 per cent of the respondents with Motive E are thirty-seven years or older, as against 47 per cent of the ex-members with other motives. The similarity between the two motives is also suggested by their quantitative positions.

Although Motive C only ranks third in frequency, its rank average suggests that it is a rather important complaint. Measured by the combined

indices, it reaches a rank average of 5·25, the highest of the seven motives.[1]
Disappointment with the union's service to the individual with regard to
on-the-job problems turns out to be one of the most serious factors in the
erosion of union membership.

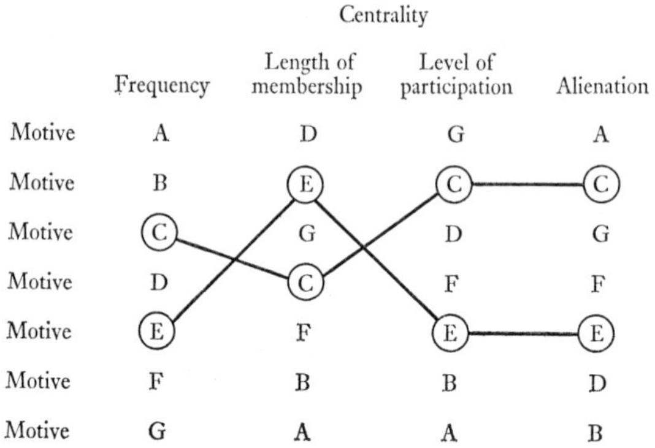

CHART 2. Ranking of Motives C ('insufficient assistance in individual problems at work')
and E ('I did not like the way the union treated me') compared with other motives for resigning.

The effect of this disappointment probably reaches beyond the frequency with which it occurs. The disappointing experiences with the
organization are usually reported to others, for example, to friends,
relatives and colleagues, and such reports are very effective in spreading a
negative image of the union.

Motives C and E: qualitative analysis

For many workers, especially those of middle-age and heads of households,
conflict with management is a rather traumatic experience. It is a threat
to the worker's self-confidence and to the social status of his family and,
as such, will often evoke strong feelings of insecurity and anxiety.[2] In
this threatening situation the worker will turn to the union for protection:

'I have cried for help, two times.'

Ex-members who gave Motive C for resigning complained that the
union failed in its support at the critical moment. Their reactions are
bristling:

'They've let me down.'

'I had to handle it myself.'

'They only took a shot at it.'

'They put me off with empty promises.'

'I'll *never* join again.'

[1] Computed as: $\left(\dfrac{5+4+6+6}{4}\right) = 5\cdot25.$

[2] E. W. Bakke, *The Unemployed Man* (New York, E. P. Dutton & Co., 1934), pp. 79–80.

These workers had some positive attachment to the organization and paid their weekly dues, confident that the union would support them in on-the-job problems. They interpret its neglect as a breach of trust and although they accept trade unions *in principle* they decide to resign from membership. We shall now describe three typical situations.

(*a*) *Action outweighs effect.* Some answers to our questions indicate that the security of belonging to an organization which is willing to protect one's interests is psychologically more important than the outcome of this protection. The following ex-members, for example, do not complain about lack of success, but about lack of effort:

'I had a conflict with my boss, and I went to the union. But as far as I know they *haven't moved a finger.*'

I've been to the union, more than once. In my case I got no support. They *haven't shown any attention* to my difficulties.'

'I don't mind if they sometimes say "no". But I do mind if they even *fail to respond.*'

These answers leave unclear whether the union failed to act or whether it failed to inform the member of its action. The first case suggests a policy problem, and the necessity of intensifying the union's assistance in the individual problems of its members. In the second case, there would be a communication gap between the members and the organization, even at the relatively low level of the local branch. And our analysis of Motive D will confirm that communication is one of the crucial problems between the workers and the organization.

(*d*) *Dysfunctions of bureaucracy.* As a system of social security is extended over larger and larger groups of persons, a greater number of individuals run the chance of becoming entangled in its complicated network of rules and regulations.[1] Applying abstract rules objectively to individual cases is one of the skills of the bureaucratic official. His incapacity to view an individual problem in the context of its idiosyncratic complexity, however, is one of his drawbacks.[2]

The fact that blue collar workers often lack the clerical training to present their personal problems in a convincing way provides the trade union with the opportunity to act as 'human' intermediary between them and the bureaucracy. The following answers from ex-members suggest,

[1] The Dutch economist Jan Pen considers its bureaucratic traits to be one of the limiting factors of the welfare state. Many officials of our modern social-security systems create such an impenetrable mass of administrative jargon, regulations, and forms that they almost serve as paid propagandists against the welfare state. See J. Pen 'De Grenzen van de Welvaarsstaat', *Sociologische Gids.*, x, No. 2 (1963), p. 76.

[2] R. K. Merton, *Social Theory*, p. 151, considers this 'trained incapacity' a serious dysfunction of modern bureaucracies.

however, that many a union official is not able to escape occupational deformation himself:

'I had to come back about a hundred times. Felt like a beggar, nothing for me. They don't really care for you.'

'I'd always paid my dues, not knowing it was not the full contribution. Now I don't get compensation.'

'Over and again they told me to come back. And always those forms to fill out.'

'Those bureaucrats of the union, they always come up with another excuse.'

When the worker decides to turn to his union, after an encounter with his supervisor or a public official, he is looking for more than another administrator. In addition to expertise, he is in need of some deeper concern for his own personal problems.[1] What he seeks is the rare combination of a specialist's objective rationalism and a fellow worker's personal understanding.[2]

This seems to be a general requirement of the union official in advanced industrial society.[3] The bureaucratization of the union's individual assistance to its members is a threat to one of its essential functions in the welfare state.

(*c*) *Individual and collectivity.* Motive E ('the union has too little concern for the individual member') radiates a similar sense of alienation. Emerging spontaneously in the interviews, this image of the unconcerned trade union has a high degree of reality in the workers' eyes. In the strain that arises between the union's long-range aims and the individual worker's daily needs, one recognizes a trend described in Chapter 2: the expansion of the union's macroscial functions, and their diminishing relevance for the individual's immediate situation. Some typical reactions are:

'The union thinks in terms of large groups. *Not in terms of the individual.* You wonder whether you get your share. In my case, I didn't.'

'The union is not interested in *individual problems.* It is only good for big conflicts.'

---

[1] 'Feelings of sympathy to the union official, and reciprocated by him, are often a prerequisite for his handling of grievances at all.' Michael H. Miller, 'The Approach to the Adjudication of Grievances as a Selective Indicator of Steward Future Job Orientation' (unpublished term paper, based upon research among shop stewards in the Buffalo area, 1967), p. 15.

[2] K. Mannheim, *Man and Society in an Age of Reconstruction* (London, Routledge and Kegan Paul, 1940), pp. 323–4.

[3] Compare the observation of a student of Austrian trade unions: 'Wenn es überall nur Ämter und Amtston, überall nur Büros und Bürokraten, Schalter und Parteien und nirgends Menschen gibt, wird der Verängstigte noch furchtsamer und der Gleichgültige noch abweisender und eigensüchtiger werden.' Fritz Klenner, *Die Österreichischen Gewerkschaften, Vergangenheit und Gegenwartsprobleme*, III (Wien, 1953), p. 1785.

'A union is fine in large plants. *For the single worker, it's no use.* I am alone here, and the union has no concern for me.'

'Unions work *for large groups*, for example, the steelworkers. For small groups and individuals, they do nothing.'

'It's pretty clear to me, they *only function for the masses*. But if little me is in in trouble, they couldn't care less.'

'They are only after big results. No union is interested *in small grievances*.'

Lack of concern for the individual, one of the bureaucratic dysfunctions of the welfare state, is a functional justification of trade union membership.[1] The implication is that if its functions are subject to the same process of bureaucratization, one reason for joining a labor organization has disappeared.

The image of a powerful bureaucratic organization, deeply integrated in industrial society and neglecting the daily needs of the individual worker, is attractive in its simplicity. Apart from whether or not it is a true image, it suits the sense of alienation many workers experience in twentieth-century society.

Motive D, the 'service' motive

Motive D ('I did not like the way the union treated me') has several characteristics in common with Motives C and E. It also refers to the relationship between individual and organization, it is also an expression of disappointment, and it is also based upon the worker's experiences. But while Motives C and E reflected criticism of the adequacy of the handling of individual grievances, Motive D is primarily concerned with the psychological content of the relationship of member and union.

Motive D: quantitative analysis

The hope of finding in the union official a helpful colleague, who can be approached as an equal and who responds as a fellow member, is often disappointed. Almost one-quarter (24 per cent) of the ex-members stated that the union: did not respond to a question or request; did not explain or clarify its assistance; did not inform the member of whether it had taken any action; did not explain why no assistance was given; did not respond when the member left or threatened to leave the union; treated the member in a cold, official, or disinterested way.

---

[1] 'For many, the loss of self-respect is too high a price for legalized assistance', R. K. Merton writes. 'In this struggle between alternative structures for fulfilling the nominally same function of providing aid and support to those who need it, it is clearly the machine politician who is better integrated with the groups which he serves than the impersonal, professionalized socially distant and legally constrained welfare worker.' Merton, *Social Theory*, p. 74. With regard to industrial relations, 'trade union official' can be substituted for 'machine politician'.

This Motive D appears equally strong among all groups of members, with such variables as status and age showing no correlation with its frequency. It is mentioned more often than the other motives by workers who were in the union longer and its alienating effect is relatively low:

| | Frequency | Centrality | | Alienation |
		Length of membership	Level of participation	
Motive	A	(D)	G	A
Motive	B	E	C	C
Motive	C	G	(D)	G
Motive	(D)	C	F	F
Motive	E	F	E	E
Motive	F	B	B	(D)
Motive	G	A	A	B

CHART 3. Ranking of Motive D ('I did not like the way the union treated me') as compared with other motives for resigning.

Of average relative frequency, Motive D has a higher organizational centrality than all other motives, which suggests that it occurs less at the periphery of the rank and file and that the ex-members for whom it operated had a positive relationship with the organization. Its low alienating effect implies that their attachment to the organization has not entirely vanished. That they, nevertheless, severed their ties with the union indicates that it is a powerful motive.

Motive D: qualitative analysis

The various answers in respect to this motive reveal three typical situations.

(*a*) The organization did not respond to the member's question or request.

(*b*) The organization did not react when the member left or threatened to leave;

(*c*) The member was treated by the organization in a cold, official, or disinterested manner.

Each of these situations is subjected below to an analysis of its content and its impact upon the members.

(*a*) *The union did not respond.* In Chapter 4 we saw that the majority of both blue collar workers (76 per cent) and white collar workers (65 per cent) joined the union for support in an individual conflict at work. For 40 per cent and 22 per cent, respectively, this was the major reason for joining. A number of these members may be expected to turn to the union for help. But the fact that 'individual service' is the major motive for its members does not imply that it is also the organization's major goal:

'I wrote them. I wrote them two times. They never answered.'

'But they never gave me an answer, and that is why I quit.'

'. . . and after that they just ignored me.'

'. . . that's why I objected, at the union. But no action. I mean, they never answered. They did not even say: "We have done all we could, but to no avail." No, they just played dumb.'

If an organization whose major attraction lies in the area of individual service fails to respond to a simple question, doubts will arise as to whether it will act in more serious situations. This lack of action is easily interpreted as unconcern, with the result that the worker resigns from membership.

(*b*) *No reaction after resigning.* For a member of a voluntary organization, discontinuing one's membership is the strongest possible way to show one's disappointment. In some cases, members use this as a means of protest. Examples of this 'provocative resignation' can be seen in such reactions as:

'But what happened was that nobody tried to keep me as a member.'

'They did not even come to me, when I tentatively quit.'

'I feel they should have come after I resigned. They should fight to keep you as a member.'

These members, from the start in doubt about the individual benefits of union membership, became disappointed in its service, and decided to leave the organization. After making this decision, they look for signs that will confirm the wisdom of their act. Such confirmation is provided by the fact that the organization does not even try to win them back. Only after this final proof of the organization's lack of concern, their quitting becomes a psychological reality to these workers.

(*c*) *The union gave no 'service'.* 'Service' is a social technique which substitutes for personal elements in an essentially nonpersonal relationship. Used by large commercial organizations (department stores, air lines, oil companies, banks), it serves to compensate for the lack of person-to-person contacts with a large number of clients.

A characteristic of the affluent society is that blue collar workers increasingly conceive of themselves as consumers.[1] As part of this re-orientation, they are rapidly becoming appreciative of service and, conversely, resent a lack of service—even from the union:

[1] R. Dubin, 'Behavioral Science Analysis and Collective Bargaining', *Proceedings of the 1965 IRRA Spring Meeting* (Buffalo, N.Y., 3–4 May 1965), pp. 504–5.

'The union said I should have cared for that myself. But is an old member like me not entitled to some service?'

'. . . this lack of service made me decide to quit.'

'It's better to put one's dues in a bank account, each month. For that money one can hire a lawyer, in case of a conflict. Of course, you have to pay a little more then, but you get much better service.'

In Chapter 1 we described the changing blue collar subculture. Its 'class consciousness' and its sense of solidarity have shifted to the background, while individual status aspirations have moved into the foreground of the workers' world. Although the union may still approach them as partners in a social conflict these workers view themselves increasingly as 'clients', entitled to 'service' from the organization. This is another aspect of the psychological gap between the leaders and the rank and file in modern labor organizations.

Some conclusions

A need for on-the-job security is the main reason for union membership for many workers (see Chapter 4). Of the ex-members, however, 28 per cent complain about the way in which the union fulfills this need. And the effects of this reach far beyond the complainers themselves. When reported to other workers, an anti-union climate can easily be created in a plant:

'. . . and some said: "Why did you join the union? Why don't you quit? It's just throwing good money away." One tells you to join, and the other tells you to quit. But I decided I'd better quit.'

Possessing a high degree of reality, and communicated from person to person, negative experiences with the union are especially effective in disaffecting younger workers, who are already doubtful about the benefits and goals of trade unions. A positive side of these complaints—different from that of the structural motives—is that they are not embedded in an indeterminate sense of indifference and apathy. Specific as these experiences are, they offer real opportunities to the union for therapeutic measures.

THE POLICY MOTIVES

There is some degree of disjunction between union officers and the rank and file even in locals with effective leadership and democratic practices.[1] It is not surprising, therefore, that Motive F ('objections to the union's leadership') is mentioned by members as well as ex-members of the union. Asked about the degree of democracy in their union (Appendix

[1] D. C. Miller and W. H. Form, *Industrial Sociology* (New York, Harper & Row, 1964), p. 339.

C, q.58), 16 per cent of the members and 42 per cent of the ex-members were of the opinion that the officers wielded too much power (P<0·001). Although this indicates a correlation between a negative opinion of the leaders and resignation from membership, it by the same token shows that, even among the ex-members, a majority had *no* complaints about the leadership.

In Chapter 4 we saw that policy motives played a minor role among the reasons for joining a union; this also proves to be the case with the reasons for resigning. Motive G ('objections to the union's policy or principles') has the lowest frequency of all of the motives for leaving the organization. This is upheld by the fact that this motive involves two diametrically opposed views, one being that the union is too conservative, the other that it is too radical. Losing members both at the left *and* at the right of the organization is probably typical for integrated trade unions.

Motives F and G: quantitative analysis

In response to an open question on complaints about the union, only 6 per cent of the members and 11 per cent of the ex-members referred to the officials (Motive F). Asked for what reasons they were leaving the union, 19 per cent of the ex-members mentioned the power or affluence of the union's leaders among their motives. Only Motive G, which refers to policy or principles, has a lower frequency.

A trait found also among new members is that policy arguments (Motive G) are mentioned more often by white collar (23 per cent) than blue collar workers (8 per cent). (P<0·001). One of Motive G's most interesting aspects is that these ex-members, although lowest in number, showed the highest degree of participation:

| | | Centrality | | |
	Frequency	Length of membership	Level of participation	Alienation
Motive	A	D	G	A
Motive	B	E	C	C
Motive	C	G	D	G
Motive	D	C	F	F
Motive	E	F	E	E
Motive	F	B	B	D
Motive	G	A	A	B

CHART 4. Ranking of Motives F ('objections to the union's leadership') and G ('objections to the union's policy') compared with the other motives for resigning.

Although members who resigned out of discontent with the union's policy or its leadership are few in number, they were relatively active in the organization. We saw that they belonged predominantly to the white collar group. Their disappointment with the organization has evoked some resentment, ultimately resulting in a relatively high degree of alienation. They are less important because of their numbers than because of their desirability as members and because of their negative feelings as ex-members.

Motives F and G: qualitative analysis

About the union's officers

Complaints about the union officers involve mainly the social distance that separates them from the rank and file. This is manifested, in the eyes of the latter, in such status symbols as 'expensive cars', 'trips abroad', and 'big cigars'. The statements show little variation. They differ only in that some are confined to a simple observation:

'Union officers have a pretty good life, with trips and luxuries.'

while others draw the conclusion that, *consequently*, the officers have little interest in the union's members:

'The officers get highly paid. From our dues. With high living, travels, and dinners. But at the same time, they can't work very hard for their members.'

The low frequency and relatively mild formulation of these complaints suggest that a 'negative leadership-image' is hardly an independent variable in membership erosion. It is harmful only in the framework of an organization whose functions are not geared to the problems of its members. Disillusion about the organization is a fertile soil for an image of leaders living in luxury and neglecting their members' needs. It makes the rank and file both more vulnerable and more prone to criticism of the union's leadership.

About the union's policy

Ex-members complaining that the union's policy is too conservative are found in the shop as well as in the office. One type among such ex-members is the older worker, often with socialist leanings, who rejects the trend towards welfare unionism for both political and emotional reasons. His words reveal the class-consciousness of an older generation:

'In the past the unions took a stronger line. They were more aggressive. The leadership was in better hands. After the war they've only been compromising.' —Steelworker.

Born and raised in the social climate of the class conflict, these older activists still harbor strong resentments against the capitalist system, even in its modern form. And they hold the unions' integration into that system to be at cross-purposes with the workers' true and fundamental interests.

The objections of a younger generation are more pragmatic: its members reject the integration of the unions because it interferes with their role as pressure group. A trade union, they argue, should work for special interests rather than for the common good:

'A union should naturally be one-sided. Not general or neutral. First it should fight for the workers, and only second for the country.'—Technical designer.

Both types of reaction are symptomatic of resistance among the rank and file to the unions' integration in the welfare state, which they assume leads to neglect of the workers' true interests. Without being aware of it, they are representatives of the 'conflict theory' of industrial relations.

There is an opposite opinion also. Another group of members, of about the same size and of mixed age, argue that the unions are too socialistic and their policies too radical. All are white collar workers, and some of them take the view of management:

'The union . . . professes to be neutral, but in reality it is radical. These ideas of the workers getting part of the profits go too far. The union demands everything from the employer, and nothing from the workers. It goes too far and that's why I quit.'—Accountant.

'The employers nowadays have too many obligations, put upon them as compared with the workers.'—Clerical worker.

Although one must beware of the 'status fallacy' of attributing all political opinions to individual status and status-frustrations,[1] it seems hardly coincidental that this opinion is found only among white collar workers. Here, we are probably confronted with another manifestation of 'anticipatory socialization' and its negative effect upon union membership among the new middle class.[2] It would be worthwhile to verify whether this form of conservatism also occurs among manual workers[3] and whether it is on the increase among the younger generations of the affluent society. If so, the implication would be that the 'cooperation theory' of industrial relations is gaining adherents in the labor force.

[1] For a critique of this type of sociological interpretation, see R. Samuel, 'Lipset's Nightmare', *The New Statesman*, LX, No. 1553 (1960), pp. 983–4.   [2] See also p. 106.
[3] 'Working-class conservatism' is, according to R. T. McKenzie, an important factor in British political life. See R. T. McKenzie and A. Silver, 'Conservatism, Industrialism and the Working Class Tory in England' (Paper presented at the fifth World Congress of the International Sociological Association, Washington, D.C., 3 September 1962). See also W. G. Runciman, 'The Working Class Conservatives', *Relative Deprivation and Social Justice* (London, Routledge and Kegan Paul, 1966), pp. 170–87.

THE SHAPE OF MEMBERSHIP EROSION

Conditional variables

Motivation analysis confines itself almost exclusively to such subjective factors as needs, values, perceptions, opinions, and attitudes. Its procedure is usually to explain social phenomena by reducing them to psychological variables.[1] But one would be mistaken to view membership erosion only as a psychological process.

Table 6 showed, for example, that use of the union's services—and the conditions leading to it—are instrumental in keeping members in the organization. Another sociological condition is that ex-members of the union are more often rooted in higher status groups:

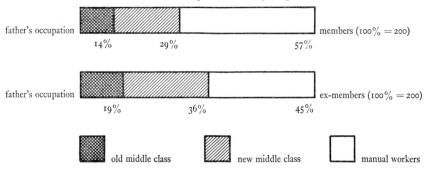

df = 2; 0·05>P>0·02

FIGURE 19. Social background of members and ex-members.

Ex-members come more often than members from an old middle-class (business, independent craftsmen, professionals) milieu or a new middle-class (white collar) milieu. This suggests that influences in early youth are responsible for a self-image that leads the adult worker to resign more easily from an organization with predominantly blue collar membership.

Other social factors play a similar role. Our analysis indicates that the fact that a worker's father did not belong to a union or that the worker is promoted from a blue collar to a white collar rank has a similar negative impact on union membership. It makes the ex-members of the union sociologically distinct from members.

Volitional variables

Membership erosion consists of two distinct processes which are related to each other in the manner of concentric circles. The larger one, encompassing the other, is the *structural* process. With no less than 70 per

[1] D. Sills, 'A Sociologist Looks at Motivation', *The Citizen Volunteer*, ed. N. E. Cohen (New York, Harper & Brothers, 1960), p. 70.

cent of the ex-members resigning for Motives A or B, the perception of the union as a mass organization, with high dues and few individual benefits, is the basis of membership erosion. Central in this motivation is the doubt whether unions are still essential in the welfare state. This negative image is especially widespread among the younger workers, who have no personal experience of pre-welfare-state conditions and feel no commitment to the labor organization.

Of the ex-members younger than thirty-seven years, a majority of 56 per cent mentioned *only* structural motives, compared with 38 per cent of the older ex-members ($0.02 > P > 0.01$). The same trend is found in length of membership: 58 per cent of the structurally motivated ex-members belonged less than three years to the union, compared with 38 per cent of the functionally motivated. Related to this are differences in degree of participation: of the ex-members with structural motives, 53 per cent had never attended a meeting of the union; of those with functional motives, 34 per cent.

Within and partly overlapping with this broader trend we find the *functional* process of withdrawal. Less widespread than the former, it includes 46 per cent of the ex-members. Older and less in doubt about the role of unions in the welfare state, their motives are often rooted in specific disappointments with the organization. Although they view union membership as useful *in principle*, they denounce the way it actually functions in the life of the individual worker. Having been somewhat more involved in its action, they are less disaffiliated from the union than the structurally motivated ex-members.

CONCLUSION

A crucial problem for the unions in the welfare state is to prevent further erosion of their functions in the individual work situation. Only if they are able to prove on the basis of hard facts that their membership is beneficial will they attract and hold the new generations of workers. Unions are not the only institutions coping with this type of problem. The churches, consumer cooperatives, universities, political parties and urban communities are each in their own way struggling with similar adjustment to environmental change.

The unions even have the advantage that with technological change new social and economic problems are arising. Although the question of the impact of automation upon employment had been the subject of heated discussion,[1] a definite answer has finally emerged. It is that over the long

---

[1] See Ch. 6, 'The Great Employment Controversy', in W. Buckingham, *Automation, its Impact on Business and People* (New York, Harper & Row, 1963), pp. 101–19; G. H. Hildebrand, 'Some Alternative Views of the Unemployment Problem in the United States', in *Employment*

run, and in the labor force as a whole, automation does not appear to considerably raise the level of unemployment. Over the short run, however, and in specific plants and industries, technological change is causing the displacement of many thousands of workers.[1]

In the United States, this displacement has been high in the 1950s, especially among the unskilled and skilled workers in agriculture and mining. Between 1953 and 1957 amounting to a yearly average of 200,000, it leveled between 1957 and 1963 to an average 100,000 not including hidden unemployment and indirect displacement in competing industries and firms.[2] With the spread of electronic equipment in the office, it is now moving into the lower and middle ranks of the clerical group. The indications are that labor force displacement is becoming a semi-permanent trend in advanced industrial society.[3]

Although this lay-off of displaced workers indirectly contributes to greater efficiency in their firms,[4] the task of their readjustment has proved too immense to be coped with by industry. Retraining and relocating thousands of displaced workers demands sacrifices which lie beyond most companies' resources. This situation entails three different levels of approach for the unions.

The first approach is through government, by means of union demands for manpower training programs, government contracts in areas of dislocation, and official surveys in areas of the labor market where automation is due. Pressure for planned regional industrialization and full employment measures is part of this approach.[5]

The second approach is in the company, through collective bargaining.

Problems of Automation and Advanced Technology, ed. Jack Stieber (New York, St Martin's Press, 1966), pp. 105–28; C. E. Silberman, *The Myths of Automation* (New York, Harper & Row, 1966), pp. 1–26; E. Clague and L. Greenberg, 'Employment', *Automation and Technological Change*, ed. J. T. Dunlop (Englewood Cliffs, N.J., Prentice-Hall, 1965), p. 116.

[1] E. Clague and L. Greenberg, 'Employment', p. 130.

[2] C. E. Killingsworth, 'Structural Unemployment in the United States', in *Employment Problems*, ed. J. Stieber, p. 136; also W. Buckingham, *Automation*, p. 112–13.

[3] Although the expanding United States economy presents a favorable climate for readjustment, some groups, especially the semi-skilled at the assembly-lines of mass production industries (cars, rubber, meat-packing) and continuous processing industries (steel, chemicals, refining) have met serious difficulties in finding new employment. See Otto Eckstein, Perspectives on Employment under Technological Change, in *Employment Problems*, ed. J. Stieber, p. 96. Also W. Haber, L. A. Ferman, and J. R. Hudson, *The Impact of Technological Change, the American Experiment* (Kalamazoo, Mich., Upjohn Institute for Employment Research, 1963), p. 36.

[4] J. Stieber, 'Manpower Adjustments to Automation and Technological Change in Western Europe', in *Automation and Economic Progress*, ed. H. Bowen and G. L. Mangum (Englewood Cliffs, N.J., Prentice-Hall, 1966), p. 165.

[5] On the different role of full employment policies in Europe and the United States, *ibid*. p. 60. For an excellent review of 'active manpower policies' see S. Barkin, 'Programming of Technical Changes and Manpower Adjustments', in *Employment Problems*, ed. J. Stieber, pp. 432–45.

The introduction of union–management committees, the retraining of displaced workers, the introduction of plant-wide seniority systems, pension plans permitting earlier retirement, the reimbursement of moving and relocation expenses, and the provision of severance pay will diminish the negative impact of technological change.[1]

Both public legislation and collective bargaining, however, operate at levels beyond the worker's private fight to escape the fate of structural unemployment.[2] This is the more crucial as research indicates displacement to be primarily an *individual* disaster. Aid from the community, for instance, has been found to be of little help, with most displaced workers having to find jobs through such informal channels as friends, relatives, or random applications.[3] This individual nature is confirmed by the fact that most of the newly-found jobs are temporary or of short duration, with several shifts being necessary to obtain more permanent employment. Even with successful adjustment, displacement for most workers entails some element of individual deprivation, for instance of seniority, promotion rights, status, job skills, hours, pension rights, work satisfaction, savings or level of wages. Also, it often results in a change of occupation or industry, forcing a large minority of the displaced workers to leave their community, with the additional problems of family dislocation.[4] These aspects require a third and more individualistic union approach to the problem of technological displacement.

We found in Chapter 4 that even under normal conditions many workers seek union membership in order to find individual on-the-job security. This need now will be considerably enhanced by the individual consequences of technological displacement. It is evident that to meet this increased demand, the unions' function of 'individual problem insurance' will have to be extended over the unemployed as well as over the employed.[5] The above experiences of ex-members suggest, however, that

[1] The examples are from W. P. Reuther, Congressional Testimony, in *Automation, Implications for the Future*, ed. Morris Philipson (New York, Random House, Vintage Books, 1962), pp. 267–316. For a more pessimistic view of the role of collective bargaining, see A. H. Raskin, 'The Obsolescent Unions', in *Industrial and Labor Relations*, ed. A. Fraser Isbester (Boston, Mass., E. C. Heath and Company, 1967), p. 35.

[2] It has been found, for example, that severance pay does not play a major role in finding re-employment, W. Haber, L. A. Ferman, and J. R. Hudson, *The Impact of Technological Change*, p. 24.

[3] *Ibid.* p. 30.

[4] *Ibid.* p. 38.

[5] Trade unions are often exclusively concerned with the employed, which leads Hildebrand to the criticism that: 'Much of our policies under collective bargaining today rest implicitly upon (this) orientation to the fortunate insiders, which accounts for the inability of American unionism to address itself to unemployment beyond sterile appeals to the purchasing power doctrine on behalf of wage increases.' G. H. Hildebrand, 'Some Alternative Views of the Unemployment Problem', p. 118.

the functions, organization and leadership of our contemporary labor organizations are often insufficiently adapted to this challenge. This is the lesson we draw from the data in Chapter 6: that in the age of automation, besides the existing tasks at the levels of government and company, the union's appeal will depend on their ability to create new and more adequate functions at the level of the individual worker.

Appendix A. The method of research

This study is based on seven surveys. A survey is a comprehensive analysis of a social phenomenon—a social group or a social process—in its contemporary form, based upon empirical research.

That the survey is a method in its own right is evident from the fact that it can be distinguished from other scientific methods. Compared with the method of theoretical deduction, it is predominantly empirical and inductive. Compared with the sociopsychological experiment, it is concerned less with the causal relationship between two variables than with the structure and functions of a system of interdependent variables. Compared with this statistical method, it is fundamentally 'verstehend' in character, allowing more scope for qualitative analysis, and revealing more of the emotional background of observed behavior.

Although distinct from other methods, the survey also has much in common with them. Designing the survey, formulating the hypotheses, and analyzing the data, for instance, involves logical deduction. The method of the *ex post facto* experiment can also be applied to survey data, and statistical techniques have actually become an inseparable part of the modern survey. It is even claimed that this very complexity turns the survey into a special method of its own.[1] The possibilities and problems of this method can be illustrated by three contradictions it has overcome in recent years, viz. (1) between the macro-social and the microsocial approach, (2) between quantitative and qualitative analysis, and (3) between empirical and theoretical results.

Macrosocial and microsocial approaches

For a long time, one of the major objections to the survey method was its unsuitability for studying large populations. Since World War II, this restriction has been largely overcome by the introduction of random sampling, a technique which has made it possible to draw conclusions about a macrosocial population, such as the membership of a national organization, from a comparatively small sample.

In the present study, sampling has been combined with case studies of both representative and deviant groups. In the former, a sample has been drawn from a limited population that was assumed to be of average character. The surveys of new members (Chapter 4), participants (Chapter 5), and ex-members (Chapter 6) of the Dutch Federation of Trade Unions in Utrecht are of this type. Statistically, Utrecht has been proven to be a 'normal' community, and its local union branches are fairly representative of the whole country. An example of the latter is our survey of a local branch of a political party (Chapter 5). There,

---

[1] W. Gee, *Social Science Research Methods* (New York, Macmillan, 1950), Ch. 10.

an exceptional population was chosen, where the process under investigation (the influx of white collar workers) manifested itself in an extreme form.[1]

The introduction of sampling required the use of inferential statistical tests. Among the available devices we have made a choice of the widely known χ^2 test, and of the rarely used 'test for the equality of probabilities against trend', developed by Van Eeden and Hemelrijk.[2] Use of the latter, as in the Figures 16 and 20, is indicated by the w/σ symbol.

Quantitative and qualitative analysis

The choice of technique in a survey depends largely on the nature of the data required. There are a number of possibilities: systematic observation; content analysis; projective techniques; many types of interview, ranging from non-structured to fully structured; and the personally administered or mailed questionnaires. One of the instruments used in this book is the personally administered questionnaire, with fixed questions and a choice of fixed answers. An example is our survey of about 22,363 union members in Rotterdam, results of which are presented in Table 20 and Figure 17. Another method, used in Chapters 4, 5 and 6, is the semi-structured interview, developed by Rogers,[3] Kahn, Cannell[4] Merton and others,[5] with the purpose of preserving the affective aspects of the answer, while retaining the advantage of quantification. Such semi-structured interviews, again, make use of fixed basic questions, but the replies are left open. The interviewer encourages the respondent to be spontaneous and introspective and in addition asks his own independent and indirect questions. This technique is based on 'rapport', the atmosphere of trust and frankness between interviewer and respondent, and on a schedule of open-ended questions (see, for example, App. C). After each basic question, our interviewers were trained to probe into the following dimensions:

(1) *Range*, to ascertain whether the respondent has more knowledge, responses or motives.

(2) *Specification*, to encourage the respondent to elaborate his responses.

(3) *Depth*, to try to lay bare the affective background to the responses.[6]

The drawbacks to this technique are that, for each survey, the interviewers must undergo rigorous training, sometimes lasting as long as several weeks (for the survey in Chapter 4, even as long as six months); and high standards are set for the construction of the code system and, subsequently, for coding the

[1] For an example of a deviant case study of a social organization, see S. Lipset, M. A. Trow, and J. S. Coleman, *Union Democracy: the Internal Politics of the International Typographical Union* (Glencoe; Ill., Free Press, 1956).

[2] Constance van Eeden and J. Hemelryk, 'A test for the equality of probabilities against a class of specified alternative hypotheses, including trend', *Proc. Kon. Ned. Akad. v. wetenschappen*, A 58, Indag. Math. 17, 191 and 301 (1955).

[3] C. R. Rogers, 'The Non-directive method as a technique for social research', *American Journal of Sociology*, Vol. LI, pp. 143–4.

[4] R. L. Kahn and C. F. Cannell, *The Dynamics of Interviewing: Theory, Techniques and Cases* (New York, Wiley, 1957), *passim*.

[5] R. Merton, M. Fiske, and P. L. Kendall, *The Focused Interview: a Manual of Problems and Procedures* (Glencoe, Ill., Free Press, 1956), *passim*.

[6] R. Merton, M. Fiske, and P. L. Kendall, *The Focused Interview*, p. 12.

answers.[1] But the advantage is that, when quantitative analysis of the data can go no further, the material still presents opportunities for qualitative analysis from which new hypotheses and even conclusions can be derived. Chapters 5 and 6 provide several illustrations of this procedure.

Empirical and theoretical results

The objection that former surveys were little more than descriptions of concrete facts—or, in Merton's phrase, 'social bookkeeping'[2]—applies not only to the United States, but also to Europe. It has been pointed out, for example, that European sociographic surveys have contributed little to the construction of sociological theory.[3]

Since World War II, however, the survey method has gained greater theoretical depth in two ways, viz. by the introduction of operational concepts and by the verification of *a priori* hypotheses. Because of their general character, reaching beyond the concrete data, operational concepts can put the survey on a more abstract level and function as a bridge between facts and theory. An example is the paradigm on page 115, depicting the process of decision forming toward union membership as a system of operational concepts. Individual examples of operational concepts are in Chapter 5 'participation', 'alienation', 'sense of purpose', 'apathy', and 'retrogressive idealism', By means of such abstractions, based on facts, the researcher takes the first step toward 'middle range theories'.[4] An advantage of such operational concepts is that, unlike nominal concepts, they have no fixed and unchangeable content to which the researcher must constantly adapt himself or his material. On the contrary, they allow theory to be adjusted to facts, with the precondition that the researcher specify the indicators on which the operational concept is based.[5]

The introduction of *a priori* hypotheses brings the survey still closer to the realm of theory, since they indicate clearly what contribution the researcher hopes to make to general theory. Examples are in Chapter 4 the hypotheses I and II about the role of primary-group influences among unskilled workers, and in Chapter 5 the Marxist and revisionist hypotheses about the personality of the active trade unionist, and the psychological and sociological hypotheses of voluntary participation in democratic organizations. By means of such hypotheses it is possible to test a middle range theory under different conditions, as illustrated on pages 145 and 163. This kind of crosschecking increases the possibility of constructing a system of more general theory.

[1] M. van de Vall, 'Social onderzoek als didactische opgave', *Sociol. Gids*, III, No. 8 (1956), 141–52; and M. van de Vall, 'Wat biedt de opleiding?' *Opleiding en beroepsuitoefening van de sociaal wetenschappelijk academicus* (ISONEVO/VSWO) (Amsterdam, 1960), pp. 14–22.
[2] R. K. Merton, 'The Social Psychology of Housing', in *Current Trends in Social Psychology*, ed. W. Dennis (Pittsburgh, Penn., University of Pittsburgh Press, 1948), p. 163.
[3] S. Groenman, *Kanttekeningen bij de voortgang van het sociale onderzoek in Nederland* (Meppel, 1948), p. 14.
[4] 'Theories of the middle range', as the term implies, will apply only to limited fields of social reality of not too high a level of abstraction.
[5] See, for example, M. van de Vall, 'Das Problem der Partizipation in Freiwilligen Organisationen' in *Soziologie und Gesellschaft in den Niederlanden*, ed. Joachim Matthes (Berlin, Luchterhand Verlag, 1965), p. 255.

Having outlined the principal features of the method on which this study is based, we shall now look at each of the seven surveys used. Only their major aspects will be considered; the details can be found in the appropriate reports.

THE SURVEY USED IN CHAPTER 4

The new members in this study joined the Utrecht branch of one of the trade unions affiliated with the Dutch Federation of Trade Unions. Utrecht was selected because the surveys of 'passive members' and 'ex-members' (see Chapters 5 and 6) had also been carried out there, with the effect that cultural and sociogeographical variables were kept constant.

Members were considered 'new' only if they were joining for the first time or if they had been out of the union so long that their names no longer appeared in the register of former members. In this way transfers and brief breaks in membership were eliminated from the sample, so that each new member surveyed had actually undergone a process of decision-forming. During the sampling there was no evidence of special circumstances with regard to the labor situation.

Some weeks after joining, each of the 204 persons in the sample was given a motivation interview by a sociology major who had been trained for the purpose. The interviewers, all of whom had previous interviewing experience, followed a six-month practical course during which they studied trade unions and received an intensive training in interviewing techniques. The intensity of the interview was increased with the aid of pictures, strips of card to be placed in sequence, and sentence completions. The interview (see App. B) took an average of one-and-a-half hours and was held at the respondent's home. Based upon the procedure of post-coding, all data were coded twice; divergent cases three times. The project was subsidized by the Dutch Federation of Trade Unions.

THE SURVEY USED IN CHAPTER 5

The passive and participating members studied in this chapter live in Utrecht and are members of the Utrecht branch of the General Dutch Metalworkers' Union (ANMB) or of the 'Mercurius' union of clerical workers. The two samples, each of 100 individuals, were selected with the help of a list of random numbers. The two unions were selected after consultation with union officials at various levels. It may be assumed that by and large they differ little from the other unions in the Federation. Not only in the sociogeographic sense, but sociologically as well, the city of Utrecht is known to have something of an 'average' statistical character. This applies also to the trade union movement, the Utrecht branches of which can be classed as statistically normal, having no extreme features. With regard to their hold on members, for example, the Utrecht branches were found to be neither unusually weak nor unusually strong.[1]

---

[1] For a similar solution, see W. L. Warner and P. S. Lunt, 'Criteria Used in Selecting the Community', *The Social Life of a Modern Community* (New Haven, Conn., Yale University Press, 1941), Ch. 3.

This survey was also subsidized by the Dutch Federation of Trade Unions and was carried out as an 'instructional survey', as part of the sociology curriculum at Utrecht University. The interviews (see App. C) were conducted by sociology majors who, as part of a required course on social research, had received a two week field work training in interviewing.

THE SURVEY USED IN CHAPTER 6

This project was carried out concurrently with the one described above. From the Utrecht branches of each of the two unions, ANMB and Mercurius, 2 times 100 members who had recently resigned were interviewed, using an interview schedule that differed from the previous one in details. The method employed was the semistructured interview survey, and a copy of the questionnaire can be found in Appendix C. Coding was done in duplicate; sorting and counting were carried out, after control punching, by Bull countersorters. The calculations were made by computer and checked at the Sociological Institute, Utrecht.

THE SURVEY USED ON PAGES 31 AND 187

As part of an 'instructional survey', the Sociological Institute of Utrecht University has carried out 473 semistructured interviews of young (under 30) office workers employed by Philips' Gloeilampen-fabrieken at Eindhoven, the Dutch Mother company of the North American Philips Company in the

TABLE 24. *Representativeness of the sample in Table 20 and Figure 17*

Trade union	Percentage of members in Rotterdam	Percentage of members in sample
ANMB	23·6	26·0
ABVA	20·8	21·6
CBT	16·0	14·0
ANB	8·4	9·4
Mercurius	6·3	6·7
ABC	5·3	4·7
ANGB	4·8	4·8
NVVP	3·7	3·6
AVVG	3·2	3·4
CKO	2·6	— (on boats)
ABMH	2·3	2·4
NBH	1·8	— (at work)
Eendracht	1·1	3·3
ANTB	0·04	0·05
ANAB	0·04	0·03
NTB	0·05	0·02
AAAB	0·03	—
Alg. Bedrijfsbond	0·03	0·02
VVT	0·02	—
NOMA	—	—
NBS	0·01	0·01
TOTAL	100% = (48,213)	100% = (22,363)

United States. The random sample was tested for representativeness with regard to age, marital status, and occupational group. Four reports were published in all.

THE SURVEY QUOTED ON page 158, Table 20, and page 160, Figure 17

The author supervised a survey of 22,363 members of the Rotterdam federation of union branches (NVV); this survey included several questions about participation in the union. Table 24 on the previous page shows the representativeness of the sample.

The information in Figure 17 (voluntary officials) is also derived from this sample. To avoid duplication in this graph, most respondents were asked to state only their highest unpaid post in the union. Since they have been ordered according to this post and since it is to be expected that a large proportion of these officials also held posts at lower levels, the conclusion to be drawn is that Figure 17 understates, rather than exaggerates, the actual trend.

THE SURVEY QUOTED IN Chapter 5 on pages 164 ff.

The results are based upon a semistructured interview survey in the Amersfoort branch of the Dutch labor party. This branch was relected as 'deviant', having recently been subject to a large scale influx of white collar members. A stratified random sample of 150 party members were given an interview consisting of 85 questions. The survey from which the qualitative data in the above sections are derived, was funded and published by the Wiardi Beckman Foundation.

THE SURVEY QUOTED IN Table 1, page 5

This survey was conducted in the Arnhem branch of the Dutch Consumer's Cooperative Movement (Co-op). It was based upon semistructed interviews with 470 housewives, members of Co-op Holland. Its results were published in M. van de Vall, 'Clients, Consommateurs ou Coopérateurs?' in *Coopération*, 22ᵉ Année, avril, mai et juin, 1962.

Appendix B. Text of the interview conducted among 204 newly joined members of the NVV at Utrecht (Chapter 4)

1. How long have you been living in Utrecht? ———years.
2. How long have you been working with your present firm? ———years.
3. What firm are you with?
4. Roughly, what sort of work do you do?
5. Job or grade:
6. Would you personally consider yourself more of a blue collar worker or a white collar worker (if you had to make a choice)?

(Question 7 and 8 only for the 'blue collar workers' in question 6.)

7. Do you belong to one of these three collective contract groups: unskilled, semiskilled or skilled? If so, which?
8. If not, in which category would you place yourself?
9. Which trade union did you recently join?
10. Could you say roughly what you think is, at present, the most important activity of the trade unions (together with any criticism)?
11. Is this activity also the *purpose* of the trade union movement? (If not, what is?)
12. Would you explain in as much detail as possible what motives and circumstances led you to join the union?
13. Were there any particular people who influenced your decision?
14. Who is this person: fellow-worker, superior, friend, etc.
15. If a member of the firm: What kind of position does he occupy in the firm?
16. What do you think of him as a person? (ONLY if a member of the firm.)
17. What was the literal content of your conversation with him about the union? What did he say, and what did you reply, and so on?
18. When was the first time in your life that you heard of the existence of trade unions? (Favorably/unfavorably.)
19. (If the *parental home* was *not* named in the previous answer.) Was the trade union movement ever discussed in your home? (Favorably/unfavorably.)
20. When was the first time in your life that the possibility of your becoming a *member* of a trade union occur to you? (Why and how?)
21. Did you then join at once? (If not, why not?)
22. Have the other employees in your firm any particular attitude toward people who are *not members* of the union?

23. Have they any particular attitude toward people who *do belong* to the union?

(Questions 24 and 25 only if not yet stated.)

24. Did you discuss your intention of joining the union with your wife/parents? If so, what was the literal content of the conversation?

25. Was her/their reaction favorable or unfavorable?

26. Before becoming a member, had you ever read anything about the union? If so, what?

27. Had you ever heard a radio talk about the union? If so, by whom, about what, and what did you think of it?

28. How much, approximately, is your weekly subscription to the union?

29. Could you name a specific characteristic of the trade union members in your firm? Is there some quality they have in common?

30. Why did you not join a Catholic or Protestant union?

31. In your firm, are there still differences between members of these unions and members of your union?

32. Would you not have preferred to join a different NVV union and why?

33. Do you think you will shortly *turn to the union* for some reason? What?

34. Most of the people who join a union leave again within one or two years. Why do you think this is?

35. And what do you think will happen in your own case and why?

Now, for a few personal data:

36. Male/Female.

37. Age.

38. Religion.

39. Education.

40. Was your father a union member? If so, what union?

41. On each of these six slips is written a reason for joining a union. Would you place them in their order of importance in your own case. First the reason which for you was most important, then the second most important, and so on.

Comments:

First Picture: Let me now show you this picture (sun): Would you say something about it? (E.g. what it represents, what you think of it.) And after the description: Could this man be you? Why/why not?

Second picture: And now this picture (march): Would you say something about this as well (what it represents)? After the description: if you had to point yourself out in this picture, where would you be? (Get him to point.) Why not there? (Indicate individual or procession. Note whether respondent pointed to procession or individual.)

Would you complete the following sentences. The idea is not to spend a long time thinking, weighing the pros and cons, but to write down straightaway what comes into your mind when you read the incompleted sentence.

1. I pay my union subscription mainly because —————————————

2. Union meetings are ————————————————————

3. The union leaders ——————————————————————

4. The NVV should really ————————————————————

5. In the future I ———— expect to be involved in a strike.

6. Where I work it is mainly the ———— employees who belong to a union.

7. One of the major tasks of the trade union is ——————————

8. I would ———— like to sit on my union's branch committee.

9. The firm's management thinks the union is ——————————

10. Politically the NVV is ————————————————————

11. In the union magazine I mainly read ————————————

Appendix C. Text of the interview conducted among 200 members and 200 ex-members of the NVV at Utrecht (Chapters 5 and 6)

First of all, some questions about yourself, places you have lived, your career and such:

1. How long have you been living in Utrecht? ———years.
2. At what places have you lived up to now?
   Up to the age of 21:
   And since then:
3. When were you born?
4. What education have you had?
5. Other training, etc.
6. Marital status:

(Questions 7-10 only if married, or formerly married.)

7. How many children do you have?
8. What are their ages?
9. How many of them are fully dependent on you?
10. What is (was) the occupation of your father-in law? (In detail.) (For married women: husband's occupation.)
11. What is (was) your father's occupation? (If more than one, underline the one in which you knew him best.)
12. Was he a manual worker, a supervisor, a technician, a clerk, a civil servant, or self-employed?

Now, for a few questions about your own occupation and the work you are now doing:

13. What is your occupation? (Detailed description, with grade, type of firm, etc.)
14. Do you come under a collective contract (CAO)? If so, which one?
15. Do you come within any particular occupational group (skilled, unskilled, etc.) work grade, job classification, etc.?
16. Compared with your father's occupation, do you think your position is now equal to his and why?
17. Have you always been in your present occupation, or did you previously have others?
18. Other occupation(s) before 1950; other occupation(s) since 1950.

19. Since the war, have you always been with your present firm, or have you also worked for other firms since 1950? Other firms since 1950.

20. Do you feel you have made enough progress since the beginning of your career? (Details.)

21. Have you ever been unemployed: If so, for how long?

22. Do you think you might ever become unemployed? If not, why not? If so, why?

23. Do you think your position at work may improve or worsen? If 'improve' or 'worsen' in what respect and in what way?

24. How many people are employed at the firm where you work?

25. What percentage of them, at your own estimate, belongs to a union? (And which one?)

26. What are your net earnings, including piece rates and merit rating?

27. What do you think of this income, compared with other people's? (And whose do you compare it with?)

28. (For heads of families only.) What is your family's average income (including working members of the family who contribute to the family budget)?

29. Do you belong to a trade union? If so, which one?

30. How much are your union dues?

31. (For married men only.) Does your wife ever object to this expense? If so, why?

32. What does the union do with this money?

And now I should like to ask a few questions about other groups to which you belong:

33. Do you belong to a church, ethical society, etc.? If so, specify.

34. Roughly, how often do you attend the meetings or services?

35. Would you state to which other organizations, societies, clubs or groups you belong (including card clubs or other groups of friends, in fact, any group outside family and firm in which it is possible to play an active part)?

36. If since last year September you have not attended any *union* meeting.

    a. but you *have* attended meetings of *other* societies/organizations: Why did you go to the meetings of ———— and not to those of the union?

    b. Nor any meeting of other societies/organizations: Why did you not attend the union meeting? ————

If since last year September you *have* attended union meetings

    c. *and* meetings of other societies or organizations. Did you prefer going to the meetings of the union or those of ———— and why?————

    d. but *not* the meetings of other societies or organizations: Why did you attend the union meetings, but not those of ————?

37. Only if you have attended union meetings:
    a. If you say nothing at union meetings but *do* speak at other meetings: Why do you speak at the meeting of ——————— but not at the union meetings? ————————————————————————
    b. If you do not speak either at union meetings or at other meetings: Why do you not speak at union meetings? ———————————————
    c. If you speak both at union meetings and other meetings: Where do you prefer to speak, at union meetings or the meetings of ——————— ——————————— and why? ———————————————
    d. If you *do* speak at union meetings but *not* at other meetings: Why do you speak at the union meeting but not at the meeting of ——————— ?

38. In which of the societies, organizations, or clubs to which you belong would you most like to serve on the committee? Why this particular one? ———

39. (Only if the union was not named in the answer to previous question.) Why not in the union? ———————————————————————

40. What do you think of the relationship *in general* between workers and employers in the community? ———————————————————

41. Has this relationship changed since the war? ———————————

42. Do you think that in the future there will have to be a different relationship between workers and employers in the community? If so, could you say why, and roughly what this relationship should be? ———————

43. A large firm intends to give skilled workers the same status as office staff (e.g. the same holiday rights and working hours, no fines, coffee and tea in the morning and afternoon, no more clocking in, salary, etc.) What do you think of this and why? ———————————————————

44. On each of these six slips is written a trade union aim. Would you please arrange them in their order of importance as you see it:
    (*a*) Achieving *higher wages*.
    (*b*) Winning *more respect* for the worker in society.
    (*c*) Spreading knowledge about wage policy, codetermination, piece rates, etc.
    (*d*) Preventing future *unemployment*.
    (*e*) Providing employees with codetermination in industry.
    (*f*) Taking the *high profits* away from the employers.

45. Which of the above tasks do you consider completely unimportant? ————————————————————————————————

46, Do you think any task has been left out here? ———————————If so, what? ————————————————————————————————

(Questions 48 and 49 only for those who joined before 1940.)
48. Before the war were you less, equally, or more interested in the union, as compared with now? ———————————————————

49. If less:

    a. Why does the union now interest you more? ———————————

    If more:

    b. Why does the union now interest you less? ———————————

50. Did your father also belong to a union? ——————————————

(Questions 51 and 52 only for those who joined after 1950.)

51. Was your father less interested in the union than you, equally, or more interested? ——————————————————————————

52. If less:

    a. Why are you more interested than your father? ———————————

    If more:

    b. Why are you less interested than your father? ———————————

53. Would you care to say what you *personally* get from being a union member? ——————————————————————————————

54. If you had your way in the union, to what would you devote the most attention *in your firm*? ————————————————————————

55. Have you any grievances about the union? ————————————————

56. Have you ever left the union? ——— If so, for what reason? ——————— Why and how did you join again? ———————————————————

57. If not, have you ever considered leaving the union? ————————— If so, for what reason? ——————————————————————— Why did you not leave? ——————————————————————

58. Do you think the *members* have enough influence in the union or do you think the *union leaders* have too much say? ——————————————

59. Do you consider that blue and white collar workers (i.e. supervisory, technical, and clerical staff) have enough common interests to belong to the same union? ——— If so, what interests? ——————————————— If not, why not? ——————————————————————

60. Would you call yourself a blue or a white collar worker? ——————————

61. Do you think it possible that you will at some time be involved in a strike? ——————————————————————————————

62. There is a proposal to make strikes illegal in future. What do you think of this? ————————————————————————————————

63. Do you know what codetermination stands for and what it implies? (If not, what do you think?) ——————————————————————

64. Do you know what job classification is? ——————————————————

65. Do you think the union should encourage this? Why? (Or, why not?) ——————————————————————————————————

66. Do you know why the trade union is organized on an industry basis? ——————————————————————————————————

67. Do you know what attitude the NVV adopted towards the abandonment of the controlled wage policy? ——————————————————

68. Would you prefer a joint consultative committee or a works council in your firm—and why? —————————————————————————

69. To conclude, may I ask you a few questions about acquisitions for your household?

In your house do you have a:

vacuum cleaner —————————	car —————————————
radio set —————————————	gramophone and records ———
gas or electric stove —————	television set ————————
washing machine ———————	

70. (If not already stated.) What firm do you work with? ———————————

Appendix D. Check on the validity of the inverse correlation between participation and frustration in Chapter 5, pp. 161-4

For methodological reasons, we need to check whether the negative correlation found between 'frustration' and 'participation' is genuine or not; it is possible that the difference between participants and nonparticipants may be due to an antecedent variable that also causes the difference in levels of frustration. In that case, the correlation would be spurious.

The analysis revealed two variables, age and occupation, which might be responsible for such a relationship. A check must be made, therefore, to see whether or not the correlation holds if these variables are kept constant. In order not to have to check for each question separately, each answer to each of the six questions was rated as follows: an answer indicating frustration was graded $+1$, a neutral answer o, and an answer which indicated absence of frustration -1. By applying the formula $Xi+6/2$, a 'frustration index' was worked out for each respondent. A high frustration index means that the respondent answered the questions negatively (the question on unemployment in the affirmative), and so reveals a pronounced frustrated attitude.

The first variable against which we check is age, since the blue collar participants are older than the nonparticipants.

TABLE 25. *Age of blue collar participants*

Age*	Nonparticipants %	Participants %
up to 37	58	39
37 and over	42	61
	100% (43)	100% (43)

*Based on the question: 'When were you born?'

Age may be positively correlated with participation, since it is not unlikely that the older person, more familiar with the early stages of the labor movement as he is, takes more interest in his trade union. Or, there is the possibility that union members are more inclined to delegate the responsibility of an unpaid union post to an older colleague than to a younger one. At the same time, however, age may be inversely correlated with frustration: as people grow older, they often become more resigned and, perhaps, less aggressive; whereas youth still has high expectations and, so, stands a greater chance of being frustrated.

There is a possible connection, therefore, between age and participation and a possible connection between age and frustration. We shall investigate whether or not the relationship found between frustration and participation holds if the age variable is eliminated. This by again correlating the frustration and participation variables, but this time *within* each of the two separate age groups.

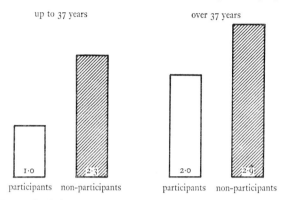

FIGURE 20. Frustration index among blue collar union members in two age groups.

Figure 20 shows that, within the categories of younger and older workers, the participants are less frustrated than the nonparticipants. In other words, the inverse correlation between participation and frustration is not affected by the fact that the nonparticipants, as a group, are younger than the participants. Indeed, the fact that Figure 20 shows: (participant/−37) < (participant/37−) and (nonparticipant/−37) < (nonparticipant/37−), suggests rather that, at the same participatory levels, the older members are more frustrated than the younger ones.

With regard to the second variable, i.e. occupation, the participants proved to belong more frequently to the skilled blue collar group, while most of the nonparticipants were semiskilled or unskilled.

TABLE 26. *Occupational level of blue collar participants*

Occupation*	Nonparticipants %	Participants %
Unskilled or semiskilled	58	42
Skilled	42	58
	100% (43)	100% (43)

* Based on the questions: 'What is your occupation?', 'Have you any particular rank?' 'In what kind of firm?' 'What education have you had?' 'Do you come under a collective contract?' 'If so, which one?' 'Do you come within any particular occupational category, work grade, job classification, etc?' 'If so, which?' 'Would you consider yourself in the skilled, semiskilled, or unskilled group?'

It has also been observed elsewhere,[1] that trade union participants are more often found among skilled workers. Although this certainly needs further study, this may result from the fact that they are more intelligent and active than their unskilled and semiskilled workmates. At the same time, one could argue that the unskilled and semiskilled workers, who are on the lowest wage and status level, will be more frustrated than the skilled, who enjoy a constantly rising income and prestige. Thus, there is a possible connection between skilled work and participation and between skilled work and frustration. It is now necessary to check whether or not the relationship between frustration and participation holds if the variable 'level of skill' is eliminated. This is done by correlating the variables frustration and participation, *within* the two occupational groups.

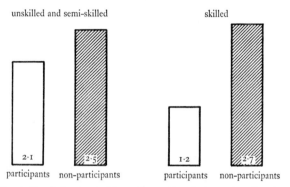

FIGURE 21. Frustration index among blue collar workers in two occupational groups.

Figure 21 shows that, in both the skilled and the semi- or unskilled categories, the participants are less frustrated than the nonparticipants. This means that the inverse correlation between frustration and participation is not affected by the fact that nonparticipants more often belong to the semiskilled or unskilled group than to the skilled. From these figures, it cannot even be assumed that unskilled workers always reveal a more frustrated attitude than skilled workers.

On the basis of this multivariate analysis, therefore, we must conclude that the inverse relationship between frustration and participation holds, and that we may speak of a genuine correlation between on the one hand integration-satisfaction and on the other hand participation in the labor organization.

[1] E. Bernstein, *Evolutionary Socialism* (Schocken, New York, 1961), p. 106.

Bibliography

Abma, E., 'De Nov en de Socioloog, verslag van een onderzoek van de Land-bouwhogeschool', *Het Schoolblad*, xv, No. 17 (May 1960).
——'Participation in Community Services', *Sociologia Ruralis*, 1 (1960).
Adorno, T. W. and M. Horkheimer, *The Authoritarian Personality* (New York, Harper & Brothers, 1950).
Agarz, V., *Landesbezirkskonferenz des DGB Bayern* (Rede) (München, 1956), in G. Triesch, *Die Macht der Funktionäre* (Düsseldorf, 1956).
Albeda, W., *De Rol van de Vakbeweging in de moderne Maatschappij* (Hoorn, Edecea, 1957).
Alg. Ned. Bouwbedrijfsbond, *Rapport Commissie Leiding en Leden* (Utrecht).
'Algemene Industrie Statistiek' (3rd Quarter, 1959), *Maandstatistiek van de Industrie*, 1, No. 12 (December 1959).
Allport, G. W., 'The Psychology of Participation', in *Readings in Group Work*, ed. D. Sullivan (New York, The Association Press, 1952).
'Angestellten', *Meyers' Neues Lexikon* (Leipzig, 1961).
'Annuaire des Statistiques du Travail', 1954, Bureau International du Travail, Genève.
Armer, Paul, 'Computer Aspects of Technological Change', in *Automation and Economic Progress*, ed. Howard R. Bowen and Garth L. Mangum (Engle-wood Cliffs, N. J., Prentice Hall, 1966).
Aron, R., 'Remarques sur les particularités de l'évolution sociale de la France', *Transactions of the Third World Congress of Sociology*, III (London, ISA, 1956).
Axelrod, M., 'Urban Structure and Social Participation', *American Sociological Review*, xxi, No. 1 (February 1956).
Bakke, E. W. *The Unemployed Man* (New York, E. P. Dutton & Co., 1934).
Banning, W., 'Desillusie of Verdieping?', *Tijd en Taak*, No. 43 (1 November 1950).
——'Non-participatie in de tegenwoordige Westerse samenleving', *Sociologisch Jaarboek*, XIII (Amsterdam, 1959).
——(Quoted by A. van Biemen) in *Samen op Weg* (Amsterdam, Arbeiderspers, 1958).
Barkin, S., 'Programming of Technical Changes and Manpower Adjustments', in *Employment Problems*, ed. J. Stieber.
Bavinck, J. G., *De Philips Koerier*, 4 October 1961.
Bear-Rose, C., 'Morale in a Trade Union', *American Journal of Sociology* (1950).
Beck, M., *Wirtschaftsdemokratie* (Zürich, Polygrafischer Verlag, 1962).
Bednarik, K., *Der junge Arbeiter von heute—ein neuer Typ* (Stuttgart, 1953).
Bendix, R., 'Social Stratification and Political Power', *American Political Science Review*, XLVI, No. 2 (June 1952).
——*Work and Authority in Industry* (New York, Harper & Row, 1963).
Benney, M., A. P. Gray, and R. H. Pear, *How People Vote : a Study of Electoral Behaviour in Greenwich* (London, Grove Press, 1956).

9

Bennis, Warren, *et al.* (eds), *Interpersonal Dynamics, Essays and Readings on Human Interaction*, rev. ed. (Homewood, Ill., The Dorsey Press, 1968).

Berelson, B. R., P. F. Lazarsfeld and W. N. McPhee, *Voting: a Study of Opinion Formation in a Presidential Campaign* (Chicago, University of Chicago Press, 1954).

Bernstein, Eduard, *Sozialistische Monatshefte* (1909).

——*Die Voraussetzungen des Sozialismus und die Aufgaben der Sozialdemokratie* (Stuttgart, 1899), translated as *Evolutionary Socialism* (London, Allen & Unwin, 1928).

Bernstein, J., 'The Growth of American Unionism 1945-1960', in *Labour History*, Vol. 2, No. 1 (1961).

Bibliographie Zur Mitbestimmung und Betriebsverfassung (Köln, Deutsches Industrie Institut, 1963).

Biemen, A. van, *Samen op Weg* (Amsterdam, Arbeiderspers, 1958).

Bjerke, Kjeld, 'Changes in Danish Income Distribution, 1939-1952', *Income and Wealth*, VI (London, 1957).

Blanpain, R., *De Syndikale Vrijheid in Belgie* (Antwerp, 1963).

Bonger, W. A., *Problemen der Demokratie, een sociologische en psychologische studie* (Amsterdam, 1936).

Braun, K., 'Cultural Activities of West European Organized Labor', *Monthly Labor Review*, LXXXVI, No. 4 (1963).

Brickman, H., 'Freedom of Association in Eight European Countries', *Monthly Labor Review*, LXXXVI, No. 9 (1963).

Briefs, G., *Das Gewerkschaftsproblem, Gestern und Heute* (Frankfurt am Main, Fritz Knapp Verlag, 1955).

Britain, an Official Handbook (London, Central Office of Information, 1964.)

British Trade Unionism, Political and Economic Planning (London, 1948).

Broeder, A. L. den, *De Ontwikkeling van het Ledental der ANMB* (report to the Dutch Metal Workers' Union, The Hague, 1961).

Brooks, G. W., 'The Security of Worker Institutions', *Monthly Labor Review*, LXXXVI, No. 6 (1963).

Broom, L., and P. Selnick, *Sociology* (Evanston, Ill., Row, Peterson, 1955).

Brown, J. A. C., *The Social Psychology of Industry* (London, Penguin Books, 1954).

Brugmans, I. J., *De arbeidende klasse in Nederland in de 19e eeuw* (The Hague, 1929).

Bruin, J. J. de, *Het Funktioneren van de Ondernemingsraden* (report) (Amsterdam, 1962).

Buckingham, W., *Automation, its Impact on Business and People* (New York, Harper & Row, 1963).

Buiter, J. H., C. Poppe, and H. Wallenburg, 'Lager Vakbondskader als Communicatieschakel', *Socialisme en Demokratie* (January 1962).

Burnham, J., *The Managerial Revolution* (London, Penguin Books, 1954).

Burns, Robert K., 'The Comparative Economic Position of Manual and White Collar Employees', *Journal of Business*, XXVII (October 1954).

Burtt, E. J., Jr., *Labor Markets, Unions, and Government Policies* (New York, St Martin's Press, 1963).

Caplow, T., *The Sociology of Work* (Minneapolis, University of Minnesota Press, 1954).

Carr, E. H., *Conditions of Peace* (London, 1942).

Cartter, A. M., *Theory of Wages and Employment* (Homewood, Ill., Irwin, Inc., 1959).

Cartwright, Dorwin, 'Influence, Leadership, Control,' in *Handbook of Organizations*, ed. J. G. March (Chicago, Rand McNally, 1965).

'Census of England and Wales', 1951.

Het Centrum, 19 January 1957.

Chamberlain, Neil W., 'Collective Bargaining in the United States', in *Contemporary Collective Bargaining in Seven Countries*, ed., Adolf Sturmthal (New York State School of Industrial and Labor Relations, Cornell University, Ithaca, N.Y., 1957).

Chamberlain, W., *Industrial Relations in Germany, 1914–1939* (Stanford, Stanford University Press, 1942).

Christmann, A., 'Mitbestimmung und sozialer Konflikt, löst die Mitbestimmung die sozialen Gegensätze?' in *Das Mitbestimmungsgespräch*, 9 Jahrgang, Nos. 5/63 and 6/63.

——and O. Kunze, *Wirtschaftliche Mitbestimmung im Meinungsstreit* (Koln, Bund-Verlag, 1964).

Churchill, Sir W. S., 'Trade Unions in a Changing World', *The Political Quarterly*, xxvii, No. 1 (1956).

Clague, E., and L. Greenberg, 'Employment', *Automation and Technological Change*, ed. J. T. Dunlop (Englewood Cliffs, N. J., Prentice-Hall, 1965).

Cole, G. D. H., *Self Government in Industry* (London, 1919).

Collaboration between Public Authorities and Employers' and Workers' Organizations at the Industrial and National Levels (Geneva, ILO, 1958).

Collinet, M., *Essai sur la condition ouvrière* (Paris, 1951).

Cook, Alice H. and Agnes M. Douty, *Labor Education Outside the Unions, a Review of Postwar Programs in Western Europe and the United States* (School of Industrial and Labor Relations, Cornell University, Ithaca, N.Y., 1958).

Croner, F., *Die Angestellten in der Gesellschaft* (Frankfurt am Main, Humboldt Verlag, 1954).

Crossland, C. A. R., 'De socialistische partijen en de toekomst', *Socialisme en Democratie* (11 November 1959).

Crossman, R. H. S., 'Towards a Philosophy of Socialism', *New Fabian Essays* (London, Turnstile Press, 1953).

Cushman, Edward L., 'Management Objectives in Collective Bargaining', in Arnold R. Weber, *The Structure of Collective Bargaining* Glencoe, Ill., The Free Press, 1961).

Cyriax, C. and R. Oakeshot, *The Bargainers, A Survey of Modern British Trade Unionism* (New York, Praeger, 1961).

Dahl, R. A., 'Hierarchy, Democracy and Bargaining in Politics and Economics', *Research Frontiers in Politics and Government* (Washington, D. C., Brooking Institution, 1955).

——and C. E. Lindblom, *Politics, Economics and Welfare : Planning and Politico-economic Systems resolved into basic social Processes* (New York, Harper & Brothers, 1953).

Dahrendorf, R., *Class and Class Conflict in Industrial Society* (Stanford, Stanford University Press, 1959).
——*Das Mitbestimmungsproblem in der deutschen Sozialforschung, Eine Kritik* (Tübingen, 1956).
Daudt, H., 'Wij varen niet zo wel als U denkt', *Ariadne*, No. 11 (20 October 1961).
David, Marcel, 'Le Monde Ouvrier', in Georges Vedel, ed., *La Dépolitisation, Mythe ou Realité?* (Paris, Libr. Armand Collin, 1962).
Dean, L. R., 'Social Integration, Attitudes and Union Activity', *Industrial and Labor Relations Review*, VII (1954).
Deleon, A., *The Yugoslav Worker* (Belgrade, 1962).
Derber, M., 'The Idea of Industrial Democracy in America, 1898–1915' *Labor History*, No. 3 (Fall, 1966).
——W. E. Chalmers, and M. T. Edelman, *Plant Union–Management Relations: from Practice to Theory* (Urbana, Ill., Institute of Labor and Industrial Relations, 1965).
——'Union Participation in Plant Decision-Making', *Industrial and Labor Relations Review*, XV.
DGB Auslandsdienst, No. XII (November 1956).
Directory of National and International Labor Unions in the United States, 1961, Bulletin No. 1320 (Washington, D.C., U.S. Dept. of Labor, Bureau of Labor Statistics, 1962).
Dodge, R. W., 'Some Aspects of the Political Behavior of Labor Union-Members in the Detroit Metropolitan Area' (mimeograph).
Dollard, J., *Frustration and Aggression* (London, Routledge & Kegan Paul, 1944).
Doorn, J. A. A. van, *De Proletarische Achterhoede* (Meppel. Boom, 1954).
Drucker, P. F., *The Concept of a Corporation* (New York, Mentor, 1964).
——'The Employee Society', *American Journal of Sociology*, LVIII (1953).
——'Labor in Industrial Society', *The Annals of the American Academy of Political and Social Science*, Vol. 274 (March 1951).
——*The New Society* (New York, Harper & Bros., 1950).
Dubin, R., 'Behavioral Science Analysis and Collective Bargaining Research', *Proceedings of the 1965 IRRA Spring Meeting* (Buffalo, New York, 3–4 May 1965).
Dudra, M., 'Approaches to Union Security in Switzerland, Canada and Colombia', *Monthly Labor Review*, LXXXVI, No. 2 (1963).
Dunlop, J. T., 'The Social Utility of Collective Bargaining', in *Challenges to Collective Bargaining*, ed. L. Ulman.
——*Wage Determination under Trade Unions* (New York, Augustus M. Kelley, Inc., 1950).
Duverger, M., *Les Partis Politiques* (Paris, 1951).
Eckstein, Otto, 'Perspectives on Employment under Technological Change', in *Employment Problems*, ed. J. Stieber.
Eeden, Constance van, and J. Hemelryk, 'A test for the equality of probabilities against a class of specified alternative hypotheses, including trend', *Proc. Kon. Ned. Akad. v. wetenschappen*, A 58, Indag Math. 17, 191, and 301 (1955).

'Einkommen und Verbrauch in nordrhein-westfälischen Haushalten 1950–1959', *Beiträge zur Statistik des Landes Nordrhein-Westfalen*, No. 135 (Düsseldorf, 1961).

Ellis, T. L., 'Cooperation Provisions in Major Agreements', *Monthly Labor Review*, LXXXIX, No. 3 (1966).

Engelfriet, J., *Algemeen Handelsblad*, 'Bank en Verzekeringswezen' edition, 19 January 1960.

Engle, Earl L., 'Coordinated Bargaining, A Snare—and a Delusion', *Proceedings of the 1968 Annual Spring Meeting of the Industrial Relations Research Association* (Columbus, Ohio, 1968).

Etzioni, A., *Modern Organizations* (Englewood Cliffs, N. J., Prentice Hall, 1964).

Festinger, L., 'Informal Social Communication', in L. D. Cartwright and A. Zander, *Group Dynamics* (Evanston, Ill., Row, Peterson, 1960).

Festinger, L. A., *A Theory of Cognitive Dissonance* (Evanston, Ill., Row, Peterson, 1957).

Fitzwilliams, Jeanette, M., 'Size Distribution of Income in 1963', *Survey of Current Business*, April 1964.

Foote, N. N., 'The Movement from Jobs to Careers', *Transactions of the Third World Congress of Sociology* (Amsterdam, I.S.A., 1956.)

——'The Professionalization of Labour in Detroit', *American Journal of Sociology*, LVIII, No. 4 (January 1953).

Fourastié, J., *Le Grand Espoir du XXe Siècle*.

——*Machinisme et Bien-Etre* (Paris, Ed. du Minuit, 1951).

Fourier, C., *Le Nouveau Monde Industriel et Sociétaire* (Paris, 1929).

Freedom and Welfare, Social Patterns in the Northern Countries of Europe, ed. G. R. Nelson (Copenhagen, 1953).

Friedmann, G., 'The Social Consequences of Technical Progress', *International Social Science Bulletin*, IV, No. 2 (1952).

Friis, H., 'The application of sociology to social welfare planning and administration', *Transactions of the Fourth World Congress of Sociology* (Milan-Stresa), II (London, International Sociological Association, 1959).

Fromm, E., 'Zum Gefühl der Ohnmacht', *Zeitschrift für Sozialforschung*, VI (1937).

Fürst, G. *et al.*, 'Zur Frage der Einkommensschichtung', *Wirtschaft und Statistik*, No. 6 (1954).

Furtwängler, F. J., *Die Gewerkschaften, ihre Geschichte und Internationale Auswirkung* (Hamburg, Rowohlt, 1956).

Gadourek, I., *A Dutch Community* (Leiden, 1956).

Galan, C. de, *De Invloed van de Vakbeweging op de Loonshoogte en Werkgelegenheid* (Leiden, Stenfert Kroese, 1957).

Galbraith, J. K., *The Affluent Society* (New York, Mentor Books, 1958).

——*Economics and the Art of Controversy* (Boston, Beacon Press, 1965).

Gallagher, 'Voluntary Associations in France', *Social Forces*, XXXVI, No. 2 (December 1957).

Garbarino, T. W., 'The Unemployed Worker during a Period of Full Employment', in *A Source-book on Unemployment Insurance in California*.

Gee, W., *Social Science Research Methods* (New York, Macmillan, 1950).

Gesetzbuch der Arbeit (Berlin, Staatsverlag der Deutschen Demokratischen Republik, 1963).

Gillin, John, 'Personality Formation from the Comparative Cultural Point of View', *Personality in Nature, Society and Culture*, ed. C. Kluckholn and H. A. Murray (New York, A. A. Knopf, 1949).

Gleitze, B., *Wirtschafts- und Sozialstatistisches Handbuch* (Köln, 1960).

Golden, C. S. and J. J. Ruttenberg, *The Dynamics of Industrial Democracy* (New York, Harper & Brothers, 1942).

Goldsmith, S., G. Jaszi, K. Kaitz and M. Liebenberg, 'Size Distribution of Income since the Midthirties', *Review of Economics and Statistics*, XXXVI, No. 1 (1954).

Goldstein, J., *The Government of British Trade Unions* (London, 1952).

Göseke, G., *Verteilung und Schichtung der Einkommen der privaten Haushalte in der Bundesrepublik 1955 bis 1959* (Berlin, Duncker & Humblot, 1963).

Gottlieb, S. B., 'The Union Intellectual in the Labor Movement' (Panel Remarks, *IRRA Convention*, Boston, Massachusetts, December 1963).

Gouldner, A. W., *Wildcat Strike* (New York, Harper Torchbooks, 1965).

Goudsblom, J., *De nieuwe volwassenen, een enquête onder jongeren van 18 tot 30 jaar* (Amsterdam, 1959).

Grant, A., *Socialism and the Middle Classes* (London, Lawrence & Wishart, Ltd., 1958).

Groenman, S., *Correspondentieblad der Centrale van Hogere Rijksambtenaren*, No. 346.

——*Kanttekeningen bij de voortgang van het sociale onderzoek in Nederland* (Meppel, 1948).

Haber, William, Louis A. Ferman and James R. Hudson, *The Impact of Technological Change, the American Experiment* (Kalamazoo, Mich., Upjohn Institute for Employment Research, 1963).

Hamelet, M. P., 'Le syndicalisme au carrefour', *Le Figaro* (August-September 1958).

Het Handelsblad, 9 May 1956.

Harle, R., 'The Role of Trade Unions in Raising Productivity', *The Political Quarterly*, XXVII, No. 1.

Harris, H., 'Why Labor Lost the Intellectuals', *Harper's Magazine* (June, 1964).

Haveman, J., *De ongeschoolde Arbeider* (Assen, van Gorcum, 1952).

Heek, F. van, 'Klassen en Standenstructuur als Sociologische Begrippen' (Speech given in Leiden, 1948).

Heneman, H. G., Jr. and Dale Yoder, *Labor Economics* (Cincinatti, South-Western Publishing Co., 1965).

Herold, L. J. M., 'Psychologische Beschouwingen over de Wet op de Ondernemingsraden', *Mens en Onderneming*, IV (1950).

Heyde, L., 'Der Arbeitskampf', in *Handwörterbuch der Sozialwissenschaften*.

Hildebrand, George H., 'Coordinated Bargaining, An Economist's Point of View', *Proceedings of the 1968 Annual Spring Meeting of the Industrial Relations Research Association* (Columbus, Ohio, 1968).

Hildebrand, George H., 'Some Alternative Views of the Unemployment Problem in the United States', in *Employment Problems of Automation and Advanced Technology*, ed. Jack Stieber (New York, St Martin's Press, 1966).

Hirsch-Weber, W., *Gewerkschaften in der Politik, von der Massenstreikdebatte zum Kampf um das Mitbestimmungsrecht* (Cologne, Westdeutscher Verlag, 1959).

Hofstee, E. W., 'Changes in Rural Stratification in the Netherlands', *Transactions of the Second Congress of Sociology* (London, ISA, 1956).

Holst-van der Schalk, H. Roland, *Revolutionnaire Massa Aktie* (Rotterdam, 1918).

Holter, H., 'Disputes and Tensions in Industry', *Scandinavian Democracy*, ed. J. A. Lauwerijs (Copenhagen, 1956).

Homans, G., *The Human Group* (London, Routledge and Kegan Paul, 1951).

Horney, K., *The Neurotic Personality of our Time* (New York, W. W. Norton & Co., 1937).

Hudig, J. D., *De vakbeweging in Nederland 1866–1878* (Amsterdam, 1904).

Hughes, E. J., *The Ordeal of Power* (New York, Dell, 1963).

Hyman, Herbert H., *Political Socialization: A Study in the Psychology of Political Behavior* (Glencoe, Ill., Free Press, 1959).

——'The Value System of different Classes, a Social Psychological Contribution to the Analysis of Stratification', in *Class, Status and Power*, ed. Reinhardt Bendix and Seymour Lipset (Glencoe, Ill., Free Press, 1953).

ICFTU, *Workers' Participation in Industry* (study guide) (Brussels, August 1954).

ILO, *Consultation and Cooperation between Employers and Workers at the Level of the Enterprise* ('Labour-Management Series', No. 13) (Geneva, 1962).

Ijzerman, A. W. 'De groei van de nieuwe middenstand', *De Socialistische Gids* (1934)

Incomes in Postwar Europe: A Study of Policies, Growth and Distribution, prepared by the Secretariat of the Economic Commission for Europe (Geneva, 1967).

Industrial and Occupational Manpower Requirement, 1964–75, Bureau of Labor Statistics, U.S. Dept. of Labor.

De Informatiefunctie van de Ondernemingsraad (report), (Antwerp, Centrale voor Productivitetsbevordering, 1964.

International Yearbook of Labor Statistics, 1960.

Jansen, G. K., in *Over en Weer*, 1955.

Jenkins, Howard, Jr., 'Trade Union Elections', in *Regulating Union Government*, ed. Marten S. Estey, Philip Taft and Martin Wagner (New York, Harper & Row, 1964).

Joint Consultation in British Industry (London, National Institute of Industrial Psychology, 1952).

'Joint Consultation Devices in Collective Bargaining', *Monthly Labor Review*, LXXXVIII, No. 2 (1965).

Jong, F. de, *Om de Plaats van de Arbeid*.

Kahn, R. L. and C. F. Cannell, *The Dynamics of Interviewing:* Theory, Techniques and Cases (New York, Wiley, 1957).

Kairat, H., 'Die Soziale Rolle des Arbeitsdirektors', *Soziale Welt*, No. 1 (1966).

Kaiser, J. N., *Die Repräsentation organisierter Interessen* (Berlin, 1956).
Kassalow, E. M., 'New Union Frontier: White Collar Workers', *Harvard Business Review*, XL, No. 1 (January-February, 1962).
——'White Collar Unionism in the United States' (mimeographed 1962).
Katona, G., *The Powerful Consumer* (New York, McGraw-Hill, 1961).
Katz, E., 'The Two-Step-Flow of Communication: an Up-to-Date Report on Hypothesis', *Public Opinion Quarterly*, XXI, No. 1 (Spring 1957).
——and P. F. Lazarsfeld, *Personal Influence, the Part Played by People in the Flow of Mass Communications* (Glencoe, Ill., Free Press, 1955).
Kautsky, K., *Die proletarische Revolution und ihr Program* (Berlin, 1922).
Kavčič, S., *Self-Government in Yugoslavia* (Beograd, 1961).
Kelley, Stanley, Jr., *Professional Public Relations and Political Power* (Baltimore, Johns Hopkins Press, 1966).
Kerr, Clark, *Labor and Management in Industrial Society* (New York, Doubleday-Anchor Books, 1964).
Kerr, Clark, 'Productivity and Labor Relations', in *Labor and Management in Industrial Society* (New York, Doubleday-Anchor Books, 1964).
——J. T. Dunlop, F. Harbison, and C. A. Myers, *Industrialism and Industrial Man* (New York, Oxford University Press, 1964).
Killingworth, Charles K., 'Structural Unemployment in the United States', in *Employment Problems of Automation and Advanced Technology*, ed. Jack Stieber (New York, St Martin's Press, 1966).
Klages, H., *Der Nachbarschaftsgedanke und die nachbarliche Wirklichkeit in der Grosstadt* (report) (Cologne, 1958).
Klenner, F., *Die Oesterreichischen Gewerkschaften, Vergangenheit und Gegenwartprobleme*, III (Vienna, 1953).
Kloos, A. H., *De Metalkoerier*, No. 19 (23 September, 1961).
Kluth, H., in H. Schelsky, *Arbeiterjugend, gestern und heute* (Heidelberg, 1955).
Knowles, K. H. G. C., 'Strike-proneness and its Determinants', *American Journal of Sociology*, 1954.
König, R., *Soziologie Heute* (Zürich, 1949).
Koning, J. de. *De lezers van Het Metaalbedrijf* (Utrecht, Sociological Institute of the Federation of Protestant Unions, 1957).
Kornhauser, W., *Scientists in Industry: Conflict and Accommodation* (Berkeley, University of California Press, 1962).
Kravis, Irving B., *The Structure of Income* (University of Pennsylvania, 1962).
Krech, D. and R. S. Crutchfield, *Social Psychology, Theory and Problems* (New York, McGraw-Hill, 1948).
——*Theory and Problems of Social Psychology* (New York, McGraw-Hill, 1948).
Kruijt, J. P., 'Arbeiders en nieuwe middenstand' (Amsterdam, De Arbeiderspers, 1947).
Kuiper, G., 'Terreinverkenning voor het sociografisch onderzoek naar de sociale afstand tussen leiding en leden' (speech given in Amsterdam, 1954).
Kuylaars, A. M., 'Medezeggenschap in de Onderneming', in *Mens en Onderneming*, IV (1950).

Kuznets, S., 'Economic Growth and Income Inequality', *American Economic Review*, XLV, No. 1 (1955).
——'Income Distribution and Changes in Consumption', *The Changing American Population*, ed. H. S. Simpson (New York, Arden House Conference, 1962).
——'Quantitative Aspects of the Economic Growths of Nations', *Economic Development and Cultural Change*, XI, No. 2 (1963).
Lammers, C., *De Vakbeweging en haar problemen* (Amsterdam, Arbeiderspers, 1951).
Lane, R. E., *Political Life: Why People Get Involved in Politics* (Glencoe, Ill., Free Press, 1959).
Laserre, G., *Les Expériences Françaises de Participation des Travailleurs* (report) (Vienna, 1958).
——'Le Fonctionnement de la démocratie coöpérative', *Revue des études coöpératives*, XXIX (April-June 1957).
Laski, H. J., 'The Pluralistic State', in *The Foundation of Sovereignty and Other Essays* (New York, Harcourt, Brace and Company, 1921).
——*Trade Unions in the New Society* (New York, Viking Press, 1949).
Lasser, David, 'Coordinated Bargaining, a Union Point of View', *Proceedings of the 1968 Annual Spring Meeting of the Industrial Relations Research Association* (Columbus, Ohio, 1968).
Lauterbach, A., *Man, Motives and Money: Psychological Frontiers of Economics* (Ithaca, New York, Cornell University Press, 1954).
Lazarsfeld, P. F., 'Methodological Problems in Empirical Social Research', *Transactions of the Fourth World Congress of Sociology*, II.
——,B. Berelson and H. Gaudet, *The People's Choice: How the Voter Makes up His Mind in a Presidential Campaign* (New York, Columbia University Press, 1955).
——and M. Rosenberg, *The Language of Social Research* (Glencoe, Ill., The Free Press, 1955).
Lefranc, G., *Les expériences syndicales en France de 1939 à 1950* (Paris, 1950).
Leger, C., *La Démocratie Industrielle et les Comités d'Entreprise en Suède* (Paris, Librarie Armand Collin, 1950).
Leibbrand, J. G., unpublished report of a survey of Luxembourg trade unionism (1957).
Leon, D. van, in a letter to the Dutch Federation of Trade Unions (NVV), 6 July 1960.
Lering en Leiding, XXVII, Nos. 8, 9, 10.
Lester, R. A., *As Unions Mature* (Princeton, N.J., Princeton University Press, 1958).
Lindsay, A. D., *The Modern Democratic State*, I (London, Oxford University Press, 1947).
Linton, R., *The Study of Man* (New York, 1936).
Lipset, S. M., and J. Gordon, 'Mobility and Trade Union Membership', in *Class, Status and Power: A Reader in Social Stratification*, ed. R. Bendix and S. M. Lipset (Glencoe, Ill., Free Press, 1953).

Lipset, S. M., M. A. Trow and J. S. Coleman, *Union Democracy: the Internal Politics of the International Typographical Union* (Glencoe, Ill., Free Press, 1956).

Lockwood, D., 'The New Working Class', *Archives Européennes de Sociologie*, No. 2 (1960).

Lohmar, D., in H. Schelsky, *Arbeiterjugend, gestern und heute* (Heidelberg, 1955).

McCarthy, W. E. J., *The Closed Shop in Britain* (Berkeley, University of California Press, 1964).

MacDonald, D. F., *The State and the Trade Unions* (London, Macmillan, 1960).

McKee, J. B., 'Status and Power in the Industrial Community: A Comment on Drucker's thesis', *American Journal of Sociology*, LXI, No. 6 (1956).

McKenzie, R. T. and A. Silver, 'Conservatism, Industrialism and the Working Class Tory in England' (Paper presented at the Fifth World Congress of the International Sociological Association, Washington, D.C., 3 September 1962).

McMurry, R. N., 'The Case for Benevolent Autocracy', in *Human Relations in Management*, ed. I. L. Heckman, Jr., and S. G. Huneryager (Chicago, South-Western Publishing Co., 1960).

McNair, Malcolm P., 'Thinking Ahead: What Price Human Relations?' *Harvard Business Review*, XXV, No. 2 (March-April 1957).

Mallet, S., *La Nouvelle Classe Ouvrière* (Paris, Editions du Seuil, 1963).

Man, H. de, *The Psychology of Socialism* (London, Allen & Unwin, 1928).

Mannheim, K., *Man and Society in an Age of Reconstruction* (London, Routledge & Kegan Paul, Ltd., 1940).

Manpower Report of the President, U.S. Dept. of Labor, Washington, D.C., transmitted to the Congress, April 1967.

March, J. G. and H. A. Simon, *Organizations* (New York, Wiley, 1959).

Marenco, C., 'Psycho-sociological incidences of office work rationalization on employee status', *Trade Union Information*, no. 35 (Organization for Economic Cooperation and Development).

Marx, C. H. and E. H. de Waal, *De Toekomst van de Ondernemingsraad* (Alphen a/d Rijn, Samson NV, 1960).

Marx, Karl, *Capital*, ed. F. Engels, 2nd impression (Moscow, Foreign Languages Publishing House, 1962).

——*The Communist Manifesto* (Chicago, Henry Regnery Company, 1965).

——*Economic and Philosophic Manuscripts of 1844* (Moscow, Foreign Languages Publishing House, n.d.).

Mausolff, A., *Gewerkschaft und Betriebsrat im Urteil der Arbeitnehmer* (Darmstadt, 1952).

Meadows, Martin, 'A Managerial Theory of Unionism', in *The American Journal of Economics and Sociology*, XXV (1966).

Melman, S., 'The Rise of Administrative Overhead in the Manufacturing Industries of the United States, 1899–1947', *Oxford Economic Papers*, III (1951).

Merton, R., M. Fiske, and P. L. Kendall, *The Focused Interview: a Manual of Problems and Procedures* (Glencoe, Ill., Free Press, 1956).

Merton, R. K., 'The Social Psychology of Housing', in *Current Trends in Social Psychology*, ed. W. Dennis (Pittsburgh, Penna., University of Pittsburgh Press, 1948).

——*Social Theory and Social Structure*, revised and enlarged edition (Glencoe, Ill., Free Press, 1957).

——and A. S. Kitt, 'Contribution to the theory of reference group behavior'. *Continuities in Social Research* (Glencoe, Ill., Free Press, 1950).

Metzger, B. L., *Profit Sharing in Perspective* (Evanston, Ill., Profit Sharing Research Foundation, 1964).

Michels, R., *Zur Soziologie des Parteiwesens in der moderne Demokratie* (Leipzig, 1911).

Mikardo, I., 'Trade Unions in a Full-employment Economy', *New Fabian Essays*, ed. R. H. S. Crossman (London, F. A. Praeger, 1953).

Miller, D. C. and W. H. Form, *Industrial Sociology* (New York, Harper & Row, 1964).

Miller, G. W. and J. E. Young, 'Member-Participation in the Trade Union Local: A Study of Activity and Policymaking in Columbus, Ohio', *American Journal of Economics and Sociology*, xv, No. 1 (October, 1955).

Miller, H. P., *Income of the American People* (New York, John Wiley & Sons, 1955).

——*Income Distribution in the United States*, U.S. Dept. of Commerce, Washington, D.C., 1960.

——*Rich Man, Poor Man* (New York, Crowell, 1964).

Miller, Michael H., 'The Approach to the Adjudication of Grievances as a Selective Indicator of Steward Future Job Orientation' (unpublished term paper, based upon research among shop stewards in the Buffalo areas, 1967).

Miller, S. M. and F. Riessman, 'The Working Class Subculture: A New View', in A. B. Shostak and W. Gombers, *Blue-Collar World* (Englewood Cliffs, N. J., Prentice-Hall, 1964).

Mills, C. W., *White Collar: the American Middle Classes* (New York, Oxford University Press, 1951).

Moderne jeugd op weg naar volwassenheid (The Hague, Staatsuitg., 1953).

Morgan, T. B., 'Is Labor on the Skids?' *Look* (11 September 1962).

Mulder, M., *Group Structure, Motivation and Group Performance* (The Hague, Mouton 1963).

Murdoch, I., *Conviction* (London, MacGibbon & Kee, 1958).

Murphy, G., 'The Internalization of Social Control', in *Freedom and Control in Modern Society*, ed. M. Berger, T. Abel, and C. H. Page (New York, Van Nostrand, 1954).

——*Personality, a Bio-Social Approach to Origins and Structure* (New York, Harper & Brothers, 1947).

Myrdal, G., *Beyond the Welfare State, Economic Planning in the Welfare States and its International Implications* ('Store Lectures') (New Haven, Conn., Yale University Press, 1958).

Nader, R., 'Profits versus Engineering, the Corvair Story', *The Nation*, Vol. 201, No. 14 (November, 1965).

Naess, A., *Democracy, Ideology and Objectivity* (Oslo, 1956).

Neary, H. J., 'American Trade Union Membership in 1962', *Monthly Labor Review* (May 1964).

Nelson, G. R. (ed.), *Freedom and Welfare, Social Patterns in the Northern Countries of Europe* (Copenhagen, 1953).

Neufeld, M., 'The Historical Relationship of Liberals and Intellectuals to Organized Labor in the United States', *Annals of the American Academy of Political and Social Science*, 350 (November 1963).

Nuttin, J., *Psycho-analyse en de spiritualistische opvatting van de mens* (Utrecht, 1949).

——'De dynamische strustuur der persoonlijkheid en de psychoanalyse', *Ned. Tijdschrift v.d. Psychologie en haar Grensgebieden*, N.S.P. IV (1949).

'Omvang en samenstelling van de Nederlandse beroepsbevolking' (31 October 1959), *Maandschrift van het CBS* (Zeist, De Haan, 1961).

Omvang der Vakbeweging, CBS, 1967.

Omvang der vakbewging in Nederland op 1 January 1961 (CBS) (Zeist, 1962).

'Onrust in Denemarken', *Nieuwe Rotterdamsche Courant* (26 April 1956).

Ornati, Oscar, 'Fewer Strikes, Smaller Wage Hikes', *Challenge*, November 1960.

Osch, A. J. M. van, *Tijdstudie over de werkzaamheden van de Districtsbestuurders van de Nederlandse katholike Metaalbewerkersbond St Eloy* (stencil) (Utrecht, 1960).

Ostergaard, G. N. and A. H. Halsey, 'Democracy in British Retail Cooperatives', *Archives Internationales de Sociologie de la Coopération*, I (1957).

Parsons, T., 'The Social Structure of the Family', in *The Family, Its Function and Destiny*, ed. R. N. Anshen (New York, Harper & Brothers, 1959).

Pen, J., De Grenzen van de Welvaarsstaat', *Sociologische Gids.*, X, No. 2 (1963).

——'The Strange Adventures of Dutch Wage Policy', *British Journal of Industrial Relations*, I, No. 3 (1963).

Philip, A., 'La Pensée Politique des Partis Ouvriers', *Les nouveaux comportements politiques de la classe ouvrière*, under the direction of L. Hamon (Paris, Presses Universitaires de France, 1962).

Plaats en Taak van de Bestuurdersbonden (Amsterdam, NVV, n.d.).

Plant, C. T., 'Some sociological problems raised by the introduction of electronic computers in offices', *Trade Union Information*, No. 35.

Polak, F. L., 'Gedachten over het Socialisme van de toekomst', Socialisme en Demokratie (1959), No. 9 and No. 10.

Popitz, H., H. P. Bahrdt, A. E. Jüres, and H. Kesting, *Das Gesellschaftsbild des Arbeiters* (Tübingen, 1957).

Poppe, S., *Conceptrapport over het bij onze enquête naar het ledenverloop verzamelde materiaal* (The Hague, ANMB).

Le Populaire Dimanche (17 June 1951).

Potthoff, E., 'Zur Geschichte der Mitbestimmung', in E. Potthoff, O. Blume, and H. Duvernell, *Zwischenbilanz der Mitbestimmung* (Tübingen, 1962).

'Poverty and Deprivation in the U.S.', *Conference on Economic Progress, Washington, D.C., April, 1962*.

Price, J., *Functions of Trade Unionism in Relation to Welfare Policy* (The Hague, Van Keulen, 1958).

'The Profits Explosion and Inflation', *AFL-CIO American Federationist*, LXXIII, No. 9 (1966).

Purcell, T. V., *The Worker Speaks his Mind on Company and Union* (Cambridge, Mass., Harvard University Press, 1953).

Putten, W. M. van, *De Menselijke Achtergronden van de Ondernemingsraad* Bussum, 1955).

De Ramp (Amsterdam, 1953).

Rapport van de Commissie ter bestudering van het vraagstuk van het verplichte lidmaatschap van de financiele lasten van de vakbeweging, 8 February 1949.

Rapport van de Commissie Ondernemingsraden van het NVV (Amsterdam, n.d.).

Rapport naar de oorzaken, de achtergronden en het verloop van de staking van het Amsterdamse gemeentepersoneel, maart-april 1955 (Amsterdam, Committee of the Dutch Labor Party, 1955).

Raskin, A. H., 'Collective Bargaining and the Public Interest', in *Challenges to Collective Bargaining*, ed. L. Ulman.

——'The Obsolescent Unions', in *Industrial and Labor Relations*, ed. A. Fraser Isbester (Boston, Mass., D. C. Heath and Company, 1967).

Reder, M. W., *Labor in a Growing Economy* (New York, John Wiley & Sons, 1957).

Rees, A., *The Economics of Trade Unions* (Chicago, University of Chicago Press, 1963).

Reuther, Walter P., Congressional Testimony, in *Automation, Implications for the Future*, ed. Morris Philipson (New York, Random House, Vintage Books, 1962).

——*Report of President Walter P. Reuther to the 19th UAW Constitutional Convention, Part Two: Economic Conditions* (Atlantic City, N.J., 20–7 March, 1964).

——*Selected Papers*, ed. H. M. Christman (New York, Pyramid Books, 1964).

Reynolds, L. G. and G. H. Taft, *The Evolution of Wage Structure* (New Haven, Conn., Yale University Press, 1956).

Richtlinien für die Vertrauenskörper in der Industriegewerkschaft Metall für die Bundesrepublik Deutschland (Frankfurt am Main, 1958).

Riesel, Victor, 'Reuther Held Aiming for Seats on Firm Boards', *Courier Express* (Buffalo, 13 September 1967).

Roberts, B. C., *Unions in America, a British View*, Industrial Relations Section, Princeton University, Research Series No. 97 (Princeton, N.J., 1959).

Robertson, D. J., *The Economics of Wages and the Distribution of Income* (London, Macmillan & Co, 1961).

Robson-Brown, W. and N. A. Howell-Everson, *Industrial Democracy at Work, A Factual Survey* (London, Pitman, 1950).

Rogers, C. R., 'The Non-directive method as a technique for social research', *American Journal of Sociology*, Vol. LI.

Ross, A. M. and P. T. Hartman, *Changing Patterns of Industrial Conflict* (New York, John Wiley & Sons, 1960).

Ruitenberg, L. H., 'De Klassieke Jeudgbeweging', *Wending*, XI (1956–7).

Rümke, H. C., *De levenstijdperken van de man* (Amsterdam, 1950).

Runciman, W. G., 'The Working Class Conservatives', *Relative Deprivation and Social Justice* (London, Routledge & Kegan Paul, 1966).

Russell, B., 'Pitfalls in Socialism', *Political Ideals* (London, Allen & Unwin, 1963).

Ruygers, G., 'Socialistische Bezinning', *De Grondslagen van het Socialisme*, ed. Dr Wiardi Beckman Stichting, Research Bureau, Dutch Socialist Party (Amsterdam, Arbeiderspers, 1947).

Samuel, R., 'Lipset's Nightmare', *The New Statesman*, LX, No. 1553 (1960).

Sanford, F. H., 'Public Orientation to Roosevelt', *Public Opinion Quarterly*, XV, No. 2 (1951).

Saxena, S. K., *Nationalization and Industrial Conflict, the Example of British Coal Mining* (The Hague, Nijhoff, 1951).

Sayles, L. R., and J. E. Young, 'Member-Participation in the Trade Union Local: A Study of Activity and Policymaking in Columbus, Ohio', *American Journal of Economics and Sociology*, XV, No. 1 (October 1955).

Schelsky, H., *Arbeiterjugend, gestern und heute* (Heidelberg, 1955).

——*Die skeptische Generation* (Düsseldorf, 1958).

——*Wandlungen der Deutschen Familie in der Gegenwart*, quoted in J. Idenburg, *Op het keerpunt der onderwijsgeschiedenis* (Groningen, Wolters, 1957).

'Die Schichtung der privaten Haushalts-einkommen in der Bundesrepublik', *Wochenbericht des deutschen Institut für Wirtschaftforschung* (Berlin, 11 May 1962) XXIX, No. 19.

Scott, J. C., 'Membership and Participation in Voluntary Associations', *American Sociological Review*, XXI, No. 1 (February 1956).

Scott, W. G., *The Management of Conflict* (Homewood, Ill., Richard Irwin, Inc., and Dorsey Press, 1965).

Seidman, J., J. London, and B. Karsh, 'Political Consciousness in a Local Union', *Public Opinion Quarterly*, XV, No. 4 (1951).

Shanks, M., *The Stagnant Society* (London, 1961).

Shaw, M. M., 'A Comparison of Individuals and Small Groups in the Rational Solution of Complex Problems', in *Readings in Social Psychology*, ed. Maccobby, Newcomb and Harley (New York, Holt, 1958).

Sherif, Muzafer, and Hadley Cantril, *The Psychology of Ego-Involvements* (New York, John Wiley & Sons, 1947).

Shore, P., 'In the Room at the Top', in *Conviction*, ed. N. Mackenzie (London, Monthly Review Press, 1958).

Siegel, A. F., 'The Extended Meaning and Diminished Relevance of "Job Conscious" Unionism', *Proceedings of the 18th Annual Meeting of the Industrial Relations Research Association*, ed. Gerlald Somers (Madison, 1966).

Siegel, S., *Nonparametric Statistics for the Behavioral Sciences* (New York, McGraw-Hill, 1956).

Silberman, C. E., *The Myths of Automation* (New York, Harper & Row, 1966).

Sills, D., *The Volunteers: Means and Ends in a National Organization* (Glencoe, Ill., Free Press, 1957).

Simkin, William E., 'Refusals to Ratify Contracts', address at the Graduate School of Business, University of Chicago, 17 November, 1967.

Smits, P., *Kerk en Stad* (The Hague, 1952).

Solomon, B., 'The Growth of the White Collar Work Force', *Journal of Business*, XXVII, No. 4 (October 1954).

Spinelli, A., 'Le Socialisme, idée et Mouvement', *Preuves*, No. 106 (December 1959).

Spinrad, W., 'Correlations of Trade Union Participation', *American Sociological Review*, xxv, No. 1 (February 1960).

Starr, E. H., 'Promethean Constellations', *Psychological Clinic*, xxii (1933).

Statistical Abstracts of the United States: 1960.

'Statistisch Zakboek' (Den Haag, Staatsuitgeverij, 1966).

Statistisch Zakboekje (Zeist, De Haan, 1959).

'Statusgroeperingen, een studie over de ontwikkeling van de sociale status en rechtspositie van handarbeiders en lagere beambten bij de N. V. Philips' (report) (Eindhoven, 1955).

'Statuten en reglementen van het Nederlands Verbond van Vakvereningingen', *Doel en Beginselen* (1959).

Stephenson, T. E., 'The Changing Role of Local Democracy: the Trade Union and Its Members', *The Sociological Review*, N.S. v, No. 1 (July 1957).

Stieber, J., 'Collective Bargaining in the Public Sector', in *Challenges to Collective Bargaining*, ed. Lloyd Ulman (Englewood Cliffs, N.J., Prentice Hall, Inc., 1967).

——'Manpower Adjustments to Automation and Technological Change in Western Europe', in *Automation and Economic Progress*, ed. H. Bowen and G. L. Mangum (Englewood Cliffs, N.J., Prentice-Hall, 1966).

——(editor), *Problems of Automation and Advanced Technology* (New York, St Martin's Press, 1966).

Stinchcombe, Arthur L., 'Social Structure and Organizations', in *Handbook of Organizations*, ed. James G. March (Chicago, Rand McNally, 1965).

Stouffer, Samuel A., 'Communism, Conformity and Civil Liberties', in *Sociological Research*, ed. Mathilda White Riley (New York, Harcourt, Brace and World, 1963).

Strauss, A. L. and L. Rainwater, *The Professional Scientist, A Study of American Chemists* (Chicago, Aldine Publishing Co., 1962).

Strauss, G., 'Control by Membership in Building Trade Unions', *American Journal of Sociology*, lxi, No. 6 (May 1956).

——'The Shifting Power Balance in the Plant', *Industrial Relations*, 1 (1962).

Sturmthal, A., 'National Patterns of Union Behavior', *Journal of Political Economy*, lvi, No. 5 (December 1948).

——*Unity and Diversity in European Labor* (Glencoe, Ill., Free Press, 1953).

——*Workers' Councils* (Cambridge, Mass., Harvard University Press, 1964).

Sultan, P. E., *The Disenchanted Unionist* (New York, Harper & Row, 1963).

Survey of the Participation of Trade Unions in the Determination of Economic and Social Policies in their Countries, International Confederation of Free Trade Unions, Executive Board, Brussels, 2–5 December 1963, Agenda Item 9.

Tagliacozzo, 'Trade-union Government, Its Nature and Its Problems, A Bibliographical Review, 1945–1955', *American Journal of Sociology*, lxi, No. 6 (May 1956).

Tannenbaum, Arnold S., 'Unions', in *Handbook of Organizations*, ed. James G. March (Chicago, Rand McNally, 1965).

——and R. L. Kahn, *Participation in Union Locals* (New York, Row, Peterson, 1958).

Tannenbaum, R. and F. Massarik, 'Participation by Subordinates in the Managerial Decision-Making Process', *The Canadian Journal of Economics and Political Science*, XVI (August, 1950).

Taylor, George W., 'Collective Bargaining', in *Automation and Technological Change*, ed. John T. Dunlop (Englewood Cliffs, N.J., Prentice Hall, 1965).

Teuteberg, H. J., *Geschichte der Industriellen Mitbestimmung in Deutschland* (Tübingen, Mohr, 1961).

Telderstichting, B. M., *De publiekrechtelijke bedrijfsorganisatie in Nederland* (The Hague, 1958).

Theodore, R., 'Union Security Provisions in Major Union Contracts', *Monthly Labor Review*, LXXXII, No. 12 (1959).

Thoenes, P., *The Elite and the Welfare State* (London, Faber & Faber, 1964).

Thomas, Norman, 'Humanistic Socialism and the Future', *Socialist Humanism, an International Symposium*, ed. Erich Fromm (New York, Doubleday, 1965).

Thönessen, Werner, letter 1 February 1961.

Thorel, G., 'Masse et Militants', *Esprit*, XIX, Nos 180–1 (July–August 1951).

Tilburg, W. F. van, in *Tijdschr. v. Efficientie en Documentatie*, XXXII, No. 13 (November 1962).

The Times, London, 7 October 1940.

Titmuss, R. M., *Essays on the Welfare State* (London, Allen & Unwin, 1958).

Tjebbes, M. and H. A. Wigbold, 'Wordt de P.v.d.A. de partij van de Dreestrekkers?' *Vrij Nederland* (15 November 1958).

The Trade Union Situation in the United States (Geneva, ILO, 1960).

Trade Unions and Productivity, London, British Trades Union Congress, n.d.

Triesch, G., *Die Macht der Funktionäre* (Düsseldorf, 1956).

Trocchi, A., *The Outsiders* (New York, Signet Books, 1961).

Tweëntwintigste Verlag van de werkzaamheden van het Nederlands Verband van Vakvereningen, 1959–61 (Amsterdam, 1962).

Twentieth Century Socialism, the Economy of Tomorrow (London, Socialist Union, 1956).

'Union Aide Predicts White Collar Gains,' *New York Times*, 8 June 1967.

Uyl, J. M. den, 'Theorie en Beweging', *Socialisme en Demokratie* (1956).

Vall, M. van de, 'Blue Collar and White Collar Workers in Industry—the Institutionalization of a Dichotomy', Paper presented at the Sixth World Congress of Sociology (Evian, 4–11 September 1966).

——'Clients, Consommateurs ou Coopérateurs, une enquête Néerlandaise', *Coopération, Idées, Faits, Techniques*, April, May, June 1962.

——'Jonge beambten bij de N. V. Philips' Gloeilampenfabrieken te Eindhoven' (report) (Utrecht, 1959).

——'Non participatie in Vakbeweging', *Sociologisch Jaarboek*, XIII (Amsterdam, Het Koggeschip, 1959).

——'Das Problem der Partizipation in freiwilligen Organisationen', in J. Matthes, *Soziologie und Gesellschaft in den Niederlanden* (Berlin, Luchterhand Verlag, 1965).

——'Social onderzoek als didactische opgave', *Sociol. Gids.*, III, No. 8 (1956).

——'Sociografie van een doorbraakafdeling' (Report for the Dutch Labor Party) (Amsterdam, 1953).

Vall, M. van de, 'Trade Unions of the Welfare State as Seen by their Members', *Trade Union Information*, No. 38 (OECD, Paris).

——'Voluntary Participation in Democratic Organizations', *Studies in Sociology*, ed. Milton C. Albrecht, *Buffalo Studies*, III, No. 2 (December 1967).

——'Wat biedt de opleiding?' *Opleiding en beroepsuitoefening van de sociaal wetenschappelijk academicus* (ISONEVO/VSWO) (Amsterdam, 1960).

——'The Workers' Councils in Western Europe: Aims and Results', in *Proceedings of the Seventeenth Annual Meeting, Industrial Relations Research Association*, ed. G. G. Somers (Chicago, 1965).

——and R. W. Boesjes-Hommes, *Een Onderzoek naar de Situatie van Enkele Lagere Technische Scholen* (Groningen, Wolters, 1961).

——and J. Roelands, *De jonge Philipsbeambte, zijn cao en devakbond* (report) Utrecht, 1959).

Vall, W. van de, 'Een paar losse herinneringen aan de arbeidersbeweging in Groningen bij de eeuwwisseling', *Cultureel Maandblad*, III, No. 8 (October, 1962).

Ven, F. J. H. M. van der, 'Het arbeidsconflict', *Sociale Wetenschappen*, II, No. 3 (April 1959).

Ventejol, G., *Le Conseil d'Entreprise et les Problèmes Économiques de l'Entreprise* Paris, OECD, 1956).

'Verenigingsleven', *Vrijetijdsbesteding in Nederland, Winter 1955-56* (Zeist, De Haan, 1957).

Verhandlungen des Deutsches Soziologen-Tages (1948–9).

Verwey-Jonker, H., 'Commissie Ondernemingsraden, inzake de verenigingen van Hoger Personeel' (Memorandum), *Sociaal Economische Raad* (mimeographed), 5, May 1959.

——'Vijfentwintig jaar socialistische theorie', *Ir. J. W. Albarda, een kwart eeuw parlementaire werkzaamheid* (Amsterdam, Arbeiderspers, 1938).

Vliegen, W. H., *Die onze kracht ontwaken deed* (Amsterdam, Arbeiderspers).

Vrankrijker, A. J. C. de, *Een groeiende gedachte, de ontwikkeling der meiningen over de sociale kwestie in de 19e eeuw in Nederland* (Assen, Van Gorcum, 1959).

Wagenfeld, H., *De toestand van de vakbeweging in de Tielerwaard* (report of the Gelders Komgronden Commissie).

Wages, Prices, Profits, and Productivity (American Assembly, Columbia University, June 1959).

Wakefield, Joseph C., 'Expanding Functions of State and Local Governments, 1965–1970', in *Monthly Labor Review* 1 (July 1967).

Waris, Heiki, 'Workers' Participation in Management in Scandinavian Industry' in *Transactions of the Fourth World Congress of Sociology* (London, ISA, 1961).

Warner, W. L. and P. S. Lunt, 'Criteria Used in Selecting the Community', *The Social Life of a Modern Community* (New Haven, Conn., Yale University Press, 1941).

Webb, S. and B., *History of Trade Unionism* (London, 1894).

Weber, M., 'Parlamentierung und Demokratisierung', *Gesammelte Politische Schriften* (Munich, Drei Masken Verlag, 1921).

Weber, M., 'Politik als Befur', *Gesammelte Politische Schriften* (Munich, Drei Masken Verlag, 1921).

——*The Protestant Ethic and the Spirit of Capitalism* (New York, Charles Scribner's Sons, 1958).

——'Der Sozialismus', *Gesammelte Aufsätze zur Soziologie und Sozial-politik* (Tübingen, Mohr, 1924).

——*Sozialistische Monatshefte*, 1909.

Weisenfeld, Allan, 'Collective Bargaining by Public Employees in the U.S.', in *Collective Bargaining in the Public Service*, Proceedings of the Annual Spring Meeting, IRRA (Milwaukee, Wisc., 1966).

Weisser, G., 'Soziale Sicherheit', *Handwörterbuch der Sozialwissenschaften*.

Wigham, E., *What's Wrong with the Unions?* (London, Penguin Books, 1961).

Wingerden, C. W. van, in *Preface to the 22nd Report of the Dutch Socialist Trade Unions, Covering the Period from 1 January 1959 to 31st December 1961* (Amsterdam, 1962).

Wit, J. J. de, *Correctie op de Eeuwgrens, het anachronisme van de Ommelanden, sociaal-psychologisch beschouwd* (Assen, Van Gorkum, 1957).

Wit, J. W. W. A., 'De verdeling van de gezinsinkomens in Nederland in de jaren 1949 en 1954', *Statistische en Econometrische Onderzoekingen* (4th Quarter, 1956).

Wolf, S. de, *Voor het land van belofte, een terugblik op mijn leven* (Bussum, 1954).

Work Stoppages in Fifty States and the District of Columbia, 1927–62, BLS Report, No. 256 (Washington, D.C., 1964).

Wuthe, G., *Gewerkschaften und politische Bildung* (Hannover, Verlag f. Literatur u. Zeitgeschehen, 1962).

Wyant, R. and H. Herzog, 'Voting via the Senate Mailbag—Part II', *Public Opinion Quarterly*, v, No. 4 (1941).

'Yearbook of Labour Statistics', 1966, International Labour Office, Geneva.

Zahn, E., *Die Soziologie der Prosperität* (Berlin, 1960).

Zeelenberg, H. D., 'Sociale waardering voor hoofd- en handarbeid', *Mens en Onderneming*, IV (1950).

Zestig Jaren Statistiek in Tijdreeksen (Zeist, De Haan, 1959).

Zweig, F., *The British Worker* (London, Pelican, 1960).

——'The New Factory Worker', *The Twentieth Century* (May 1960).

Index of Names

Index of Subjects

typists, 20
Typographical Union, 166

UAW, 59, 73
unemployment, 9, 21, 59; cycles of, 45; insurance, 85; office, 189; prevention of, 118; structural, 207
Unilever, 13
Union, aid, 83; boss, 78; bureaucratic, 1; branch, 30; delegates, 71; *see also* trusted members; democracy, 90; elections, 89; goals, 13; image, 116–25; labels, 59; leaders 12; leaders, voluntary, 68; *see also* officials; movement, 37; office, 159–60; officers 202; officials, 196 ff.; security, 83; structure and functions, 115
Union Carbide Corporation, 78
unionism, active new, 11; economic, 12; political, 12
unions, Catholic, 29, 42, 88–9; company, 69; conservative, 201; craft, 59; denominational, 50, 88, 93; established, 113; European, 119; industrial, 11, 28, 32, 59; legitimacy of, 92; obsolescent, 136; professional, 28–9, 79; Protestant, 29, 42, 88–9; radical, 210; socialist, 29, 42, 93; superfluous, 41; theory, 63; traditional, 79; United States', 119; weaker and stronger, 77
United States, 41, 46, 47, 56, 59, 61, 62, 83, 87, 88, 90, 96, 104, 133, 144, 152, 155, 156, 163, 166, 175, 178, 180, 183, 206; bargaining in, 79; building trades, 75; Congress, 89; joint consultation in, 72–3; unions, 77, 81
universities, 205
university teachers, 33; professors, *see* professors
urban communities, 205
urbanization, 1, 38; and participation, 154–5
Utrecht, 154
utopia, social, 35
utopian ideals, 51
utopianism, 47–8, 61; *see also* socialism

vacuum, social, 136
value, incongruity and congruity, 101
values, conflict of, 63; and norms, 136–40; personal, 101

value structure, of U.S. labor relations, 72
'Verelendung', *see* impoverishment; pauperization
Vorwärts, 86
voters, 103

wage, and price levels, 118; determination, 74; demands, 58, 106; drift, 75; earners, 9; increases, 10; level, 10
wage earners' share of GNP, 74
wage policy, union, 73
wages, 141; and prices, 75; city, 6; loss of, 21; minimum, 74; weekly, **22**
walkout, 95; *see also* labor stoppage; strike(s)
want creation, industry, 17; techniques of, 12
wars, 177
way of life, 14
wealth, accumulation of, 3; distribution of, 3
Weimar, Republic of, 61
welfare, capitalism, 43; employees, 79; industrial, 81, 133; social, 45, 53
welfare State, 1–52, 118; pluralistic, 154
wife, influence of, 143; *see also* housewife
wildcat, action, strikes, 58, 75
window clerks, 20
Windsor, U.S., 58
wives, employed, 9; working, 24
white collar, 14, 147; *see also* workers
wholesale trade, 21
'Wohlfahrtskapitalismus', 13
women, 21, 24, 186
work, clerical, 22; community of, 64; environment, 162; mental, 22; office, 22; physical, 22; satisfaction, 207
worker, level of, 118–20
workers, blackcoated, 20; blue collar, 5, 105–6, 156–61; displaced, 21; factory, 6, 75; farm, 9; female, 17, 24, 30; male, 17; manual, 59; nonunionized, 76; office, 28, 30, 33, 59; rural, 6; skilled, 9, 23, 137–9; unskilled, 23, 137–9; white collar, 10, 96, 105–6, 156–61; younger, 88
Workers' Council, 55; Party, 170; world, 78
working population, 92
working-to-rule, 95

Yugoslav industry, 65
Yugoslavia, 22
Yorkshire, 98